# BOARDING PASS

Anglais

1re Séries technologiques

B1 ▸ B2

Brigitte LALLEMENT
Nathalie HATOY
Isabelle TRAMOY

hachette
ÉDUCATION

Nos remerciements à Jill Danger et Michael Combier
pour leur aide et leurs relectures.

**Maquette intérieure, couverture et mise en page :** Anne-Danielle Naname

**Iconographie :** Candice Renault

**Dessins :** Juliette Baily (pp. 27, 45, 81, 99, 117, 135, 153, 171) et Johann Misset (pp. 28, 46, 82, 100, 110, 118, 136, 154, 172)

**Cartographie :** Légendes Cartographie

**Relecture :** Nadine Lucas

**www.hachette-education.com**



ISBN : 978-2-01-399802-4

# BOARDING PASS

## Une carte d'embarquement pour les élèves des sections technologiques

**BOARDING PASS** a été spécialement conçu pour les élèves des séries technologiques. Son orientation concrète et pratique, des guidages qui facilitent la tâche des élèves, un choix de documents courts et accessibles à la majorité sont autant de facteurs propres à motiver les élèves et à les aider à progresser.

### Les thématiques

Elles s'insèrent strictement dans les quatre notions du programme. Elles abordent soit des sujets de société liés aux questions actuelles (jeux vidéo, surveillance, etc.), soit des sujets liés à des connaissances culturelles (esclavage, légendes écossaises, etc.).

### Les problématiques

Chaque *Unit* est organisée pour développer une problématique annoncée en page d'accueil et récapitulée en dernière page. Les documents se complètent et se répondent pour emmener les élèves dans un parcours interactif rigoureusement programmé.

### Les stratégies

Dans chaque *Unit*, une page est consacrée à l'entraînement à une compétence ou une sous-compétence.

**BOARDING PASS** intègre l'approche actionnelle recommandée dans le Cadre européen commun de référence. Avec une très large place accordée aux activités orales, tant en compréhension qu'en production, il permet aux élèves de s'entraîner au baccalauréat. À chaque étape, une *Action* implique les élèves dans une communication réelle et les invite à comprendre, négocier et exprimer du sens. Ces *Actions* conduisent naturellement au *Project* de fin de séquence.

**BOARDING PASS** a pour ambition d'accompagner tous les élèves au niveau B2 correspondant à l'examen.

### Compléments de l'ouvrage

- Le **cédérom vidéo** comporte neuf documents vidéo authentiques liés aux thèmes des *Units*.
- Les **2 CD audio** contiennent, pour chaque *Unit*, un *podcast* (court document informatif), des documents pour l'entraînement à la compréhension de l'oral (avec des exercices de prononciation) et l'enregistrement des textes principaux accompagné de leur résumé.
- Des **fichiers MP3** sont accessibles aux élèves *via* des flashcodes tout au long des *Units*. Ils sont aussi téléchargeables sur le site www.ressources.hachette-education.com/boardingpass/1re.
- Le **eWorkbook**, outil numérique et interactif, est le complément indispensable du manuel. Il propose des questionnaires détaillés qui guident les élèves dans la découverte des documents vidéo ou sonores et dans la lecture des textes principaux (niveau A2+), ainsi que des exercices variés et interactifs.
- Des **fiches d'auto-évaluation** en ligne permettent à chacun de se positionner par rapport aux attentes du CECRL.

**Les auteurs**

# PRÉSENTATION DE L'OUVRAGE

## Welcome to Grade 11

Quatre pages pour prendre contact avec la classe de première et vous aider à réviser quelques notions de base en grammaire et en vocabulaire.

## Ouverture du chapitre

La problématique du chapitre.

Le menu de l'unité pour voir d'un coup d'œil le contenu du chapitre.

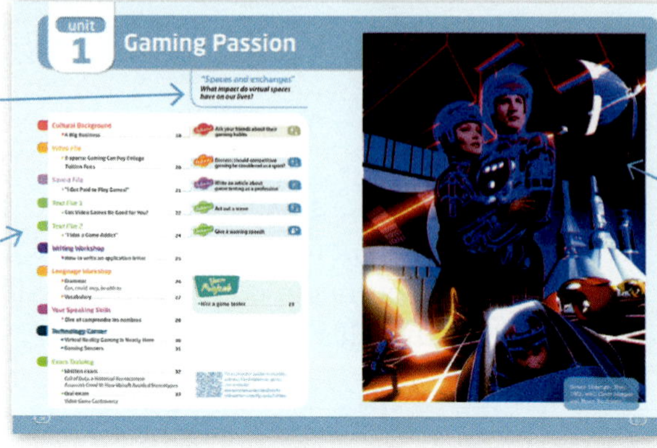

Une grande photo pour prendre contact avec le thème de l'unité.

## Cultural Background

**Vous prenez contact avec un pan de la civilisation ou de la culture des pays anglophones.**

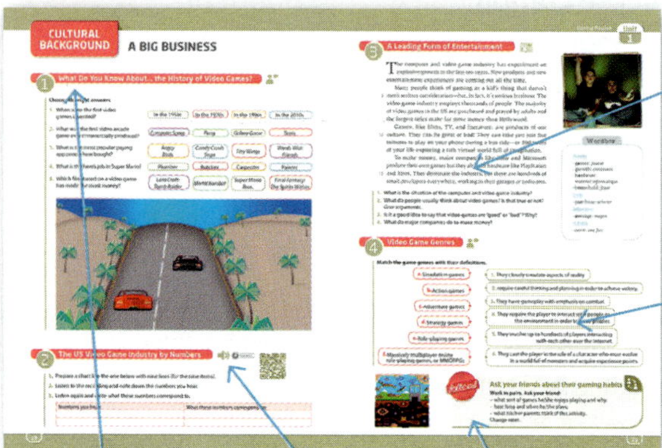

Un **texte** vous apporte des informations supplémentaires.

Un **document visuel** vous invite à vous poser des questions.

**What Do You Know About…** Vous faites le point sur ce que vous savez du thème.

**Pocast** – Une mini-conférence enregistrée.

*Action!* Vous réalisez une tâche pour utiliser ce que vous avez appris.

## Video File

## Sound File

**Vous vous préparez à voir et écouter les documents en commentant la photo, le titre et parfois une introduction.**

Des **documents vidéo authentiques** pour vous informer.

Des interviews, des reportages.

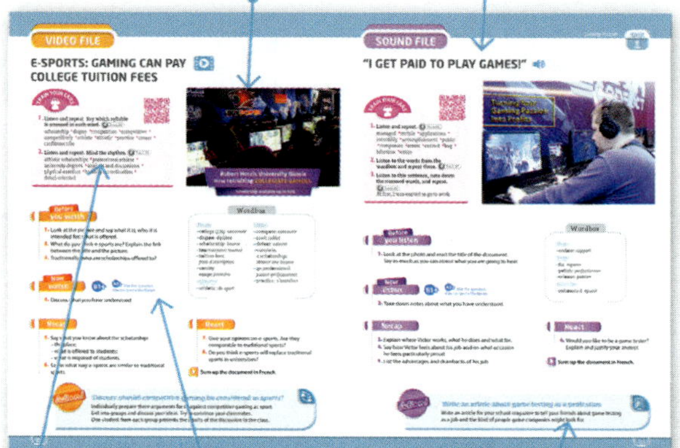

**Train your ears** Des exercices pour mieux prononcer et mieux comprendre.

**eWorkbook** Un questionnaire détaillé si vous êtes de niveau A2+.

*Action!* Vous utilisez ce que vous avez vu et entendu pour jouer un rôle, préparer une affiche, organiser un débat, etc.

## Text File 1

**Un texte pour vous entraîner à la lecture.**

Vous prenez contact avec le texte.

Vous vérifiez vos suppositions.

**eWorkbook** Un questionnaire détaillé si vous êtes de niveau A2+.

Des questions vous guident si vous êtes de niveau B1+.

On vous invite à donner votre avis.

Des exercices vous aident à comprendre et à retenir les mots.

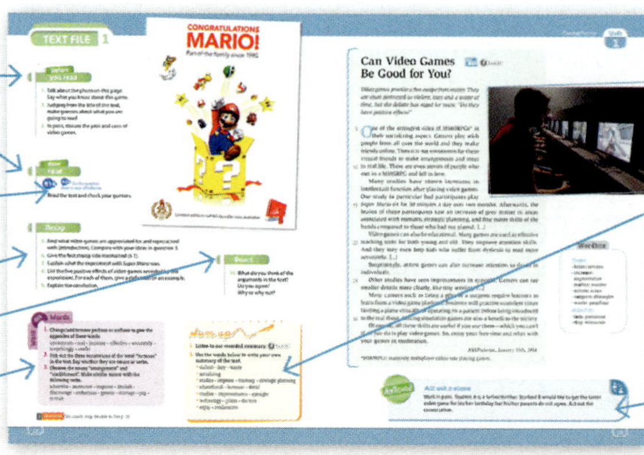

Vous écoutez un résumé enregistré puis vous le résumez avec vos propres mots.

*Action!* Vous utilisez ce que vous avez lu pour faire un discours, jouer un rôle ou discuter.

## Text File 2

**Pour apprendre à lire l'anglais, il faut lire beaucoup… ce texte est l'occasion de vous entraîner.**

## Writing Workshop

**Cette page de préparation à l'écrit vous entraîne à la réalisation d'une production grâce à un modèle.**

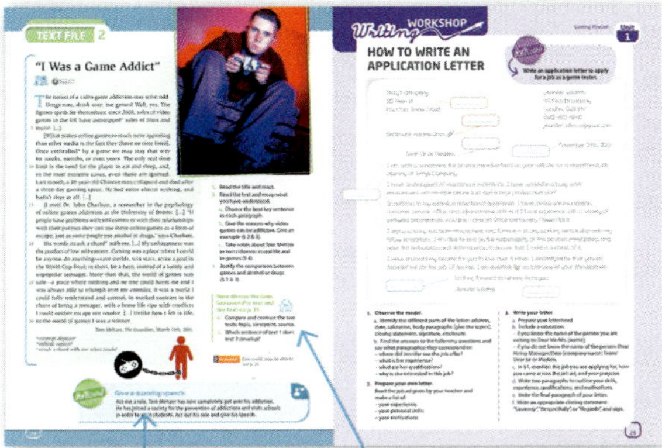

Action! Vous utilisez ce que vous avez lu pour mettre en scène la situation, organiser un débat, discuter, etc.

Des questions vous font faire le lien entre les Text Files 1 et 2 pour vous entraîner au bac.

## Language Workshop

**Grammar** – Vous observez le fonctionnement de la langue et vous déduisez des règles que vous mettez ensuite en pratique dans les exercices.

**Vocabulary** – Les mots indispensables pour parler du thème de l'unité. Des exercices vous aident à les mémoriser.

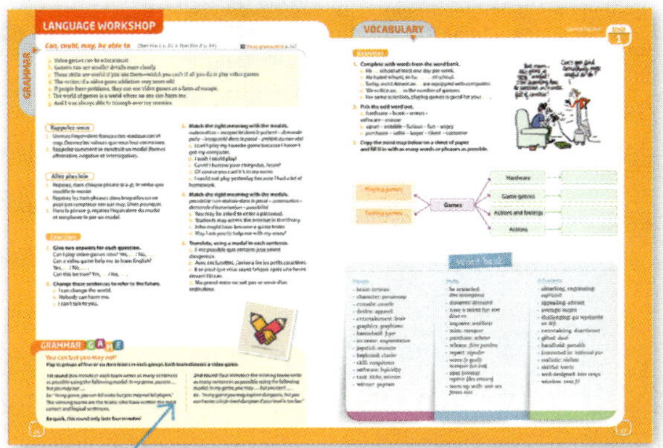

Vous utilisez un point de langue dans un jeu de communication.

Retrouvez tous les exercices interactifs dans votre eWorkbook.

## Skills Training

**Une méthode pour travailler des points spécifiques de la langue anglaise. Observez, et entraînez-vous !**

## Your Project

**On travaille en groupes, on se répartit les tâches pour aboutir à une véritable production. Les Actions de l'unité vous ont préparé à réaliser cette tâche finale.**

## TECHNOLOGY CORNER

## ART HISTORY CORNER

**Une double page en rapport avec votre domaine de compétences pour entrer dans les évolutions de la technologie, ou une double page artistique pour observer comment le monde de l'art s'est saisi du thème que nous traitons.**

## Exam Training

**Des sujets d'examen pour vous entraîner au baccalauréat.**

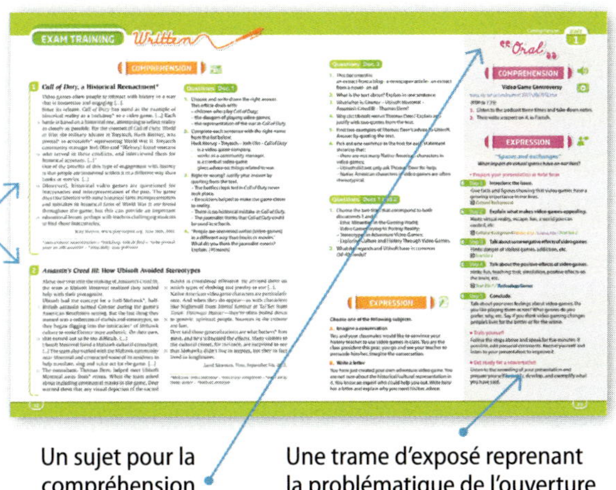

Un sujet pour préparer l'épreuve écrite (compréhension et expression).

Un sujet pour la compréhension de l'oral.

Une trame d'exposé reprenant la problématique de l'ouverture d'unité pour vous préparer à l'épreuve d'expression orale.

# SOMMAIRE

THE IDEA OF PROGRESS

unit 3

## Food Matters



unit 4

## Silicon Valley

Places and Forms of Power

unit 5

# A Nation of Gunfighters



unit 6

# Big Brother Is Watching Us



unit 7

# Scotland the Brave

MYTHS AND HEROES



unit 8

## Slaves Who Dared



unit 9

## Sport Is More Than Just a Game

# WELCOME to GRADE 11

1. Speak English
2. Write in English
3. Listen to English
4. Read in English

# 1. Speak English

## Task 1 Show how good your memory is

**Work in large groups. Start chain speaking to recap your shopping list.**

Student A starts; student B recaps and adds an item; student C recaps and adds an item. On goes the game until somebody forgets an item and gets eliminated. When only one person is left, he/she is the winner.

Yesterday, I went to the supermarket. I bought a melon. A.

Yesterday,I went to the supermarket. I bought a melon and a pair of shoes. B.

Yesterday, I went to the supermarket. I bought a melon, a pair of shoes, and a vacuum cleaner. C.

## Task 2 Bingo!

**Ask people in the class questions until you can replace each X by a student's name. You can use each person's name only once!**

eWorkbook **for a grid.**

| | | | | |
|---|---|---|---|---|
| X has a dog and a cat. | X went on holidays abroad this year. | X does a martial art. | X has already touched a snake. | X walks to school every day. |
| X can give the name of three US presidents. | X has already had a summer job. | X likes the same music/singer as I. | X can play the guitar. | X has already been to London. |
| X has a sister. | X has a pair of green trousers. | X was born the same month as me. | X will have lunch at the canteen today. | X is an only child. |
| X was not in the same class as me last year. | X can draw well. | X does not like tomatoes. | X has a grandparent of foreign origins. | X has eyes the same color as mine. |
| X has ever won a medal. | X has read a book in English. | X plays MMORPG online. | X likes reading. | X is good at maths. |

**The winner is the student who has completed a vertical, horizontal, or diagonal line first!**

# 2. Write in English

## Task 1 Make a name tag

- Fold a paper and write your name vertically on one side.
- Make beautiful letters and use your favorite color to write it. Find words corresponding to your personality, your tastes, or your mood that start with each letter of your name. Write them horizontally, in another color.
- Put this label on your table so that your teacher and your friends have an idea of who you are.

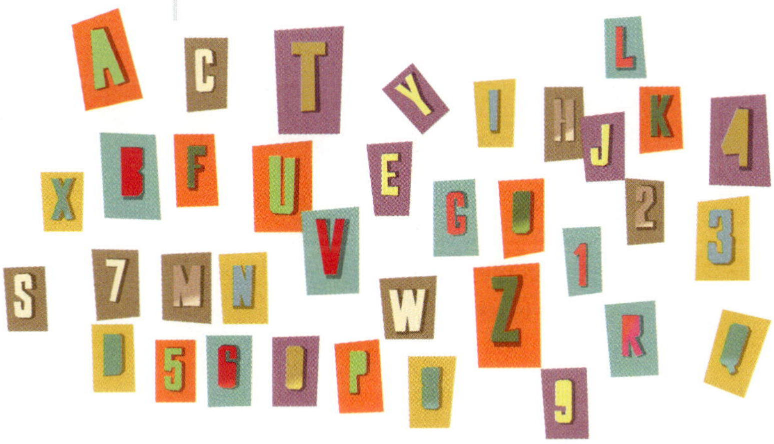

## Task 2 Talk about your friend

- Write a short paragraph about a student you know in the class: report a funny event that happened to him/her in the past.
  Do NOT write his/her name!
- The stories will be put on the wall so that everybody can read them and guess who the stories are about.

## Task 3 Write a story

- Each student starts a story on a sheet of paper: he/she adds two words (or more!) to the following sentence: "Last year, I was … when …"
  Don't worry if the sentence is not complete!
- He/she then passes the paper to his/her right-hand neighbour and completes his/her left-hand neighbour's story with a few words. He/she then passes the paper to his/her right-hand neighbour and completes his/her left-hand neighbour's story.
- On goes the game until the stories are finished.
- You can then read the strange stories you have all written together.

# 3. Listen to English

## Task 1 Listen and read a poem out loud

**Listen to this funny poem.** Track 01

Most native English speakers can't get very far without mispronouncing a word.
Can YOU do that? Good luck!

### English is a strange language!

English is a strange language!
Dearest creature in creation,
Study English pronunciation.
I will teach you in my verse
Sounds like corpse, corps, horse, and worse.

Just compare heart, beard, and heard,
Dies and diet, lord and word,
Sword and sward, retain and Britain.
But be careful how you speak;
Say break and steak, but bleak and streak.

Blood and flood are not like food,
Nor is mould like should and would.
And your pronunciation's OK
When you correctly say croquet.

Ear, but earn and wear and tear
Do not rhyme with here but ere.
Seven is right, but so is even,
Hyphen, roughen, nephew Stephen,

Finally, which rhymes with enough—
Though, through, plough, or dough, or cough?
Hiccough has the sound of cup.
My advice is to give up!

Excerpted from G. Nolst, *The Chaos*, 1922

## Task 2 Is that your last word?

**Work in pairs. Listen and choose the right answer to the following questions (you have 6 seconds to agree on each answer).** Track 02

1. What is the capital of Scotland?
2. What is the flag of the UK called?
3. Whose statue is on Trafalgar Square in London?
4. Which English king had six wives?
5. Where is Loch Ness?
6. Where in the UK is the Lake District?
7. Which is the symbol of Scotland?
8. Where is Hyde Park?
9. What is the name of the guards in the Tower of London?
10. Who invented the sandwich?
11. What do they celebrate in Britain on November 5th?
12. What is the longest river in the UK?
13. What is the name of a famous shopping street in London?
14. What is the capital of the Republic of Ireland?
15. Who wrote *Romeo and Juliet*?

**The winning pair is the pair with most correct answers.**

# 4. Read in English

## Task 1 Want to be my friend?

**In pairs, complete quotations *1* to *9* with words from the lists. Translate into French and compare your translations with other pairs'.**

1. Truly great friends are hard to ... , difficult to ... , and impossible to ... . *(G. Randolf)*
2. If you make friends with yourself, you will never be ... . *(M. Maltz)*
3. Life is partly what we ... it, and partly what it is made by the friends we ... . *(T. Williams)*
4. Friendship is like a ... ornament; once it is ... it can rarely be put back exactly the same way. *(Anonymous)*
5. A friend is one who ... us, but ... us anyway. *(Fr. J. Cummings)*
6. The best way to destroy an ... is to make him a friend. *(A. Lincoln)*
7. Friendship is like ..., easier made than ... . *(S. Butler)*
8. Only your ... friends will tell you when your ... is dirty. *(Proverb)*
9. A true friend is someone who overlooks your ... and ... your success! *(D. Larson)*

enemy failures money glass face
choose find forget knows leave
loves make tolerates real alone
broken kept

## Task 2 Solve the mystery

**Read the story and find out how Max knows the surprise visitor is a crook.**

### The Surprise Visitor

Max was going to visit Miss Fritz, his old music teacher who had invited him for dinner, when the clock in the courthouse ahead of him began ringing for six o'clock. He noticed a tall man with a brief case walking towards him. When the clock rang, the man turned around to look at it and quickly walked on. Max also quickened his step—he didn't want to be late.

"I'm glad you could come," Miss Fritz said. "I've made a salad for us." She gestured Max to a chair. "Good thing I prepared ahead. A surprise visitor has just left."

"Who visited?" Max asked.

"A teacher from the School for the Deaf. He was totally deaf himself; poor man."

"Why was he here?"

"Well, the school needs money. I was glad to help out. I had just cashed my social security check so I gave him five hundred dollars."

"Did he just leave? Was he a tall man with a brief case?"

"Yes."

"We'd better call the police. I know this man wasn't deaf."

unit 1

# Gaming Passion

## "Spaces and exchanges"

***What impact do virtual spaces have on our lives?***



To access our audio resources, use our Flashcodes or go to our website:
www.ressources.hachette-education.com/boardingpass/1re/units/unit1.html

Steven Lisberger, *Tron*, 1982, with Cindy Morgan and Bruce Boxleitner.

## CULTURAL BACKGROUND

# A BIG BUSINESS

## 1 What Do You Know About... the History of Video Games?

**Choose the right answers.**

1. When were the first video games invented?
   In the 1950s / In the 1970s / In the 1990s / In the 2010s
2. What was the first video arcade game ever commercially produced?
   *Computer Space* / *Pong* / *Galaxy Game* / *Tetris*
3. What is the most popular paying app people have bought?
   *Angry Birds* / *Candy Crush Saga* / *Tiny Wings* / *Words With Friends*
4. What is the hero's job in Super Mario?
   Plumber / Butcher / Carpenter / Painter
5. Which film based on a video game has made the most money?
   *Lara Croft: Tomb Raider* / *Mortal Kombat* / *Super Mario Bros.* / *Final Fantasy: The Spirits Within*

## 2 The US Video Game Industry by Numbers

Track 03

1. Prepare a chart like the one below with nine lines (for the nine items).
2. Listen to the recording and note down the numbers you hear.
3. Listen again and write what these numbers correspond to.

| Numbers you hear: | What these numbers correspond to: |
|---|---|
| | |
| | |

## 3 A Leading Form of Entertainment

The computer and video game industry has experienced an explosive growth in the last ten years. New products and new entertainment experiences are coming out all the time.

Many people think of gaming as a kid's thing that doesn't merit serious consideration—but, in fact, it's serious business. The video game industry employs thousands of people. The majority of video games in the US are purchased and played by adults and the largest titles make far more money than Hollywood.

Games, like films, TV, and literature, are products of our culture. They can be great or bad! They can take you just five minutes to play on your phone during a bus ride—or 500 hours of your life exploring a rich virtual world full of imagination.

To make money, major companies like Sony and Microsoft produce their own games but they also sell hardware like PlayStation and Xbox. They dominate the industry, but there are hundreds of small developers everywhere, working in their garages or bedrooms.

**Wordbox**

Nouns
- **gam**er: *joueur*
- growth: *croissance*
- **hard**ware: *matériel informatique*
- **hou**sehold: *foyer*

Verb
- **pur**chase: *acheter*

Adjective
- **av**erage: *moyen*

Adverb
- once: *une fois*

1. What is the situation of the computer and video game industry?
2. What do people usually think about video games? Is that true or not? Give arguments.
3. Is it a good idea to say that video games are "good" or "bad"? Why?
4. What do major companies do to make money?

## 4 Video Game Genres

**Match the game genres with their definitions.**

a. Simulation games
b. Action games
c. Adventure games
d. Strategy games
e. Role-playing games
f. Massively multiplayer online role-playing games, or MMORPGs

1. They closely simulate aspects of reality.
2. require careful thinking and planning in order to achieve victory.
3. They have gameplay with emphasis on combat.
4. They require the player to interact with people or the environment in order to solve puzzles.
5. They involve up to hundreds of players interacting with each other over the Internet.
6. They cast the player in the role of a character who must evolve in a world full of monsters and acquire experience points.

**Action!**

### Ask your friends about their gaming habits

**Work in pairs. Ask your friend:**
- what sort of games he/she enjoys playing and why;
- how long and when he/she plays;
- what his/her parents think of this activity.

Change roles.

## VIDEO FILE

# E-SPORTS: GAMING CAN PAY COLLEGE TUITION FEES

### TRAIN YOUR EARS

1. **Listen and repeat. Say which syllable is stressed in each word.** Track 04
scholarship • degree • competition • competitive • competitively • athlete • athletic • practice • career • cardiovascular

2. **Listen and repeat. Mind the rhythm.** Track 05
athletic scholarships • professional athlete • university degrees • analysis and discussions • physical exertion • hand-eye coordination • detail-oriented

### Before you watch

1. Look at the picture and say what it is; who it is intended for; what is offered.
2. What do you think e-sports are? Explain the link between the title and the picture.
3. Traditionally, who are scholarships offered to?

### Wordbox

**Nouns**
- **col**lege (US): *université*
- de**gree**: *diplôme*
- **scho**larship: *bourse*
- **tour**nament: *tournoi*
- tu**i**tion fees: *frais d'inscription*
- **var**sity: *équipe première*

**Adjective**
- ath**le**tic: *de sport*

**Verbs**
- com**pete**: *concourir*
- cost: *coûter*
- de**feat**: *vaincre*
- earn/win a **scho**larship: *obtenir une bourse*
- go pro**fe**ssional: *passer professionnel*
- **prac**tice: *s'entraîner*

### Now watch

B1+ A2+ Use the question sheet in your eWorkbook.

4. Discuss what you have understood.

### Recap

5. Say what you know about the scholarship:
   – the place;
   – what is offered to students;
   – what is required of students.
6. Say in what way e-sports are similar to traditional sports.

### React

7. Give your opinion on e-sports. Are they comparable to traditional sports?
8. Do you think e-sports will replace traditional sports in universities?

**Sum up the document in French.**

### Action!

**Discuss: should competitive gaming be considered as sport?**

Individually prepare three arguments for or against competitive gaming as sport.
Get into groups and discuss your ideas. Try to convince your classmates.
One student from each group presents the results of the discussion to the class.

SOUND FILE

# "I GET PAID TO PLAY GAMES!"

TRAIN YOUR EARS

1. Listen and repeat. Track 06
managed • mobile • applications • incredibly • accomplishment • public • companies • errors • excited • bug • hilarious • entire
2. Listen to the words from the wordbox and repeat them. Track 07
3. Listen to this sentence, note down the stressed words, and repeat. Track 08
At first, I was excited to go to work.

## Before you listen

1. Look at the photo and read the title of the document. Say as much as you can about what you are going to hear.

## Now listen

B1+ A2+ Use the question sheet in your eWorkbook. Tracks 09 to 11

2. Take down notes about what you have understood.

### Wordbox

Noun
- review: *rapport*

Verbs
- fix: *réparer*
- polish: *perfectionner*
- release: *publier*

Adjective
- exhausted: *épuisé*

## Recap

3. Explain where Victor works, what he does and what for.
4. Say how Victor feels about his job and on what occasion he feels particularly proud.
5. List the advantages and drawbacks of his job.

## React

6. Would you like to be a game tester? Explain and justify your answer.

**Sum up the document in French.**

## Action!

### Write an article about game testing as a profession

Write an article for your school magazine to tell your friends about game testing as a job and the kind of people game companies might look for.

# TEXT FILE 1

## Before you read

1. Talk about the photo on this page. Say what you know about this game.
2. Judging from the title of the text, make guesses about what you are going to read.
3. In pairs, discuss the pros and cons of video games.

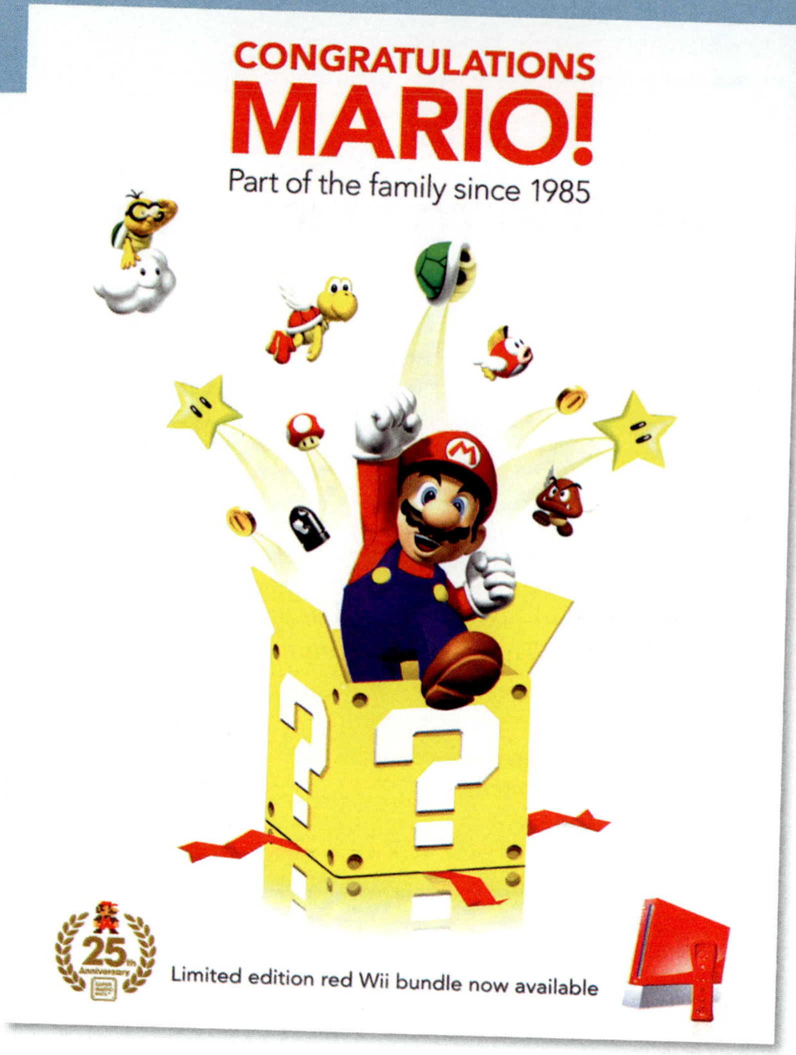


## Now read

B1+ A2+ Use the question sheet in your eWorkbook.

4. Read the text and check your guesses.

## Recap

5. Find what video games are appreciated for and reproached with (introduction). Compare with your ideas in question 3.
6. Give the first strong side mentioned (§ 1).
7. Explain what the experiment with *Super Mario* was.
8. List the five positive effects of video games revealed by the experiment. For each of them, give a definition or an example.
9. Explain the conclusion.

## React

10. What do you think of the arguments in the text? Do you agree? Why or why not?

## Work on Words

1. **Change/add/remove prefixes or suffixes to give the opposites of these words.**
   uncommon – real – increase – effective – accurately – surprisingly – useful
2. **Pick out the three occurrences of the word "increase" in the text. Say whether they are nouns or verbs.**
3. **Observe the nouns "arrangement" and "abolishment". Make similar nouns with the following verbs.**
   advertise – announce – improve – abolish – discourage – embarrass – govern – manage – pay – recruit

> Grammar *Can, could, may, be able to* See p. 26

## Sum up

1. **Listen to our recorded summary.** 1 Track 13
2. **Use the words below to write your own summary of the text.**
   - violent – lazy – waste
   - socializing
   - studies – improve – memory – strategic planning
   - educational – increase – detail
   - studies – improvements – eyesight
   - technology – pilots – doctors
   - enjoy – moderation

# Can Video Games Be Good for You?

Track 12

*Video games provide a fun escape from reality. They are often portrayed as violent, lazy and a waste of time, but the debate has raged for years: "Do they have positive effects?"*

One of the strongest sides of MMORPGs* is their socializing aspect. Gamers play with people from all over the world and they make friends online. Then it is not uncommon for these virtual friends to make arrangements and meet in real life. There are even stories of people who met in a MMORPG and fell in love.

Many studies have shown increases in intellectual function after playing video games. One study in particular had participants play *Super Mario 64* for 30 minutes a day over two months. Afterwards, the brains of these participants saw an increase of grey matter in areas associated with memory, strategic planning, and fine motor skills of the hands compared to those who had not played. [...]

Video games can also be educational. Many games are used as effective teaching tools for both young and old. They improve attention skills. And they may even help kids who suffer from dyslexia to read more accurately. [...]

Surprisingly, action games can also increase attention to detail in individuals.

Other studies have seen improvements in eyesight. Gamers can see smaller details more clearly, like tiny writing. [...]

Many careers such as being a pilot or a surgeon require learners to learn from a video game platform. Students will practise countless times landing a plane virtually or operating on a patient before being introduced to the real thing. Driving simulation games are also a benefit to society.

Of course, all these skills are useful if you use them—which you can't if all you do is play video games. So, enjoy your free time and relax with your games in moderation.

ASAPscience, January 19th, 2014.

*MMORPGs: massively multiplayer online role playing games.

## Wordbox

Nouns
- brain: *cerveau*
- incr**ea**se: *augmentation*
- m**a**tter: *matière*
- screen: *écran*
- s**ur**geon: *chirurgien*
- waste: *gaspillage*

Adjectives
- l**a**zy: *paresseux*
- t**i**ny: *minuscule*

Action!

## Act out a scene

Work in pairs. Student A is a father/mother. Student B would like to get the latest video game for his/her birthday but his/her parents do not agree. Act out the conversation.

# "I Was a Game Addict"

Track 14

The notion of a video game addiction may seem odd. Drugs sure, drink sure, but games? Well, yes. The figures speak for themselves: since 2008, sales of video games in the UK have outstripped* sales of films and music. [...]

What makes online games so much more appealing than other media is the fact they have no time limit. Once enthralled* by a game we may stay that way for weeks, months, or even years. The only real time limit is the need for the player to eat and sleep, and, in the most extreme cases, even those are ignored. Last month, a 30-year-old Chinese man collapsed and died after a three-day gaming spree. He had eaten almost nothing, and hadn't slept at all. [...]

I met Dr. John Charlton, a researcher in the psychology of online games addiction at the University of Bolton. "If people have problems with self-esteem or with their relationships with their parents they can use these online games as a form of escape, just as some people use alcohol or drugs," says Charlton.

His words struck a chord with me*. [...] My unhappiness was the product of low self-esteem. Gaming was a place where I could be anyone, do anything—save worlds, win wars, score a goal in the World Cup final; in short, be a hero, instead of a lonely and unpopular teenager. More than that, the world of games was safe—a place where nothing and no one could harm me and I was always able to triumph over my enemies. It was a world I could fully understand and control, in marked contrast to the chaos of being a teenager, with a home life ripe with conflicts I could neither escape nor resolve. [...] Unlike how I felt in life, in the world of games I was a winner.

Tom Meltzer, *The Guardian*, March 11th, 2011.

*outstrip: *dépasser*
*enthral: *captiver*
*struck a chord with me: *m'ont touché*

1. Read the title and react.
2. Read the text and recap what you have understood.
   a. Choose the best key sentence in each paragraph.
   b. Give the reasons why video games can be addictive. Give an example (§ 2 & 3).
   c. Take notes about Tom Meltzer in two columns: in real life and in games (§ 4).
3. Justify the comparison between games and alcohol or drugs (§ 1 & 3).

**Now discuss the links between this text and the text on p. 31.**

4. Compare and contrast the two texts: topic, viewpoint, source.
5. Which sentence of text 1 does text 2 develop?

**Grammar** *Can, could, may, be able to*
See p. 26

Action!

## Give a warning speech

Act out a role. Tom Meltzer has now completely got over his addiction. He has joined a society for the prevention of addictions and visits schools in order to warn students. Act out his role and give his speech.

# HOW TO WRITE AN APPLICATION LETTER

**Action!**
**Write an application letter to apply for a job as a game tester.**

Jennifer Williams,
49, New Broadway
London, SW11 1HV
(020) 4523 85612
jennifer.williams@gmail.com

Terry's Company
312 Main st
Houston, Texas 77002 ......................

......................
Enclosure: resume.docx

November 25th, 2015. ......................

......................
Dear Sir or Madam,

......................

I am writing concerning the position as advertised on your website for a receptionist job opening at Terry's Company.

I have several years of receptionist experience. I have worked in a busy work environment with multiple phone lines and a large professional staff.

In addition to my extensive receptionist experience, I have strong communication, customer service, office, and administrative skills and I have experience with a variety of software programmes, including Microsoft Office–particularly PowerPoint.

I enjoy working in a team atmosphere, and forming a strong working relationship with my fellow co-workers. I am able to take on the responsibility of this position immediately, and have the enthusiasm and determination to ensure that I make a success of it.

I have enclosed my resume for you to look over further; I sincerely hope that you will consider me for the job. Of course, I am available for an interview at your convenience.

...................... Looking forward to hearing from you,

Jennifer Williams ......................

**1. Observe the model.**

a. Identify the different parts of the letter: address, date, salutation, body paragraphs (give the topics), closing statement, signature, enclosure.

b. Find the answers to the following questions and say what paragraph(s) they correspond to:
– where did Jennifer see the job offer?
– what is her experience?
– what are her qualifications?
– why is she interested in this job?

**2. Prepare your own letter.**

Read the job ad given by your teacher and make a list of:
– your experience;
– your personal skills;
– your motivations.

**3. Write your letter.**

a. Prepare your letterhead.

b. Include a salutation:
– if you know the name of the person you are writing to: Dear Mr./Ms. [name];
– if you do not know the name of the person: Dear Hiring Manager/Dear [company name] Team/ Dear Sir or Madam.

c. In §1, mention the job you are applying for, how you came across the job ad, and your purpose.

d. Write two paragraphs to outline your skills, experience, qualifications, and motivations.

e. Write the final paragraph of your letter.

f. Write an appropriate closing statement: "Sincerely", "Respectfully", or "Regards", and sign.

# LANGUAGE WORKSHOP

GRAMMAR

## *Can, could, may, be able to* (Text File 1 p. 22 & Text File 2 p. 24)

Précis grammatical p. 197

a. Video games can be educational.
b. Gamers can see smaller details more clearly.
c. These skills are useful if you use them—which you can't if all you do is play video games.
d. The notion of a video game addiction may seem odd.
e. If people have problems, they can use video games as a form of escape.
f. The world of games is a world where no one can harm me.
g. And I was always able to triumph over my enemies.

### Rappelez-vous

1. Donnez l'équivalent français des modaux *can* et *may*. Donnez les valeurs que vous leur connaissez.
2. Rappelez comment se construit un modal (formes affirmative, négative et interrogative).

### Allez plus loin

3. Repérez, dans chaque phrase (*a* à *f*), le verbe que modifie le modal.
4. Repérez les trois phrases dans lesquelles on ne peut pas remplacer *can* par *may*. Dites pourquoi.
5. Dans la phrase *g*, repérez l'équivalent du modal et remplacez-le par un modal.

### Exercises

1. **Give two answers for each question.**
Can I play video games now? Yes, ... / No, ... .
Can a video game help me to learn English? Yes, ... / No, ... .
Can this be true? Yes, ... / No, ... .

2. **Change these sentences to refer to the future.**
a. I can change the world.
b. Nobody can harm me.
c. I can't talk to you.

3. **Match the right meaning with the modals.**
*autorisation – incapacité dans le présent – demande polie – incapacité dans le passé – prétérit du non-réel*
a. I can't play my favorite game because I haven't got my computer.
b. I wish I could play!
c. Could I borrow your computer, Jessie?
d. Of course you can! It's in my room.
e. I could not play yesterday because I had a lot of homework.

4. **Match the right meaning with the modals.**
*possibilité non réalisée dans le passé – autorisation – demande d'autorisation – possibilité*
a. You may be asked to enter a password.
b. Students may access the Internet in the library.
c. John might have become a game tester.
d. May I ask you to help me with my essay?

5. **Translate, using a modal in each sentence.**
a. Il est possible que certains jeux soient dangereux.
b. Avec ces lunettes, j'arrive à lire les petits caractères.
c. Il se peut que vous soyez fatigué après une heure devant l'écran.
d. Ma grand-mère ne sait pas se servir d'un ordinateur.

## GRAMMAR GAME

### You can but you may not!

**Play in groups of four or six (two teams in each group). Each team chooses a video game.**

**1st round** (ten minutes): each team writes as many sentences as possible using the following model: *In my game, you can ... but you may not ...*
*Ex.: "In my game, you can kill mobs but you may not kill players."*
The winning teams are the teams who have written the most correct and logical sentences.

**2nd round** (four minutes): the winning teams write as many sentences as possible using the following model: *In my game, you may ... but you can't ... .*
*Ex.: "In my game you may explore dungeons, but you can't enter a high-level dungeon if your level is too low."*

**Be quick, this round only lasts four minutes!**

## Exercises

**1. Complete with words from the word bank.**
a. He ... school at least one day per week.
b. He hated school, so he ... ... of school.
c. Today, most American ... are equipped with computers.
d. We notice an ... in the number of gamers.
e. For some scientists, playing games is good for your ... .

**2. Pick the odd word out.**
a. hardware – book – screen – software – mouse
b. upset – irritable – furious – fun – angry
c. purchaser – seller – buyer – client – customer

**3. Copy the mind map below on a sheet of paper and fill it in with as many words or phrases as possible.**

- Games
  - Playing games ...
  - Testing games ...
  - Hardware →
  - Game genres →
  - Actions and feelings →
  - Actions →

## Word bank

### Nouns
- brain: *cerveau*
- character: *personnage*
- console: *console*
- device: *appareil*
- entertainment: *loisir*
- graphics: *graphisme*
- household: *foyer*
- increase: *augmentation*
- joystick: *manette*
- keyboard: *clavier*
- skill: *compétence*
- software: *logiciel(s)*
- task: *tâche, mission*
- winner: *gagnant*

### Verbs
- be rewarded: *être récompensé*
- discover: *découvrir*
- have a talent for: *être doué en*
- improve: *améliorer*
- miss: *manquer*
- purchase: *acheter*
- release: *faire paraître*
- report: *signaler*
- score (a goal): *marquer (un but)*
- spot (errors): *repérer (des erreurs)*
- team up with: *unir ses forces avec*

### Adjectives
- absorbing, engrossing: *captivant*
- appealing: *attirant*
- average: *moyen*
- challenging: *qui représente un défi*
- entertaining: *divertissant*
- gifted: *doué*
- handheld: *portable*
- interested in: *intéressé par*
- realistic: *réaliste*
- skillful: *habile*
- well-designed: *bien conçu*
- wireless: *sans fil*

SKILLS TRAINING

# DIRE ET COMPRENDRE LES NOMBRES

## Les nombres composés

**1 Écoutez** Track 15

a. The US has a population of 316,149 million people.
b. 186 million Americans are video game players.
c. 42% of all game players are women.
d. This game costs $22 in the States and £2.50 in Britain.

**2 Concluez**

Il y a une virgule là où les Français mettent … .
On ajoute *and* entre … et … .
Dans un nombre, il n'y a pas de terminaison *-s* à la fin de *hundred*, … et … .
Les symboles *$* et *£* sont placés … mais ils sont prononcés … .

**3 Entraînez-vous** **Lisez ces phrases à voix haute.**

- *122 people applied for the job.*
- *1,253 people work in this company.*
- *In the cafeteria of this store, a hamburger costs £10.50.*

## L'accentuation

**1 Écoutez** Track 16

a. The average gamer spends about 18 hours a week playing video games.
b. My grandfather is 80 years old—and he plays video games.

**2 Concluez**

Comparez la prononciation des nombres dans ces phrases: l'accent est sur … en *a* ; et sur … en *b*.

**3 Entraînez-vous**
**Lisez ces nombres à voix haute.**

- *thirty – thirteen*
- *fourty – fourteen*
- *seventy – seventeen*

## Les dates

**1 Écoutez** Track 17

a. The first video game was invented in 1971.
b. According to a 2014 report, video games can improve memory.
c. This article was published in *The Guardian* on 25 February 2014.
d. This article was published in *The New York Times* on January 14th, 2015.

**2 Concluez**

Dites comment lire une date. En *a*, … . En *b*, … .
En anglais britannique, … . En anglais américain, … .

**3 Entraînez-vous** **Lisez ces phrases et ces dates à voix haute.**

- *Christopher Columbus discovered America in 1492.*
- Pong *was an early arcade game that came about in 1972.*
- Super Mario Kart *was released in North America on November 23rd, 2009.*
- *It was released in Europe on April 2nd, 2010.*
- *3 March 2015 – 28 June 2014 – May 4th, 1974*

## L'heure

**1 Écoutez** Track 18

a. Traditionally, the English have tea at 5 o'clock.
b. Most people play games between 8:30 p.m. and 11:30 p.m.

**2 Concluez**

Choisissez la bonne réponse :
*English-speaking people often use the* ***12-hour/24-hour*** *clock.*

**3 Entraînez-vous** **Lisez ces indications de temps à voix haute.**

*The Cavendish London opening times:*

- *Breakfast, 6:30 to 10:30*
- *Lunch, 12:00 to 14:30*
- *Dinner, 17:30 to 18:30*

# Hire a game tester

**Imagine your own video game company and hire a game tester.**

## Step 1

The class is divided into groups of applicants and groups of hiring teams.
Each hiring team imagines the game-developing company they work for (name, type of games) and writes a job ad. You can use the ad provided by your teacher as a model. The ads are put on the wall so that each applicant can read them and choose one.

TICE

You can find examples of video games companies on these sites:
http://uk.ign.com/top/video-game-makers
www.freegameempire.com/game-development-companies

## Step 2

The applicants discuss and prepare their arguments. Each applicant writes an application letter and gives it to the hiring team he/she has chosen.

Writing WORKSHOP p. 25

## Step 3

The hiring teams prepare the questions they will ask the candidates. Action! p. 19 Action! p. 21
Then they read the application forms and discuss to choose the three applicants they want to interview.

## Step 4

The groups interview the three applicants, and discuss to agree on who they will hire for their company. Action! p. 23

# Virtual Reality Gaming Is Nearly Here

## We Just Need the Right Controller*!

*Video games have long promised to offer their players "immersive experiences", but virtual reality was still a fantasy. Now with the Oculus Rift headset, gamers will [soon] be able to slip on a pair of high-tech goggles* and truly be immersed in a virtual world.*

The only problem is: how will gamers play when they get there? […] Developers are realizing [that] the standard joysticks and gamepads that gamers have been using for decades are defunct*. […]

Once I slipped on the Oculus Rift and picked up the two sticks, the virtual reality system worked so well that I found myself in a small cottage by the sea, where I could walk around and pick up various objects—not exactly with my own hands, but with the two limbs* that appeared once I successfully calibrated the controllers. […]

**The Oculus Rift might not look pretty, but it gets the job done!**

There is no substitute for the precision you get when a controller is actually in contact with your body. Holding (or wearing) a controller does have one crucial benefit when it comes to virtual reality: you don't have to be positioned directly in front of the camera for the device to accurately track your movements.

Of course, console games can already put players in beautiful environments, but with only a mouse and keyboard or gamepad for user input, they can never reflect the nuances of subtle head motions that make truly *being* in a virtual space feel authentic. At one point, I discovered I could actually crouch down in the virtual house and turn my head upwards to look up the chimney into the sky above. […] I was astounded by the visuals but the controls were another matter. When I was [almost] able to reach down to the ground and pick up a ball with my own hand in virtual reality, having to press a button to do so was abstract and arbitrary.

In virtual reality, you don't want to sit down and push buttons on a mouse. […]

"There's still a long road ahead before discovering the ideal input scheme for virtual reality," Palmer Luckey, [the creator of the Oculus Rift, said], but we'll get there eventually."

Yannick LeJacq, www.nbcnews.com, October 7th, 2013.

*controller: *commande*
*goggles: *lunettes*
*defunct: *mort*
*limbs: *membres*

# Gaming Sensors

"We've always dreamed of being able to control things with our mind..."

Sensory gaming platforms can open doors to new kinds of game design and experiences.

"There are already a number of things that are possible," said Tan Le, CEO* of neuro-engineering company Emotiv. "We've always dreamed of being able to control things with our mind, and it is possible to have some limited mental commands that have very distinct and very precise results."

[...] Emotiv's headset* can already detect if players are relaxed, frustrated or engaged. They can also reliably detect facial expressions and can differentiate between smiles, grimaces and eyebrow raises. Developers are taking advantage of this technology by giving their players Jedi-like powers, allowing them to use their minds to pick-up and throw objects in the game. This is an exciting development for the sensory gaming community, but Le has bigger ideas for ways the technology can change games. For example, what if the player's facial expressions translated into their avatar's face? And what if games recognized the player's facial expressions and responded accordingly? [...]

Le sees potential for this to be widely implemented in [...] games.

"Say you meet a character in the game and you smile at them—it seems more natural than typing something to them," she said. "Being able to convert facial gestures in the game itself is something that doesn't exist right now but it would create a level of immersion that doesn't really exist today."

Le also sees potential for neuro-gaming technology to play a role in difficulty adjustment. So instead of making players choose a level of difficulty before the game begins, the game can detect if a player is frustrated, observe when they're engaged, when they're bored, and adjust the difficulty. [...]

Developing neuro-gaming technology can be risky, though, because it's difficult to tell if it will catch on* with players. Le said there is the risk of "missing the boat*" by "being too early". But it's a risk that Emotiv and other developers are willing to explore.

"The pragmatic side says: make what the consumer wants," Le said. "But there's a passion inside me that says: let's create something I love and see where it goes."

Tracey Lien, www.polygon.com, May 23rd, 2014.

*CEO Chief Executive Officer
*headset: *casque*
*catch on: *prendre*
*miss the boat: *rater le coche*

1. **Read the article(s) and, in small groups, prepare a report in French about what you have read.**
2 **Search the Internet for information and make a short presentation for the class:**
   - **find other examples of headsets or virtual reality devices;**
   - **describe the latest gaming technologies. You can refer to gaming trade fair sites.**

# EXAM TRAINING *Written*

## COMPREHENSION

## 1 *Call of Duty*, a Historical Reenactment*

Video games allow people to interact with history in a way that is immersive and engaging [...].
Since its release, *Call of Duty* has stood as the example of historical reality as a backdrop* to a video game. [...] Each battle is based on a historical one, attempting to reflect reality as closely as possible. For the creation of *Call of Duty: World at War*, the military advisor at Treyarch, Hank Keirsey, was pivotal* in accurately* representing World War II. Treyarch community manager Josh Olin said "[Keirsey] found veterans who served in these conflicts, and interviewed them for historical accuracy. [...]"
One of the benefits of this type of engagement with history is that people are immersed within it in a different way than books or movies. [...]
[However], historical video games are questioned for inaccuracies and misrepresentation of the past. The game does take liberties with some historical facts: misrepresentation and mistakes in historical facts of World War II are found throughout the game; but this can provide an important educational lesson, perhaps with teachers challenging students to find these inaccuracies.

Katy Meyers, www.playthepast.org, June 14th, 2011.

*reenactment: *reconstitution* – *backdrop: *toile de fond* – *to be pivotal: *jouer un rôle essentiel* – *accurately: *avec précision*

### Questions Doc. 1

1. Choose and write down the right answer. This article deals with:
   – children who play *Call of Duty*;
   – the dangers of playing video games;
   – the representation of the war in *Call of Duty*.
2. Complete each sentence with the right name from the list below.
   Hank Keirsey – Treyarch – Josh Olin – *Call of Duty*
   ... is a video game company.
   ... works as a community manager.
   ... is a combat video game.
   ... gives advice on things related to war.
3. Right or wrong? Justify your answer by quoting from the text.
   – The battles depicted in *Call of Duty* never took place.
   – Ex-soldiers helped to make the game closer to reality.
   – There is no historical mistake in *Call of Duty*.
   – The journalist thinks that *Call of Duty* could be used in schools.
4. "People are immersed within [video games] in a different way than books or movies." What do you think the journalist means? Explain. *(40 words)*

## 2 *Assassin's Creed III*: How Ubisoft Avoided Stereotypes

About one year into the making of *Assassin's Creed III*, the team at Ubisoft Montreal realized they needed help with their protagonist.
Ubisoft had the concept for a half-Mohawk*, half-British assassin named Connor during the game's American Revolution setting. But the last thing they wanted was a collection of clichés and stereotypes, so they began digging into the intricacies* of Mohawk culture to make Connor more authentic. On their own, that turned out to be too difficult. [...]
Ubisoft Montreal hired a Mohawk cultural consultant. [...] The team also worked with the Mohawk community near Montreal and contracted some of its residents to help translate, sing and voice act for the game. [...]
The consultant, Thomas Deer, helped steer Ubisoft Montreal away from* errors. When the team asked about including ceremonial masks in the game, Deer warned them that any visual depiction of the sacred masks is considered offensive. He advised them on which types of clothing and jewelry to use [...].
Native American video game characters are particularly rare. And when they do appear—as with characters like Nightwolf from *Mortal Kombat* or Tal'Set from *Turok: Dinosaur Hunter*—they're often boiled down to generic, spiritual people. Nuances in the culture are lost.
Deer said those generalizations are what bothers* him most, and he's witnessed the effects. Many visitors to the cultural center, for instance, are surprised to see that Mohawks didn't live in teepees, but they in fact lived in longhouses.

Jared Newman, *Time*, September 5th, 2012.

*Mohawk: *tribu indienne* – *intricacy: *complexité* – *steer away from: *éviter* – *bother: *ennuyer*

## Questions Doc. 2

1. This document is:
an extract from a blog • a newspaper article • an extract from a novel • an ad
2. What is the text about? Explain in one sentence.
3. Who/what is: Connor – Ubisoft Montreal – Assassin's Creed III – Thomas Deer?
4. Why did Ubisoft recruit Thomas Deer? Explain and justify with two quotes from the text.
5. Find two examples of Thomas Deer's advice to Ubisoft. Answer by quoting the text.
6. Pick out one sentence in the text for each statement showing that:
– there are not many Native American characters in video games;
– Ubisoft did not only ask Thomas Deer for help;
– Native American characters in video games are often stereotypical.

## Questions Docs 1 and 2

1. Choose the two titles that correspond to both documents 1 and 2:
– Ethic Minorities in the Gaming World;
– Video Games Trying to Portray Reality;
– Stereotypes in Adventure Video Games;
– Exploring Culture and History Through Video Games.
2. What do Treyarch and Ubisoft have in common?

## EXPRESSION

**Choose one of the following subjects.**

**A. Imagine a conversation**

You and your classmates would like to convince your history teacher to use video games in class. You are the class president this year; you go and see your teacher to persuade him/her. Imagine the conversation.

**B. Write a letter**

You have just created your own adventure video game. You are not sure about the historical/cultural representation in it. You know an expert who could help you out. Write him/her a letter and explain why you need his/her advice.

# "Oral"

## COMPREHENSION

**Video Game Controversy**

www.abc.net.au/am/content/2013/s3862992.htm

*(0'00 to 1'35)*

1. Listen to the podcast three times and take down notes.
2. Then write a report on it, in French.

## EXPRESSION

### "Spaces and exchanges"

***What impact do virtual spaces have on our lives?***

• **Prepare your presentation in note form**

**Step 1 Introduce the issue.**

Give facts and figures showing that video games have a growing importance in our lives.

> Cultural Background

**Step 2 Explain what makes video games appealing.**

Hints: virtual reality, escape, fun, a world you can control, etc.

> Cultural Background / Video File / Sound File / Text File 2

**Step 3 Talk about some negative effects of video games.**

Hints: danger of violent games, addiction, etc.

> Text File 2

**Step 4 Talk about the positive effects of video games.**

Hints: fun, teaching tool, simulation, positive effects on the brain, etc.

> Text File 1 / Technology Corner

**Step 5 Conclude.**

Talk about your own feelings about video games. Do you like playing them or not? What genres do you prefer, why, etc. Say if you think video gaming changes people's lives for the better or for the worse.

• **Train yourself**

Follow the steps above and speak for five minutes. If possible, add personal comments. Record yourself and listen to your presentation to improve it.

• **Get ready for a conversation**

Listen to the recording of your presentation and prepare yourself to justify, develop, and exemplify what you have said.

unit 2

# Shop Ethical



To access our audio resources, use our Flashcodes or go to our website: www.ressources.hachette-education.com/boardingpass/1re/units/unit2.html

## "Spaces and exchanges"

***How can our values and behaviour have an impact on global exchanges? The example of shopping.***

# CULTURAL BACKGROUND

# AN UNFAIR WORLD

## 1 What Do You Know About... Consumption Figures?

**Choose the right figures to complete these sentences.**

1. ... of the world's people live in North America and Western Europe and account for ... of private consumption.
2. ... of the world's population lacks food, shelter, housing, water, and access to electricity. They account for only ... of total private consumption.
3. Companies spend more than ... on advertising in the US each year, when ... a year could provide food, clean water, and basic education for the world's poorest.
4. The world's richest countries account for ... of all meat consumption, and ... of vehicle ownership.
5. Each day, an American consumes ... liters of water while a Chinese consumes ... liters.

| | |
|---|---|
| 60% | 12% |
| 20% | 1.3% |
| $50 billion | $200 billion |
| 45% | 87% |
| 86 | 575 |

### Wordbox

Nouns
- factory farm: *ferme industrielle*
- fair trade: *commerce équitable*
- make up: *maquillage*
- purchase: *achat*
- shelter: *abri*
- struggle: *lutte*
- sweatshop: *atelier clandestin*

Verbs
- account for: *être responsable de*
- consume: *consommer*
- lack: *manquer (de)*
- spend: *dépenser*

## 2 The Vote in Your Pocket

1 Track 19

1. **Say what "the vote in your pocket" is:** With your ..., you can ...
2. **Explain what the consequences of our choices are.**
   – When we buy cheap clothes, it's a vote for ...
   – When we buy cars that consume a lot of gas, ...
   – When we buy cheap meat, ...
   – When we shop at supermarkets, ...
3. **List the small purchases that are mentioned.**
4. **Conclude:** when we favour ... produce, we vote for ... ....
   When we favour fair trade, we vote for ....

## 3 Bangladeshi Garment Workers

Around 4 million people are employed in Bangladesh's 4,500 textile factories. The garment industry generates 80% of the country's $24 billion annual exports—making Bangladesh the world's second largest clothing exporter after China. Yet wages remain as low as $37 per month for workers spending 15 hours a day in sweatshop conditions. Building collapses are common, especially in Dhaka, the capital, where construction laws are frequently ignored.

In May 2013, for example, an eight-storey garment factory collapsed in Rana Plaza, on the outskirts of Dhaka. It caused the death of 1,129 people and injured 2,500. It was the world's worst industrial accident since the Bhopal tragedy in 1984, and the worst ever in the garment industry.

The disaster caused outrage in the West and petitions were signed, calling on various companies to change. The authorities said improvements had been made. Yet, one year after the tragedy, secret investigators revealed that firms were still using child labour, beating staff, ignoring fire safety rules and threatening trade union members with murder.

1. Explain what the paradox of Bangladesh is (§1).
2. Say what happened in Rana Plaza, and what the causes of this tragedy probably were (§1 and 3).
3. Say what the consequences of this tragedy were in the West and in developing countries (§3).
4. Does this kind of accident have an impact on your consuming habits? Why or why not?

### Wordbox

**Nouns**
- garment/clothing: *vêtement*
- improvement: *amélioration*
- law: *loi*
- outskirts: *banlieue*
- staff: *personnel*
- trade union: *syndicat*

**Verbs**
- collapse: *s'effondrer*
- injure: *blesser*
- threaten: *menacer*

## 4 What Is in Our Garbage?

**Comment on the diagram.**

**Action!**

### Interview your classmates about their shopping habits

Individually, prepare five questions about your friends' shopping habits. Get into groups to choose the five best questions. Each group interviews the rest of the class and prepares a chart to present their results.

VIDEO FILE

# LIVING WITH COFFEE

## Before you watch

1. Look at the two pictures and explain what "living with coffee" means for these people.
2. Say what you know about coffee production (where, who, how, etc.).
3. What do you expect to see in the document?

## Now watch

B1+ A2+ Use the question sheet in your eWorkbook.

4. Take notes and sum up what you have understood.

## Recap

5. Say what you have learnt about coffee sales in the world and what the consumers' position is.
6. Explain what impact this position has had on the producers' lives.
7. Describe what fair trade is and how it impacts the producers' lives.

## TRAIN YOUR EARS

1. Listen to these transparent words and repeat. 1 Track 20

plant • coffee • industry • poverty • conflict • farms • hectares • export • majority • product • model • volatile • calculated • farmers • equitably • fluctuations • alternative

2. Listen to these words that belong to the same families and repeat. 1 Track 21

consume • consumer • consumerism
equal • equality • inequality
export • exporter • exportation
invest • investor • investment
people • popular • popularity
product • producer • production

### Wordbox

Nouns
- benefit: *profit*
- commodity: *marchandise*
- consumer: *consommateur*
- cost of production: *coût de production*
- needs: *besoins*
- premium: *prime*

Verbs
- ensure: *assurer*
- grow: *(faire) pousser*
- share: *partager*
- trade: *commercialiser*

Adjectives
- cheap: *bon marché*
- fair: *juste*
- global: *mondial*

## React

8. Would you be ready to buy fair-trade coffee even if it's more expensive than non-fair-trade coffee? Why or why not?

**Sum up the document in French.**

## Action! Make diagrams to illustrate the production and sale of coffee

In small groups, search the Internet to find out how coffee is produced and prepared for sale, then make diagrams to illustrate the process.

SOUND FILE

# TRADE AS ONE*—TAKE ACTION!

**Fair trade helps producers in developing countries get better trading conditions: farmers receive a fair price for their products, so they can pay their workers a fair price. They also get money that they can invest in social or environmental projects to improve their businesses and their communities.**

*Trade as One is a Californian fair trade company.

## Before you listen

1. Read the introduction and explain what fair trade is.
2. In pairs, give arguments that Trade as One could use to promote fair trade.

## Now listen

B1+ A2+ Use the question sheet in your eWorkbook. Tracks 25 to 29

3. Listen to the document and take notes.

## Recap

4. Talk about:
   - the feelings of American consumers;
   - the situation in poor countries;
   - the deal Trade as One proposes;
   - the consequences of this deal.

## TRAIN YOUR EARS

1. **Read these words out loud, then listen and repeat.** Track 22
   preoccupied • gratitude • generosity • manipulates • population • intelligent • resources • education • transform • cycles • dependency • system • access • stability • conviction • justice
2. **Listen to the words from the Wordbox and repeat them.** Track 23
3. **Which syllables are stressed? Listen to check and repeat.** Track 24
   disappears • reduced • consumers • olive • freedom • purchases • dependency

## Wordbox

Nouns
- abuse: *mauvais traitements*

Verbs
- enslave: *rendre esclave*
- escape: *se sauver*
- fix: *réparer*
- target: *viser*

Adjectives
- dignified: *digne*
- entitled: *autorisé*
- gifted: *doué*

Adverbs
- ruthlessly: *impitoyablement*
- sustainably: *durablement*

## React

5. Say what the goal of this document is.

**Sum up the document in French.**

Action!

## Encourage your friends to buy fair trade products

In pairs, prepare a podcast to encourage your friends to buy fair-trade certified goods. Then record yourselves.

# TEXT FILE 1

## Before you read

1. Look at the poster on the right. Say what it advertises and what the main argument is.
2. How can you relate the picture to the title of the text?
3. What do you expect the text to be about?

## Now read

B1+ A2+ Use the question sheet in your eWorkbook.

4. Read the text and check your guesses.

## Recap

5. Explain what "Citizen Consumerism" is (l. 7).
6. Explain what "cause-related promotions" are (l. 11-12).
7. List the cause-related promotions quoted and say what each of them defends.
8. Say what shows that this consumerism trend is developing.

## React

9. Would you say you are a citizen consumer? Why or why not?

## Work on Words

1. **Find the equivalents of these words in the text.**
   *achat – commerçant – marque – produits (financiers) – à but non lucratif*
2. **Which of these words are "real friends"? Which are "false friends"? Give the right translation.**
   merchandise (l. 10) – supports (l. 10) – bulbs (l. 25) – organic (l. 25)
3. **Observe: "Products moved from the margins into the mainstream." (l. 22-23) Which French word belongs to the same family as "margin"? Deduce the meaning of "mainstream".**
4. **Explain the construction of the words in groups *a* and *b*.**
   a. increase – increasing – increasingly
   b. purpose – purposeful – purposefully

## Sum up

1. **Listen to our recorded summary.** 1 Track 31
2. **Use the words below to write your own summary of the text.**
   - consumers – purchases – purposeful
   - choose – fair trade – merchandise – cause
   - result – retailers – cause-related
   - buy – products – money – donated – charities – schools – hospitals – jobs – causes
   - eco-friendly – spreading – retailers – boast – products
   - popularity – shopping – conscience

> Grammar La forme *be* + V-*ing* See p. 44

# Consume With a Conscience

Track 30

Jessica King, 37, has been shopping at the Ten Thousand Villages store near Lancaster, PA, since she was in grade school. "This stuff is made by these women in Bangladesh, and it's creating a job for somebody," she says. [...]

These days, more and more of us are waking up to Citizen Consumerism. Shoppers are increasingly finding ways to make more of their purchases purposeful, be it by choosing fair-trade products or merchandise that supports a cause. [...]

Many national retailers run cause-related promotions on an event basis. Shoppers can participate in programs like Macy's Go Red For Women for the prevention of heart disease, or Toys "R" Us' Autism Speaks campaign [...].

"People are really reevaluating what they're spending their money on," says Michele Loeper, marketing manager of retail and brand strategy for Ten Thousand Villages. "There's an increased popularity in shopping with a social conscience." [...]

Over the last decade, the idea of eco-friendly products moved from the margins into the mainstream. Today, many of the biggest consumer products companies boast "green" lines and products, from laundry detergent to compact-fluorescent light bulbs to organic linens. Major chains [...] have been finding ways to link those purchases to causes year-round.

Shoppers who use Target's REDcard credit card can have 1% of their purchase donated to a school in need of funding via the retailer's Take Charge of Education program. And in November, Starbucks launched Create Jobs for USA, a program designed to address the nation's economic crisis.

Starbucks customers can now buy $5 "indivisible" bracelets along with their [caffè] lattes. Proceeds will go to the Opportunity Finance Network, a nonprofit organization that supports local organizations that lend money at low interest rates to small business owners in underserved areas.

Barbara Thau, www.dailyfinance.com, January 16th, 2012.

Action!

## Present a cause-related promotion

Work in pairs. Each group selects a cause-related event (you can find them in the local paper, in advertising flyers your parents receive, or on the Internet) and presents it to the class.

## TEXT FILE 2

# Buy Nothing Today!

Track 32

*The Buy Nothing Day concept began in 1992 when a group of Canadian environmentalists, Adbusters, decided to tackle the problem of over-consumption in America.*

It's not exactly the kind of message Wall Street likes to hear. It's a campaign called Buy Nothing Day, and as its name implies, it's meant to be a call to consumers everywhere—particularly Americans—to reconsider their spending habits and take a moment to consider what rampant consumerism does to the Earth. And the event takes place on what is traditionally one of the busiest shopping days of the year: the day after Thanksgiving. [...]

"I think it's a very bad idea," says Hank Cox, a representative of the business community. "Consumer purchasing power is the one thing that has kept the economy growing."

Cox rejects the notion that consumer spending is harmful and calls the Adbusters' effort a "protest against modernity". [...]

The group's activities are not likely to lead to street fighting, but they may be a little street theater. [...] "We'll have campaigners dressing up as shopping police and handing out 'fines' to unwary shoppers with swollen bags," says Kalle Lasn, a former advertising executive. We also plan to have participants in pig masks lurking at major shopping malls, ready to snort and jeer at those they perceive as over-zealous shoppers." [...]

The campaign has, in the past, taken shots at beloved American icons [...]. For example, the organization's poster ads have featured a fattened Statue of Liberty under a banner that reads "Boycott America". [...] Lasn says that the attention-getting antics are meant to be humorous, even if they intend the underlying message to be taken seriously.

Erik Olsen, *ABC News*, November 28th, 2014.

**One million people in 65 countries participated in the Buy Nothing Day campaign!**

1. Explain what the Buy Nothing Day concept is: details, aim, etc.
2. List the actions taken on Buy Nothing Day and explain their strategies.
3. Say:
   – what you think of the actions they take;
   – what the opponents think of this campaign (develop their arguments).

**Now discuss the links between this text and the text on p. 41.**

4. What do the two texts have in common?
5. Would you say the Buy Nothing Day campaign is part of the Citizen Consumerism trend (Text File 1)? Why or why not?
6. Would you say progress has a positive or negative impact on Western societies? Develop your answers.

> Grammar L'expression de la volonté See p. 44

Action!

### Write an article about a Buy Nothing Day event

Write an article for your school magazine about the demonstration you came across on Buy Nothing Day. Your article should include:
- a short presentation of Buy Nothing Day;
- details about the event: date, activities, etc.

# HOW TO MAKE A PERSUASIVE LEAFLET

**Action!**

**Make a leaflet to promote Buy Nothing Day.**

Work in small groups.

**1. Observe the model.**

a. Have a quick look at the leaflet, then close your book and say what you remember. Then look at it again and explain what made these elements immediately clear and recognizable.

b. Read it more carefully and say what each part is composed of and what kind of information is displayed.

c. Analyze the layout of the leaflet:

– the headings: size, color, length, personal pronouns used...;

– the pictures: what they show, the link between the message and the picture, their impact...;

– the colours: background, heading, text...;

– the texts: length, fonts, type of information, type of sentences...

**2. Prepare your leaflet.**

TICE

a. Find out information about the next Buy Nothing Day campaign: www.buynothingday.co.uk

b. Discuss the information you will provide in your leaflet. Do not try to include everything. Choose one or two of the most striking things about your point.

c. Select visuals to illustrate your points and reinforce your message.

d. Discuss and make a template of your leaflet.

**3. Produce your leaflet.**

a. Write the headings for each part of your leaflet. They must be short, attractive, and clear.

b. Write the different parts of the leaflet. Give a clear idea of what the reader is expected to do to take action.

GRAMMAR

## La forme *be* + V-*ing* (Text File 1 p. 40)

Précis grammatical p. 205

a. These days, more and more of us are waking up to Citizen Consumerism.
b. People are really reevaluating what they're spending their money on.
c. Major chains have been finding ways to link those purchases to causes year-round.
d. More and more people believe in ethical shopping.

### Rappelez-vous

- Dites ce que vous savez de la forme *be* + V-*ing* : forme affirmative ; forme interrogative ; forme négative (donnez des exemples).
- Expliquez la valeur de la forme *be* + V-*ing*.

### Allez plus loin

1. Transformez l'exemple *a* pour faire référence à l'avenir, puis au passé.
2. Expliquez pourquoi la forme *be* + V-*ing* est impossible dans l'exemple *d*.
3. Référez-vous au sens du Text File 1 pour justifier la présence des nombreuses formes du présent *be* + V-*ing*.

### Exercises

1. **Give the *be* + V-*ing* form for each verb.**
   a. They + buy (*present*)
   b. They + consume (*present perfect*)
   c. He + copy (*past*)
   d. We + shop (*in the future*)
2. **Classify the following verbs into two categories.**
   create – love – prefer – shop – go – possess – find – purchase – seem – hear – decide – buy
   a. The ones that can be used in the simple present or *be* + V-*ing* present.
   b. The ones that can be used only in the simple present.
3. **Translate.**
   a. En ce moment, de plus en plus de gens choisissent les magasins qui ont une conscience sociale.
   b. Depuis quelques années, beaucoup de commerçants organisent des actions qui aident les producteurs.

## L'expression de la volonté (Text File 2 p. 42)

Précis grammatical p. 193

a. A group of Canadian environmentalists decided to tackle the problem of over-consumption.
b. They want consumers to reconsider their spending habits.
c. They choose to be humoristic.
d. They would like their message to be taken seriously.

### Observez

1. Relevez les verbes indiquant une volonté.
2. Identifiez les deux constructions que ces verbes entraînent.

### Allez plus loin

1. Expliquez la différence entre les constructions que vous avez identifiées. Énoncés *a* et *c* : ... ; énoncés *b* et *d* : ...
2. Remplacez le complément du verbe *want* par un pronom dans les exemples *b* et *d*.

### Exercises

1. **Replace the word in bold type with a pronoun.**
   a. I'd like **my sister** to join me in this campaign.
   b. Jessica wants **me and Kerry** to sign the petition.
   c. Hank Cox would like **the demonstration** to be cancelled.
2. **Translate.**
   a. Hank Cox veut défendre la consommation.
   b. Les activistes veulent que leur action ait lieu le lendemain de Thanksgiving.
   c. Ils veulent que les manifestants se déguisent en policiers.
   d. Ils leur demandent de porter des masques de porcs.
   e. Ils veulent que tout le monde soit informé.
   f. Lasn veut que son message soit entendu.

## GRAMMAR GAME

### Pictionary

**Everybody thinks of a sentence describing one or several persons doing an action of their choice.**
*Ex.: A woman is buying a box of chocolates.*
Then one student starts drawing the scene she/he has imagined and the others try to guess what is being drawn. The first student who guesses right gets one point. Another student starts drawing his/her scene, and on goes the game.

## Exercises

**1. Who does what? Match the following phrases with the right category of people (*a* or *b*).**
display the goods – go window-shopping – serve – greet – order – help – purchase – return goods – save – spend – fill shopping carts – give the bill – do their shopping
a. Customers…
b. Shopkeepers…

**2. Correct the inappropriate word in each sentence.**
a. Mrs. Ryan earned £200 at the lottery.
b. I want to put the money I have spent in the bank.
c. This good quality shirt is not expensive— it is a good affair.
d. I'd like to find a summer job to win money.
e. I don't have money. I only have my Visa Card.

**3. Find the opposites of these words in the word bank.**
out of stock – poisonous – perfect – spend

**4. Find as many expressions as you can that include the word "shopping".**
Ex.: *shopping mall*

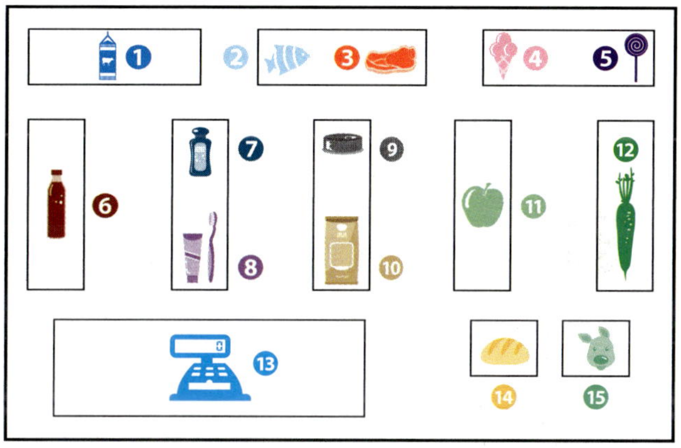


**5. Match the sections below to the number they correspond to in the picture.**
- check out line
- fruit section
- veggies section
- bakery section
- canned goods section
- dairy section
- meat section
- fish section
- frozen food section
- health and beauty section
- dry goods section
- cleaning products section
- beverages
- pet food section
- candy section

## Word bank

### Nouns
- aisle: *allée*
- bargain: *affaire*
- bill (UK), check (US): *note, facture*
- cash: *argent liquide (en)*
- till (UK), checkout (US): *caisse*
- consumer: *consommateur*
- convenience store: *petit magasin*
- customer: *client*
- discount: *réduction*
- grocery: *épicerie*
- item: *article*
- layout: *disposition*
- money: *argent (devise)*
- produce/product: *produit frais/ produit manufacturé*
- retailer: *commerçant*
- sales: *soldes*
- shelf: *étagère*
- shipping cost: *frais de port*
- shop assistant: *vendeur, vendeuse*
- shopping cart: *Caddie*
- shopping mall: *centre commercial*

### Verbs
- display: *exposer*
- earn money: *gagner de l'argent (salaire)*
- go shopping: *faire les courses*
- greet: *saluer*
- order: *commander*
- purchase: *acheter*
- return: *rapporter*
- save: *économiser*
- spend: *dépenser*
- win: *gagner (au jeu)*

### Adjectives
- available: *disponible*
- cheap, inexpensive: *bon marché*
- edible: *comestible*
- expensive, costly: *cher*

# SKILLS TRAINING

## Comprendre les mots

*Jean Tinner is an agile dancer but her partner is quite clumsy.*

### Les mots transparents

La cour d'Angleterre a parlé français pendant des siècles, après l'invasion de Guillaume le Conquérant en 1066. Il en est resté de nombreuses traces dans la langue anglaise.

Certains mots sont totalement transparents ; d'autres appartiennent à la même famille que leur équivalent français. Même s'il y a quelques différences, ou s'il y a un glissement de sens, aidez-vous de ces ressemblances.

**1 Donnez un ou des mot(s) français qui ressemble(nt) au mot en gras ; puis traduisez ce mot.**

a. *Some apps **promote** ethical purchases.*
b. *The Body Shop is **perceived** as a socially responsible company.*
c. *"The Body Shop Against Animal Testing" campaign leads to a UK-wide **ban** on animal testing.*
d. *What is the story behind The Body Shop and what **fueled** worldwide popularity?*

**2 Traduisez ce paragraphe.**

*In looking at the history and success of The Body Shop, it becomes clear that ethical campaigns can inspire loyalty from people who wish to make a difference in the world.*

### La formation des mots

Vous pouvez parfois repérer la racine d'un mot ainsi que ses préfixes ou suffixes – voire repérer deux mots accolés. Souvenez-vous que, dans un nom composé, le mot principal est toujours placé à la fin.

**3 Observez ces mots et traduisez.**

*powerful – partnership – outnumber – quick-thinking – fundraising – phone card – warship*

**4 Traduisez les mots en gras.**

a. *The store is in the **oustskirts** of London.*
b. *These problems are becoming **unmanageable**.*
c. *This is the **underlying** message.*

### Le contexte

On trouve dans le contexte des indices qui permettent de deviner le sens des mots. Par exemple, vous trouverez souvent des synonymes, des antonymes ou des mots qui se font écho.
Ex.: *Jean Tinner is an agile dancer but her partner is quite **clumsy**.* La liaison *but* indique que le mot *clumsy* est en contradiction avec le mot « agile » → maladroit.

**5 Identifiez les mots qui vous permettent de deviner la signification des mots en gras.**

a. *This is a **touchy** subject, a difficult one for an American to answer.*
b. *Instead of **squandering** their earnings on silly things, they are saving to buy a house.*
c. *Today's supermarket is like a large, hermetically **sealed** box.*
d. *I did not understand all of the details of the presentation but I did get the **gist** of it.*

### La situation

Chaque fois que cela est possible, efforcez-vous de visualiser la situation pour deviner la signification des mots.

**6 Devinez le sens des mots en gras grâce aux indices que nous vous indiquons – et que, d'ordinaire, vous devez rechercher vous-même.**

a. *I have lots of T-shirts. There are **stacks** of them in my closet.* (Comment rangez-vous vos T-shirt?)
b. *We plan to have participants in pig masks ready to **snort** at shoppers.* (Quel bruit fait un porc?)
c. *We'll have campaigners dressing up as shopping police and handing out **fines** to shoppers with **swollen** bags.* (Que donne la police à un contrevenant ? Comment est le sac de quelqu'un qui a fait des achats ?)
d. *They say that the attention-getting **antics** are meant to be humorous, even if the underlying message is serious.* (Trouvez un mot qui va avec *humorous* et qui s'oppose à *serious*.)
e. *Goods go in one end and are **dispatched** at the other.* (On parle d'une chaîne de distribution. *Dispatched* fait écho à *go in*. Or, on est à l'autre bout de la chaîne.)

# Your Project

## Organize an awareness campaign

Organize an awareness campaign to encourage your schoolmates to become conscious citizens and promote ethical consumerism. You will make leaflets and flyers that will be distributed in your school.

- **Divide the class into groups.**

### Step 1

Divide the class into groups. Each group chooses their topics.
- Fair trade.
- Labor rights.
- Ecologically-friendly products.
- Buy Nothing Day.
- An ethical shopping guide for a supermarket in your area.
- The promotion of a cause-related campaign for a brand or a shop.
- An ad for an ethical retailer or an ethical product.

### Step 2

Each group prepares a presentation of their project: the topic they have chosen, their reasons, what they want to communicate, the type of document they are going to make (a leaflet, a poster, a podcast…).
Action! p. 39

### Step 3

Each group makes an oral presentation of the project Action! p. 41: the class gives advice to improve it and decides on the event: advertising, duration, place, how the leaflets or posters will be printed and distributed; how the podcasts will be broadcast, etc.

### Step 4

The groups prepare their documents. They find information and pictures to illustrate their points, decide on the headings, and write the different paragraphs. Writing WORKSHOP p. 43

TICE

Useful help can be found on the following websites:
- www.fairtrade.org.uk
- www.buynothingday.co.uk
- www.ethical.org.au
- theartofsimple.net/shopping
- www.ethicaltrade.org

*Organize the event in your school.*
*(Don't forget to ask for the headteacher's authorization before you do so!)*

TECHNOLOGY CORNER

# Success in Store for Retailers Embracing Technology

Technology is inherent in online retail. Online merchants rely on tech and data to make sales— and keep selling. But many traditional retailers have also found ways to use technology so as to improve the in-store customer experience and boost business.

One important way is by adopting technology that helps make shopping more personalized. Apps enable customers to scan barcodes with their smartphones, build shopping lists, find stores nearby, find the merchandise they're looking for within a store, and be greeted by notifications when they approach a store that feature coupons*.

Another advancement that aids in personalization, but also in security, is chip-and-PIN* technology for credit cards. In addition to standard customer data, the chips can store information for customer loyalty* and rewards programs.

Rob Roache, *thinkgig.com*, June 10th, 2014.

*coupons: *offres commerciales*
*chip: *puce*
*PIN (Personal Identification Number): *code*
*loyalty: *fidélité*

# Chip and PIN Cards in the US

Until October 2014, Americans traveling in Europe or Canada could not use their credit cards at ATMs because their cards used magnetic stripes instead of the chip and PIN technology that had been the standard in Canada and Europe for many years. Restaurants have had to adopt the portable card readers used in Canada and Europe so patrons can pay their bill at the table rather than handing over their credit cards. Chip and PIN cards reduce the risk of fraud.

Susan Johnston, usnews.com, October 28th, 2014.

# Apps Promote Ethical Purchases

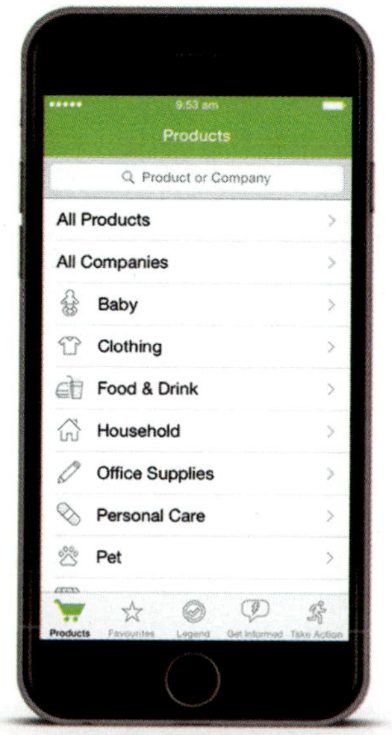


The most popular digital guide to ethical shopping in Australia, **Shop Ethical**! has been designed to provide you with the easiest way to make informed purchasing decisions in the supermarket and beyond.

Download for Android

Available on the iPhone App Store

Some feel that information technology could be a useful ally in saving the world through shopping. The future of ethical consumption lies in portable devices that can scan the items we are buying, inform us of all the benefits of buying this particular product—perhaps even show us the workers or farmers who will benefit from our decision.

Such apps already exist: you can scan a product's bar code and access health, environmental, and social performance ratings for a large variety of products.

What real impact will that extra information have on our shopping habits?

Evgeny Morozov, www.slate.com, September 30th, 2013.

## The Shop of the Future

As it stands, today's supermarket is just a large, hermetically-sealed box. Goods go in one end and are dispatched at the other. [...]

As Internet retail expands, the "box" is losing its value. In fact, it makes more sense to dedicate the space to stock for home deliveries, with fresh goods going direct to the consumer from the supplier, thus cutting down on energy and transportation costs. A number of innovative ideas are worth considering.

- The roof could play host to a rainwater-fed garden, the fruits of which are sold in the marketplace.
- We could witness a rise in urban agriculture, with vertical, climate-controlled farms taking over old high-rise car parks.
- Digital points of sale are likely to become a more common sight.
- Cameras could be used to monitor customer response to shelving and displays*, with robotics reorganizing the store according to this interaction.
- New materials could be introduced e.g. NASA-invented nanogel as a glass replacement (lets in light, but not heat in).

Of course, the foods we consume will also change over time, with bio-engineering and digital printing leading to new types of food and food tastes.

www.thevalueengineers.com, August 14th, 2012.

* shelving and displays: *agencement des marchandises*

1. Read the article(s) and, in small groups, prepare a report in French about what you read.
2. Search the Internet for information and make a short presentation for the class:
   - find other examples of in-store technologies;
   - find other retail trends that are likely to appear in the forthcoming years.

## COMPREHENSION

### The Story of My T-Shirt

On a cold day in February 1999, I watched a crowd of about 100 students gather on the Georgetown University campus. The students were passionate and, as speakers took the microphone, they cheered every sentence. They had a moral certitude, [...] and saw with perfect clarity the good and evil. Corporations, globalization, the International Monetary Fund (IMF), and the World Trade Organization (WTO) were the bad guys, ruthlessly crushing the dignity of workers around the world. [...]

I watched a young woman seize the microphone. "Who made your T-shirt?" she asked the crowd. "Was it a child in Vietnam, chained to a sewing machine without food or water? Or a young girl from India earning 18 cents per hour and allowed to visit the bathroom only twice per day? Did you know that she lives 12 to a room? That she shares her bed and has only gruel to eat? That she is forced to work 90 hours each week, without overtime? Did you know that she has no right to speak out, no right to unionize*? That she lives not only in poverty, but also in filth and sickness, all in the name of Nike's profits?"

I did not know all this. And I wondered about the young woman at the microphone. How did she know?

During the next several years, I travelled the world to investigate. I not only found out who made my T-shirt, but I also followed its life over thousands of miles [...].

[Economists in general argue that international market competition creates wealth that will lift all boats*. Meanwhile critics worry about the effects of hard market forces, especially upon workers.] Now, what my T-shirt's life suggests is that both globalizers and critics may be right. Obviously, many once-poor countries, like Taiwan, have become rich due to globalization, and many [...] countries, like China or India, are nowhere near as poor as they once were. But the poorest countries in the world, [...] largely in Africa, do not yet benefit from globalization [...]; and even in rapidly growing countries such as China, many are left behind*. My T-shirt's life is a story of the wealth-enhancing* possibilities of globalization in some settings, but a "can't win" trap* in others.

Pietra Rivoli, *The Travels of a T-Shirt in the Global Economy*,
John Wiley & Sons Inc, 2005.

*unionize: *se syndiquer*
*will lift all boats: *sera bon pour tout le monde*
*left behind: *oubliés*
*wealth-enhancing: *enrichissant*
*trap: *piège*

## Questions

1. Explain what the February 1999 demonstration was about.
2. How did the crowd react?
3. What are the two countries given as examples by the young woman?
4. Quote details about the working conditions in these countries.
5. What was the young woman's aim?
6. How does the journalist feel when she hears the woman's words? Choose the right adjective(s) and justify by quoting the text:
   - uninterested;
   - curious;
   - indifferent;
   - surprised.
7. List the arguments in favor of globalization and the arguments against it.
8. Who does Pietra Rivoli side with? Pick out the examples she gives to support her point of view.

## EXPRESSION

**A. Are you interested in the story of the clothes you buy? Why or why not?**

**B. Explain the last sentence of the text and give examples to illustrate this point:** "My T-shirt's life is a story of the wealth-enhancing possibilities of globalization in some setting, but a "can't win" trap in others".

# "Oral"

## COMPREHENSION

**Tracking Your Every Move**

www.youtube.com/watch?v=tJqKneNi6kQ

*(0:00 to 1:30)*

1. Watch the video three times and take down notes.
2. Then write a report on it, in French.

## EXPRESSION

### "Spaces and exchanges"

***How can our values and behaviour have an impact on global exchanges? The example of shopping.***

- Prepare your oral presentation in note form

Step 1 **Introduce the topic.**

Explain that trading and consuming are essential in global economic exchanges.
Briefly describe Western consumers' habits today and say what technological or social innovations have led to these changes.

Step 2 **Describe the negative impact of our shopping habits.**

Give examples and explain to what extent our shopping habits are responsible for the situation: on the environment; on poor countries; on our privacy.

> Video File / Cultural Background / Text File 1 / Technology Corner

Step 3 **Show there is a growing awareness of the situation and how people may react.**

Give examples of different actions that are taken to reduce the negative impact of consumerism. Talk about fair trade; ethical shopping; cause-related programs; Buy Nothing Day.

> Video File / Sound File / Text File 1 / Text File 2 / Technology Corner

Step 4 **Talk about the influence of new technologies.**

Show that new technologies will probably go on changing our shopping habits, with positive and negative consequences on: information; ethical buying; shopping experience.

> Technology Corner

Step 5 **Conclude.**

Say if you personally feel you are a "citizen consumer". Give your opinion about the various initiatives you have studied in this unit.

- Train yourself

Follow the steps above and speak for five minutes.
If possible, add personal comments. Record yourself and listen to your presentation to improve it.

- Get ready for a conversation

Listen to the recording of your presentation and prepare yourself to justify, develop and exemplify what you have said.

unit 3

# Food Matters



To access our audio resources, use our Flashcodes or go to our website: www.ressources.hachette-education.com/boardingpass/1re/units/unit3.html

## "The idea of progress"

***Does change always mean progress?***
***The example of eating habits.***

Ralph Goings,
*Blue Tile With Water.*

# CULTURAL BACKGROUND

# EATING HABITS

## 1 What Do You Know About ... Nutrition Basics?

**Wordbox**

Nouns
- dairy product: *produit laitier*
- food: *nourriture, aliment*
- serving: *part*

Adverb
- sparingly: *avec modération*

1. Comment on the diagram above. Which foods do you like best? Which do you like least?
2. Give examples of products that can go into each of the five food groups: vegetables, fruits, grains, dairy products, and protein products.
3. Give examples of foods that are rich in: vitamins; protein; calcium; calories.

## 2 The British at Table

Track 33

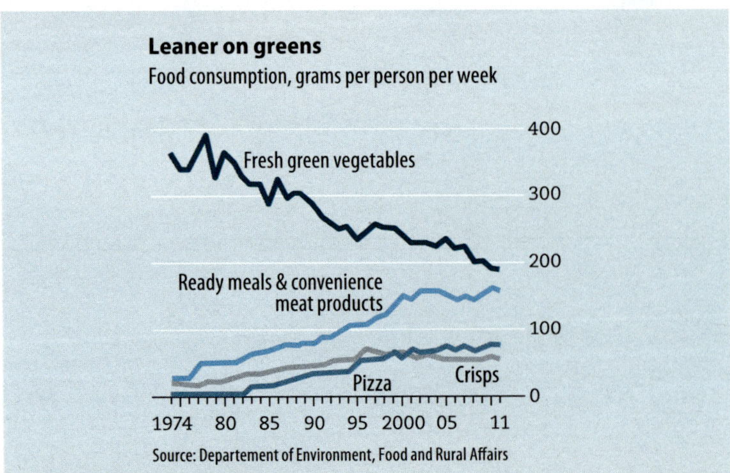


1. What is the source of information in this podcast?
2. Give the difference mentioned between French people and English people.
3. Explain what a TV dinner is.
4. Find information about English people's habits: going out; cooking; Sunday lunch.
5. Compare people's eating habits fifty years ago and now.

## 3 The Fast-Food Industry

Ray Kroc

The fast-food industry began in 1954 when Ray Kroc, an ambitious entrepreneur, bought a small chain of hot dog and hamburger restaurants run by the McDonald brothers in California. These little restaurants were inexpensive, clean, and simple, and offered a limited choice of foods. There were no waitresses and no china. Ray Kroc applied automation to food, just as Henry Ford had done to car manufacture.

Fast food quickly spread to every corner of America – with chains coming up, like KFC or Burger King. Nowadays, a quarter of the population visits a fast-food restaurant each day.

American fast-food restaurant chains have become a symbol of globalization. McDonald's now has over 30,000 restaurants in 121 countries, and serves about 46 million people a day; KFC has 11,000 restaurants worldwide.

1. Who started the fast-food industry? Where? What did he appreciate?
2. Why is Henry Ford quoted in this text?
3. Explain the sentence on l. 14-15.
4. Find the equivalents for these words: *propre, vaisselle* (§1) ; *s'étendre* (§2) ; *dans le monde entier* (§3).

## 4 New Food Trends

### New food

### Organic food

Organic food is becoming popular but it is very expensive. Restaurant chains like Panera Bread are selling healthy food but, with their 200 outlets, they cannot compete with the fast-food giants.

### Vegetarian and vegan diet

Neither vegetarians or vegans eat meat. Vegans avoid all animal products, including eggs and dairy. Vegetarians consume dairy products and eggs.

### Raw food

Disciples eat nuts, seeds, fruits, and vegetables, but nothing that has been cooked. Actress Demi Moore contributed to making this diet famous.

### Entomophagy

Eating insects is the latest food fad.

1. Find the equivalents for these words: *bio, magasin, sain, franchise* (§1) ; *régime, éviter, produits laitiers* (§2) ; *cru, noix, graines* (§3) ; *mode* (§4).
2. Which food trend are you prepared or not prepared to embrace?

**Action!**

### Interview your classmates

Individually, prepare five questions to find out about your friends' eating habits. Get into small groups and choose the best questions. Each group interviews the rest of the class and prepares a short report to present their results.

VIDEO FILE

# JAMIE OLIVER'S FOOD REVOLUTION

## TRAIN YOUR EARS

**1.** Listen to the following words and repeat until you are ready to recognize them. Track 34

potato • extreme • breast • squeeze • stabilizer • flavoring • whack • pan • experiment • expensive

**2.** Listen to these pairs of words and repeat them. Track 35

processed food • chicken breast • leftover bits • thrown away • connective tissues • bone marrow • chicken skin

## Before you watch

1. Talk about the food the child is eating: what; what it is made of; the possible consequences on health, etc.
2. Talk about the picture on the left. Guess what Jamie Oliver's "food revolution" could be.

## Now watch

B1+

A2+ Use the question sheet in your eWorkbook.

3. Take notes and sum up what you have understood.

## Recap

4. Explain what observation Jamie Oliver made in the elementary school and how he reacted.
5. Say what experiment he decided to do. Say why and how he proceeded.

## React

6. Describe the impact this experiment had on the children.
7. What is the conclusion of the video?
8. Do you often eat processed food? What is your reaction to Jamie Oliver's experiment?

**Sum up the document in French.**

### Wordbox

Nouns
- chicken breast: *blanc de poulet*
- crumbs: *miettes*
- flavouring: *arôme*
- leftovers: *les restes*
- processed food: *nourriture industrielle*
- rib: *côte*
- stabilizer: *stabilisateur*

Verbs
- mix: *mélanger*
- pour: *verser*
- squeeze: *écraser*

### Action! Convince your friends

Make a podcast to stop your friends from eating chicken nuggets (or another food of your choice).

SOUND FILE

# JUNK FOOD BLACK MARKET

**California's governor, Arnold Schwarzenegger, signed a bill to limit soda machines in schools.**

## TRAIN YOUR EARS

1. Read these transparent words. Then listen to check and repeat. (1 Track 36)
obesity • plan • governor • preference • machine • variety • transactions • campus
2. Match the words with their transcriptions and read them out loud. Then listen to check your pronunciation. (1 Track 37)
healthier • market • huge • unbelievable • seniors • diet • student • boxes
[ʌnbɪ'li:vəbl̩] • ['bɒksɪz] • ['helθɪə] • ['mɑ:kɪt] • ['daɪət] • ['stju:dnt] • [hju:dʒ] • ['si:nɪəz]
3. Pronounce the words below. Then listen and check pronunciation of the -s ending. (1 Track 38)
works • boxes • chips • supplies • transactions • teachers • backs • gates • orders • friends

## Before you listen

1. Look at the boys in the photo. Say what they are doing and what the consequences on their health might be.
2. Read the introduction and explain what Arnold Schwarzenegger did. Make guesses about his reasons.

## Now listen

B1+

A2+ Use the question sheet in your eWorkbook.

3. Listen to the document and take notes. (1 Tracks 39 to 42)

## Recap

4. Talk about:
   – the aim of the bill Schwarzenegger signed;
   – the consequences of this bill in Englewood High School, Los Angeles;
   – the black market (who? how? where?...).

## React

5. Say what you think of the bill Schwarzenegger passed.

**Sum up the document in French.**

## Action!

### Discuss: for or against soda machines in schools?

The school board considers installing soda machines in the school.
– Individually prepare three arguments for and three arguments against this project.
– Work in groups and discuss.
– One student from each group presents the results of the discussion to the class.

# TEXT FILE 1

## Before you read

1. Talk about the pictures on this page and your experience of fast-food restaurants.
2. Analyse the poster on the right-hand page and make guesses about the movie it advertises.
3. What do you expect the text to be about?

## Now read

B1+ | A2+ Use the question sheet in your eWorkbook.

4. Read the text and check your guesses.

## Recap

5. a. Explain in your own words why obesity is said to be at "epidemic" proportions in the US. (Introduction)
   b. Explain what Morgan Spurlock's "strange experiment" was (purpose, rules, etc.) (l. 8 to 15).
   c. Pick out the figures and describe Spurlock's evolution (weight, symptoms, etc.) (l. 16 to 28).

## React

6. Now answer the question: "Is fast food really that bad for you?" (l. 8).
7. Why do you think Spurlock chose McDonald's for his experiment?
8. What do you think of Spurlock's idea?
9. After learning about this experiment, have your feelings towards fast food changed?

## Work on Words

1. **Pick out the words that go with "weight".** Find extra examples.
2. **Pick out five compound nouns.** Translate them into French.
   > Grammar See p. 62
3. **Observe these words:** discomfort – unhealthy – inexpensive. Identify and give the meaning of the prefixes. Give other words that have similar constructions.
4. **Observe the word "breathlessness":** breath (*souffle*); -less (*suffixe privatif*); -ness (*suffixe qui transforme un adjectif en nom*). Translate it into French.

> Grammar **Le présent et le prétérit** See p. 62

## Sum up

1. **Listen to our recorded summary.** Track 44
2. **Use the words below to write your own summary of the text.**
   - overweight
   - health experts
   - film-maker Morgan Spurlock – experiment
   - McDonald's – 30 days
   - gained weight – health problems
   - toxic
   - 14 months – lose – 30 days

# A Strange Experiment

Track 43

*In the United States, obesity is at epidemic proportions. More than two-thirds of adult Americans are overweight and 37% of American children are carrying too much fat. There has been a meteoric rise in diabetes, heart disease, stroke, high blood pressure, etc. Health experts believe one of the major causes of this epidemic is our consumption of fast food.*

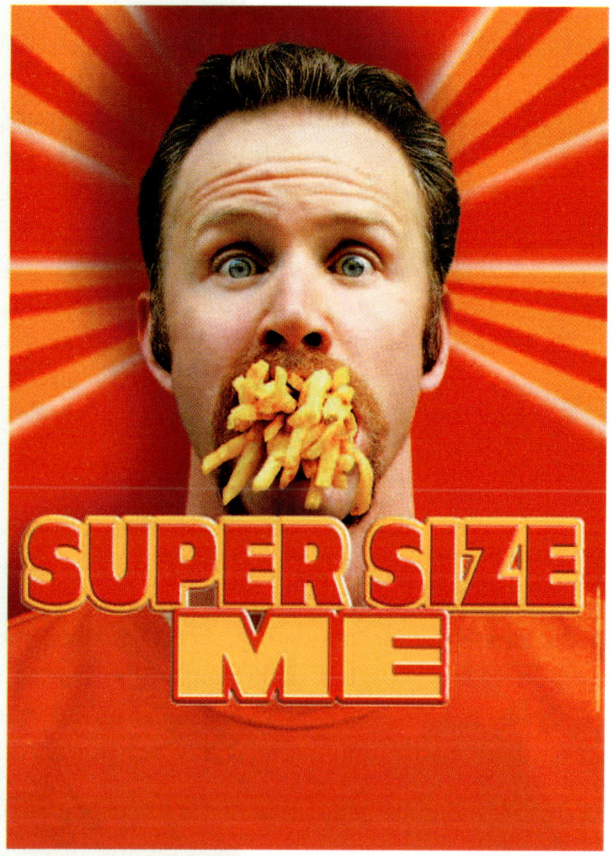


"Is fast food really that bad for you?"

To find out, [filmmaker Morgan Spurlock] decided to eat only McDonald's food for 30 days. [Finding McDonald's restaurants was no problem—there are 83 of them in Manhattan.] Spurlock made himself follow rules during his 30-day experiment. He had to eat three McDonald's meals a day—breakfast, lunch, and dinner. He could only eat what they sold over the restaurant's counter. [...]

Within the first week of his experiment, Spurlock gained 5% of his body weight. At day 9, he began having strange symptoms like chest pressure and discomfort and he felt depressed. He noticed that, even though he was taking in about 5,000 calories per day, he felt hungry soon after eating.

In 12 days, he gained 17 pounds*. [...]

By the third week, the filmmaker began to experience heart palpitations, chest pain, and breathlessness. [...]

Before his 30 days were up, Spurlock was a sick man. At 210 pounds, he was overweight (he had gained a total of 24.5 pounds in 30 days), had high cholesterol, high blood glucose, and high blood pressure. He had serious liver damage. His fat level had soared. He was often moody and exhausted.

Fast food may be inexpensive and convenient. It may taste good and even look good. Spurlock proved that it's downright toxic to the body.

*"Super Size Me" – A film by Morgan Spurlock,* www.realfoodtraveler.com.

*Nota bene: It took Spurlock 14 months to lose the weight he had gained in just 30 days.*

*1 pound = 453.5 grams

Action!

## Draw a timeline

Draw a timeline to show the impact of Spurlock's experiment on his health. Add details and make a short oral presentation.

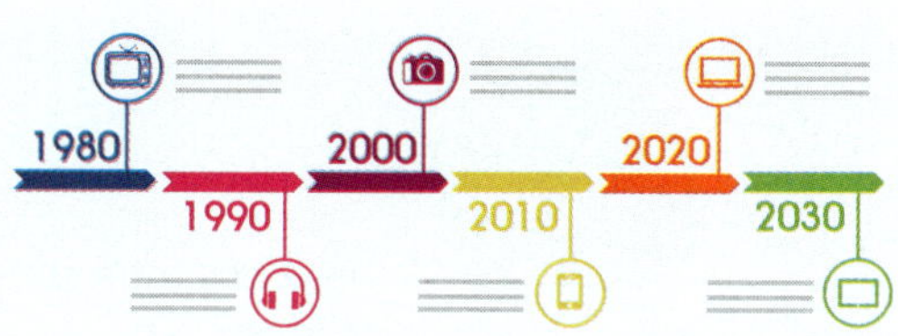

# Food Ads Target Children

Track 45

Each year, the world's food and beverage companies spend billions on marketing and advertising their products to children and teenagers. The overwhelming majority of these products are high in calories, added sugar, saturated fat and sodium—fast food, fizzy drinks, sweets, and chocolate to name just a few. Ask a child to recall a food advert and chances are that it won't be one for apples or broccoli. [...]

According to [a 2013 report by Yale University experts], children under six see three adverts for fast foods every day, while 12-17-year-olds see five adverts a day. [...]

Report author Jennifer Harris is concerned. "A lot of companies have switched their marketing target to the 12-14 age group," she says. "This is a really vulnerable time for kids; they are seeing more media and making more decisions on their own [...]."

In the UK, regulation exists to prevent adverts for unhealthy foods from being broadcast during or around programmes specifically made for children.

[British advertisers are unhappy about ads prohibition. One of them, Ian Twinn, says:] "Encouraging people to change their lifestyle rather than slapping bans on ads is what will make a difference. There are plenty of good examples of big brands changing their messages to support the message for a healthier lifestyle. Coca-Cola, for instance, only advertises its low calorie or sugar-free products."

Yet, a University of California study suggests that if governments take action to control food industries, they can help prevent obesity and its serious health consequences, including cardiovascular diseases and diabetes. This calls for more robust, government-led regulation of the industry, rather than voluntary self-regulation.

www.theguardian.com, February 25th, 2014.

1. Considering the picture and the title, say what you expect to read.
2. Read the text and classify your ideas. Which paragraphs apply to the UK and which apply to the US?
3. Explain what you understand about:
   - government regulations (where? what? details);
   - recommendation (from whom? what? why?);
   - composition of fast-food products;
   - favorite target (who? why?).

**Now discuss the links between this text and the text on p. 59.**

4. Compare or contrast the topics; the problem addressed; the means of action.
5. What are the conclusions they both come to?

Grammar Les noms composés See p. 62

Action!

## Comment on a food ad for children

Think of a food ad that targets children. Describe it and say how it attracts children.

# HOW TO MAKE AN EFFECTIVE POSTER

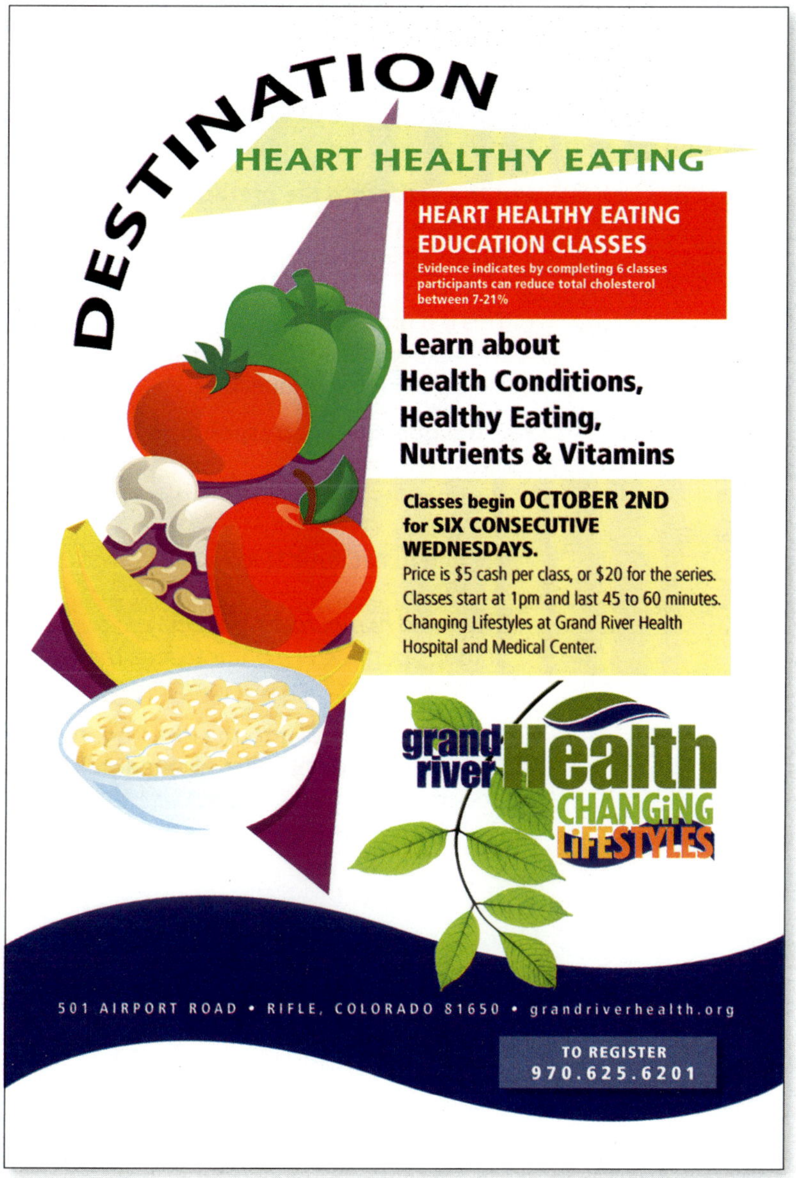


**Action!**

**Your class has decided to organize a healthy eating in your school. Make a poster to advertise it.**

Work in small groups.

1. **Observe the model.**
   a. Identify the parts of the poster:
   – the title and headings;
   – information, documentation and illustration;
   – the slogan;
   – the conclusion;
   – the references.
   b. Analyze the use of colors, space, and fonts:
   – the title bar;
   – the different colors and their impact;
   – the background;
   – the visuals;
   – the layout.

2. **Prepare your own poster.**
   a. Discuss the type of information you want to display.
   b. Write slogans, titles, and headings.
   c. Decide on the layout of your poster. Making a draft (*brouillon*) would be a good idea.
   d. Find pictures and visuals to illustrate your points.

3. **Make your poster.**
   a. Write short paragraphs corresponding to the different points you want to deal with.
   b. Create your poster.

# LANGUAGE WORKSHOP

GRAMMAR

## Présent et prétérit (Text File 1 p. 58)

Précis grammatical pp. 205, 206 et 207

a. Fast food tastes good.
b. Health experts believe our consumption of fast food is bad.
c. In 2004, Morgan Spurlock decided to eat only McDonald's food for 30 days.
d. Spurlock was often exhausted.
e. It took him 14 months to lose his extra weight.
f. Why did he do this experiment?

### Rappelez-vous

- On emploie le présent simple pour parler… ; le prétérit simple pour parler … .
- Pour mettre au prétérit un verbe régulier : … ; irrégulier : … ; *be* : … .
- Pour mettre un verbe au prétérit ou au présent à la forme interrogative … / à la forme négative … .
- Pour construire les formes négatives et interrogatives, on utilise l'auxiliaire … au présent, et … au prétérit.

### Allez plus loin

1. Identifiez le temps des verbes dans chaque exemple. Justifiez votre réponse.
2. Dites quel détail, dans l'exemple *c*, impose l'emploi du prétérit.
3. Quels exemples font partie d'un récit ? d'une présentation du présent ?

### Exercises

1. **Among these phrases, which can go with a present tense, which can go with a past tense, which can go with both?**
currently • last year • every day • right now • presently • in the 21st Century • in the 19th Century • two years ago • this month • regularly • nowadays

2. **Put the verbs into the preterit.**
a. The fast-food industry begins in California.
b. There are many fast-food restaurants on this street.
c. This is a problem.
d. This experiment exhausts Spurlock.
e. He feels hungry after eating.

3. **Ask the questions corresponding to the words in italics.**
a. Restaurants like Panera Bread sell *healthy food.*
→ What … ?
b. He had to eat *three MacDonald's meals a day.*
→ What … ?
c. They sold *hamburgers*. → What … ?
d. It took Spurlock *14 months* to lose the weight he had gained. → How long … ?

4. **Put these sentences into the interrogative form.**
a. Fast-food restaurants offer a limited choice of foods.
b. Too much fat makes you sick.
c. Doctors call for regulation of the industry.

## Noms composés (Text File 2 p. 60)

Précis grammatical p. 212

a. Some famous Yale University experts carried out a survey.
b. Health experts believe fast-food consumption is bad for us.

### Rappelez-vous

On peut relier deux ou plusieurs noms en les juxtaposant.
On place en dernier … .

### Allez plus loin

1. Dans les noms composés soulignés, quel est le nom principal ?
2. Traduisez ces noms composés en français. Que remarquez-vous ?
3. Repérez l'adjectif dans l'exemple *a.* Sur quel nom porte-t-il ?

### Exercise

**Translate into English.**
a. Une maladie de cœur.
b. L'interdiction des pubs.
c. Des programmes pour enfants.
d. Des produits basses calories.
e. Une expérience de 30 jours.
f. Un rapport de 2013.
g. Un style de vie étrange.
h. Des conséquences sérieuses sur la santé.

## GRAMMAR GAME

### Make a crazy story

**Work in groups of five or six, and sit in circles.**
Each student writes this sentence on a sheet of paper:

"Yesterday, I went to the restaurant."

Then he/she adds a sentence to continue the story. He/she then passes his/her paper to the person on his/her left and adds a sentence to the paper he/she has received, then passes it on to the person on his/her left. On goes the game until each student gets his/her own story back and discovers what it has become!

## Exercises

**1. Match the adjectives from the list with the definitions.**

| | |
|---|---|
| 1. overweight | a. too heavy, too fat |
| 2. healthy | b. very thin |
| 3. fattening | c. that you cannot stop taking once you have started |
| 4. addictive | d. good for your body |
| 5. skinny | e. likely to make you fat |

**2. Copy the mind map below on a sheet of paper and complete it with as many phrases from the word bank on this page as possible. Try to give two more words for each category.**

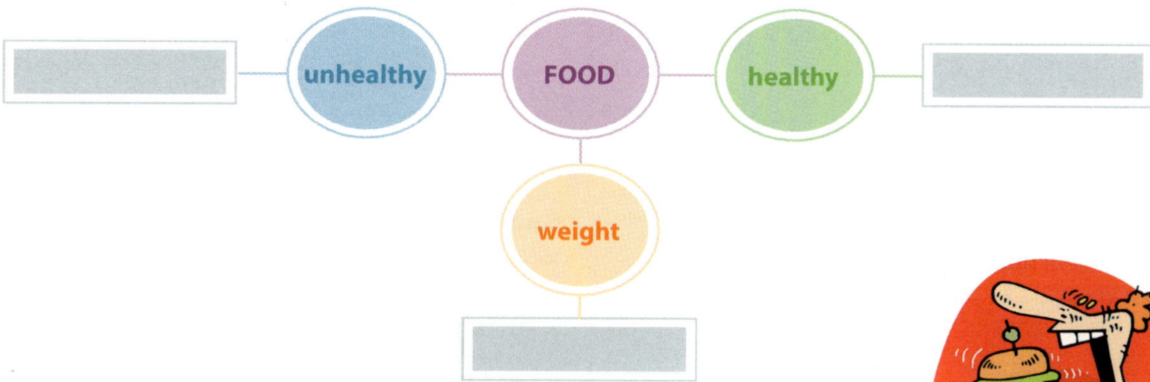

**3. Fill in the blanks with phrases from the word bank.**

Uncle Ted had a … problem. The doctor told him he was … . Indeed, he was always … and he used to love eating … food, like chips or hamburgers and he certainly didn't eat enough … . We told him to be careful, to eat … food and to … . We helped him to …: he lost 15 kilos in two months!

**4. Make short sentences to illustrate the meaning of the words below.**

overweight • balanced • exercise • slim down • candies • disease • hungry

## Word bank

### Nouns

- candies/sweets: *bonbons*
- canteen/cafeteria: *cantine*
- chips (US)/crisps (UK): *chips*
- disease: *maladie*
- dish: *plat*
- figure: *silhouette*
- fruit/a piece of fruit: *fruit*
- health: *santé*
- junk food: *malbouffe*
- meal: *repas*
- vegetable: *légume*
- weight: *poids*

### Verbs

- be hungry: *avoir faim*
- do sport/exercise: *faire du sport*
- eat out: *manger dehors*
- fast: *jeûner*
- go on a diet: *faire un régime*
- have breakfast/lunch: *prendre son (petit) déjeuner*
- put on/gain weight: *prendre du poids*
- slim down/lose weight: *perdre du poids*
- starve: *mourir de faim*

### Adjectives

- addictive: *qui crée une dépendence*
- balanced: *équilibré*
- fat: *gras/gros*
- fattening: *qui fait grossir*
- frozen: *surgelé*
- greasy/fatty (food): *gras (nourriture)*
- (un)healthy: *(mal)sain*
- low fat: *allégé*
- obese: *obèse*
- organic: *bio*
- overweight: *en surpoids*
- skinny (person): *maigre (personne)*

# SKILLS TRAINING

# COMMENTER UN DIAGRAMME

**1** **Identifiez les principaux types de diagrammes.**

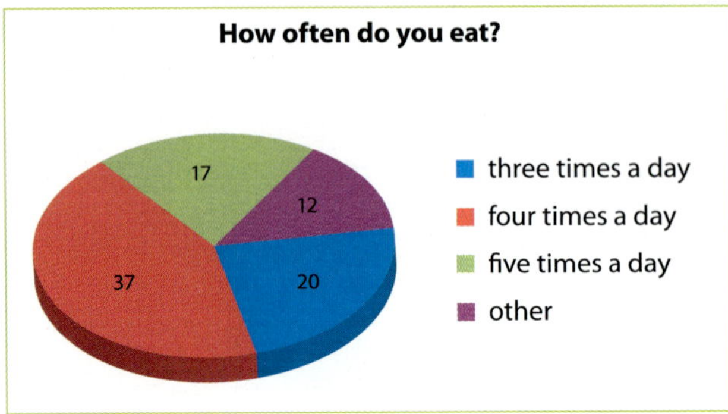


1. A pie chart

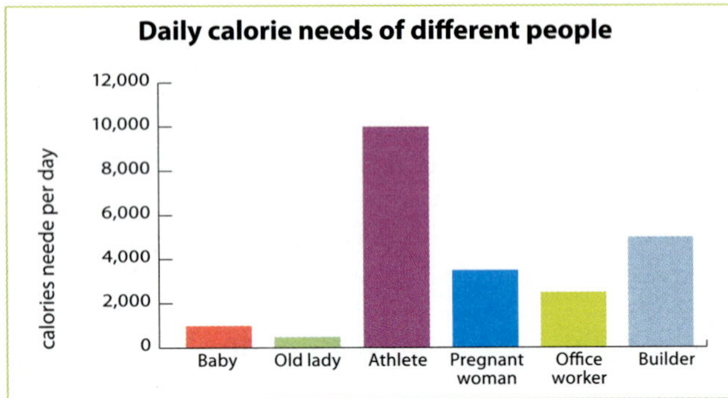


2. A bar chart

**2** **Organisez votre commentaire.**

**a. Introduction**

Reformulez et/ou développez le titre du diagramme.
Ex.: *The chart is about… . The pie chart is divided into … parts.*

**b. Message du diagramme**

Expliquez les situations ou évolutions, en termes de quantité ou pourcentages. Comparez les données. Utilisez le vocabulaire de la boîte de fin de page.
Ex.: *There are three lines in the chart. The green one shows… There twice as many… now as there were in… (year) The second largest number of…*

**c. Conclusion**

*So we can say that…*

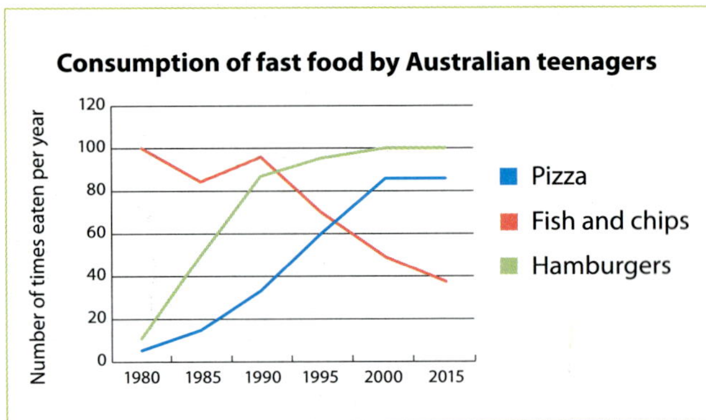


3. A line chart

➡ **Utilisez les indications ci-dessus pour commenter les diagrammes 1, 2, et 3.**

## La/les forme(s) verbale(s) dont vous avez besoin

Complétez :

a. Si le diagramme décrit le présent, utilisez le …

b. Si le diagramme décrit le passé, utilisez le …

c. Si le diagramme montre la relation entre le passé et le présent, utilisez le…

## Le vocabulaire dont vous avez besoin

**Les verbes**

- Pour indiquer une augmentation.
*rise – go up – increase – grow – surge – rocket – reach a peak – reach its highest level*
- Pour indiquer une diminution.
*fall – decline – drop – decrease – sink – go down – plunge – plummet – fall to a low – reach a bottom*
- Pour indiquer une situation stable.
*remain steady/constant/stable – not change – be unchanged – stabilize*

**Les prépositions**

*Between (date) and…*
*From (date) to…*
*Consumption of… rose from… to…*
*Consumption of… fell to… in (month/year).*
*Sales fell by x%*

**Les adverbes**

Ils servent à intensifier le mot sur lequel ils portent ou la phase qu'ils modifient.
*slightly – a little – a lot – sharply – suddenly – steeply – gradually – gently – steadily*

# Your Project

## Organize a healthy week in your school

**For a week, your class will promote healthy habits in your school. You will organize the canteen menus and prepare posters to inform your schoolmates.**

- **Divide the class into groups.**

### Step 1

Each group discusses to agree on two menus. The meals must be balanced Action! p. 55, environmentally-friendly, not too expensive – and attractive for your schoolmates! Action! p. 60
Prepare arguments to explain your choices.

TICE You may find ideas on the following websites:
- www.nhs.uk/livewell/goodfood/pages/goodfoodhome.aspx
- www.eatingwell.com

### Step 2

The groups present their menus to the class who will select the five best menus.

### Step 3

One of the groups prepares an oral presentation of the project (to ask the head teacher for example).
Action! p. 57

### Step 4

One group prepares a poster to let students know about the upcoming Healthy Week.
Writing WORKSHOP p. 61
The other groups prepare posters on one of the following topics.
- Presentation of the menus and the reasons for these choices.
- The dangers of junk food.
- The importance of balanced diets.
- Tips to plan a healthy diet.
- The benefits of sports…

The following websites may be helpful:
- www.nhs.uk/livewell/goodfood/pages/eight-tips-healthy-eating.aspx
- www.helpguide.org/life/healthy_eating_diet.htm
- www.wikihow.com/eat-healthy
- www.wikihow.com/live-a-healthy-lifestyle
- www.healthykids.nsw.gov.au/parents-carers/5-ways-to-a-healthy-lifestyle.aspx

*One week before the event, the Healthy Week is advertised in your school.*
*During the Healthy Week, the posters are put up in the school canteen so that everybody in the school can see them.*

It's a car! …
It's a van! …
It's a taco truck!

# Food Trucks Combine Fast Food and M-Commerce*

### Across the world, food trucks are everywhere!

You can find them in every major city and they're attracting more and more customers. Their secret: fresh products, the mouthwatering* scent* of barbecue, and customers who mostly pay in cash. Of course, this new trend* has aroused the anxiety of big fast-food names such as McDonald's, Burger King, and Wendy's.

### Connected burgers

[…] American food trucks are already taking advantage of new technologies. Of course, since they have to cook, serve, and cash out customers in a small space, they must make do with minimal equipment. Cash registers* are cumbersome*, and credit card readers slow down payments. That's where online payment comes in. Having the option to pay by mobile phone or online from home makes the customer experience much easier. Customers know they will be served and they just need to show a receipt or their smartphone to confirm their order. The "new technology" aspect helps attract young, trendy people looking for new culinary adventures. […]

### Fast-food giants will have to watch out

The big names in the business will have to adapt. […] They're slowly starting to see the advantages of m-marketing. For example, KFC recently launched Fast Track, which enables customers to pay for their orders by mobile phone. They can then cut the line at the store and simply pick up their order. McDonald's and Belgian chain Quick have also joined in. Their customers can now place orders using interactive stands* and avoid standing in line while waiting for their food. McDonald's is going even further with its smartphone app, which customers can use to pay for their orders prior to pick-up. The app will certainly help bring in new customers.

For anyone trying to attract new customers, new technologies are now essential. Online orders, easy payments, NFC*, m-coupons and geolocation are smart ways to appeal to more customers and a connected segment. Fast food has every interest in becoming the biggest m-payment market […].

Yann Merian, *Mobility*, September 30th, 2013.

*m-commerce: mobile commerce – *mouthwatering: *qui met l'eau à la bouche*
*scent: *odeur* – *trend: *tendance* – *cash register: *caisse* – *cumbersome: *encombrant*
*stands: *bornes* – *NFC (near field communication): *paiement par téléphone mobile*

# When It Comes to Food, Technology Is Changing the Game

Until now, food innovation happened in the laboratories of a few multinationals. But as the Internet democratizes every industry, [...] it's becoming clear that we can create a future that's decentralized, and collaborative [...].

Many sustainable food advocates believe technology is incompatible with diversified sustainable food production. [...] At Food+Tech Connect, we believe exactly the opposite.

Of course, we know that technology alone will not feed the world. But it can optimize traditional solutions, and it can help to utilize resources more efficiently, and improve communications.

To generate new ideas, we're organizing "hackathons"—events during which volunteers meet to develop tools* and solve problems—to co-create the future of food innovation.

In our latest event, people collaboratively developed new 24 technologies [...]. For example, the winning team developed CARV, a Wi-Fi software solution that captures critical data about cuts of meat*.

Danielle Gould, www.foodtechconnect.com, July 2nd, 2013.

*tools: *outils* *cuts of meat: *découpes de viande*

Technology encompasses everything: biotechnology, hardware, and information technology.

## High-Tech Farming

### Indoor farming may be taking root

A grey warehouse* in an industrial park in Indiana is home to a climate-controlled room full of perfect plants. They grow in an alien pink light, 22 hours a day, 365 days a year in 25-foot towers, untouched by pests [...]. This $2.5m techno-Eden, run by a firm called Green Sense Farms, has been made possible thanks to the thousands of blue and red light-emitting diodes (LEDs) supplied by Philips, a Dutch technology firm. The light they give off is of precisely the wavelength* required by the crops* grown here, which include lettuce, basil, and chives*.

The idea of abandoning the sun's light for the artificial sort offers plenty of advantages: no need to worry about seasons or the weather, and plants grow around the clock; [...] water can be recycled continuously, and sensors can detect which nutrients are missing and provide them accordingly. [...]

The crops grow faster, too. [...]

That could help meet demand for what was once impossible: fresh, locally grown produce, all year round. And our correspondent tasted the lettuce. It was delicious.

A new survey sets out the threats* that American agriculture is facing, such as growing numbers of insects and a rising incidence of bad weather. Indoor farming is immune* to both.

*The Economist*, May 17th, 2014.

*warehouse: *hangar* – *wavelength: *longueur d'ondes* – *crops: *cultures* – *chives: *ciboulette*
*threats: *menaces* – *be immune: *être protégé(e)*

1. Read the article(s) and, in small groups, prepare a report in French about what you read.
2. Search the Internet for information and make a short presentation for the class:
   - find what fast-food giants are doing to take advantage of m-marketing technologies;
   - find other examples of food technologies.

## COMPREHENSION

## 1 Parents Are Warned Not to Keep Children Quiet by Offering Them Junk Food

**Children's Minister, Frances Fitzgerald, has warned parents not to feed junk food to their children to keep them quiet.**

Her advice came after new figures showed one in four primary school children – around 30,000 – is overweight or obese from excessive calorie intake and lack of exercise.

Ms. Fitzgerald said it was understandable that parents were tempted to give their children junk food so they would "sit down and watch the TV and keep quiet".

However, she added: "A lot of the parents who are giving children the incorrect food do so because they don't understand the consequences. The children who are obese are likely to become obese adults. You're condemning children by doing that to a lifetime of ill-health, and that's the truth."

Ms. Fitzgerald cited the case of a child of 18 months who had to be weaned off crisps. "I have heard lots of stories of babies and young children getting completely inappropriate food," she said. Any parent giving an 18-month-old child crisps "has a huge educational issue," she added.

However, she was reluctant to blame only parents for the fact that 25% of three-year-olds are overweight or obese.

She said there was a role for schools with their safe walking routes and for the State to provide more leisure facilities.

Michael Brennan, *The Irish Independent*, April 22nd, 2013.

### Questions Doc. 1

1. This document is:
   - an extract from a blog?
   - a newspaper article?
   - an extract from a novel?
   - an ad?
2. What is the text about? Explain in one sentence.
3. Who is Frances Fitzgerald?
4. What kind of "advice" did she give? To whom?
5. Why did she decide to issue a warning?
6. What do these numbers correspond to? 30, 000 • 25%
7. Does Ms. Fitzgerald think the problem is only the parents' fault? Justify by quoting from the text.

## 2 The Model Child

At dinner that night Barbie picked carefully around the slab* of veal on her plate.

"I can't," Barbie said.

"What do you mean you can't? You just take your fork…"

"I don't eat slaughtered* baby animals."

"You can't live on potatoes," said Mrs. Marks. "You'll get fat."

Barbie was surprised when her father looked up at this. "I don't think she has to worry about getting fat," he said.

Mrs. Marks sat up straighter trying to hold in her stomach.

"It's never too early to start watching your weight. I wish someone had helped me with that before it was too late."

"Just let her eat what she wants," said Mr. Marks. "It's better that she eats her potatoes than nothing. She's getting too thin."

Barbie was glad he'd noticed. She thought it was the right time to let him know about her mother's plan.

"Mom wants me to look good for the pageant*," she said.

"What pageant?"

"The Model Child Pageant," said Mrs. Marks, glaring at Barbie. "All the little girls in it are on diets."

Barbie was hoping that her father would protest, that he would insist that there would be no pageant, no diets, no baby animals, that he would take Barbie's hand and bring her to his office with him where he would read myths to her. But instead, without looking at his daughter, he asked, "What does she think about it?"

"She's a little nervous. But it'll be so much fun, won't it, Barbie."

Barbie just stared at her mother.

"Well, it isn't healthy," her father said, wearily. He got up and left the table.

"Just ignore him, honey," said Mrs. Marks. You and I are going to have a lot of fun. It'll be just like when we played 'Supermodel' with your dolls, remember?"

She reached over and patted Barbie's head.

Francesca Lia Block, *I was a Teenage Fairy*, HarperCollins, 1998.

*slab: *tranche* *slaughtered: *abattus* *pageant: *concours*

## Questions Doc. 2

1. Who are the main characters? How are they related?
2. At what moment of the day and where does the scene take place?
3. What is on the menu? Does Barbie like the food or not? Why?
4. Right or wrong? Justify by quoting from the text.
   a. Mrs. Marks wants Barbie to eat potatoes.
   b. Barbie is overweight.
   c. Mrs. Marks feels good about her own appearance.
5. Fill in the blanks with the appropriate characters' names.
   ... wants ... to participate in a beauty pageant.
   ... doesn't seem to know about the pageant.
6. Circle the adjective(s) that best describe Barbie's feelings about the pageant.
   enthusiastic – indifferent – passionate – hesitant – excited – opposed
7. What is Mr. Marks's opinion about the pageant? Justify your answer by quoting the text.
8. Choose the right statement and justify by quoting the text.
   Barbie would like Mr. Marks to ...
   – come and support her at the Model Child Pageant.
   – ask her what she thinks about the pageant.
   – tell Mrs. Marks that Barbie will not go to the pageant.

## Questions Docs 1 and 2

1. In your opinion, what is the common theme to both documents?
2. Compare and contrast the parents' view on the way their children eat. Explain in a few sentences.
   – Parents in doc. 1 and Mrs. Marks in doc. 2.
   – Frances Fitzgerald in doc.1 and Mrs. Marks in doc. 2.
3. Do you think Mr. Marks agrees with parents in doc. 1? Explain.

## EXPRESSION

**Choose one of the following subjects.**

**A. Write a dialogue**
After the scene in doc. 2, Barbie leaves the room. Mr. and Mrs. Marks have a discussion.

**B. Tell a story**
Remember the time when you were child. Talk about the food (including sweets and drinks) you liked and disliked. Mention what your parents said and did. Say what has changed or not changed in your eating habits.

# "Oral"

## COMPREHENSION

**The First Lady Introduces Let's Move**
www.whitehouse.gov/photos-and-video/video/first-lady-introduces-lets-move

1. Watch the video three times and take down notes.
2. Then write a report on it, in French.

## EXPRESSION

### "The idea of progress"
***Does change always mean progress?***
***The example of eating habits***

**• Prepare your presentation in note form**

**Step 1** **Introduce the notion: "The idea of progress".**
Example: Fast-food has revolutionized the food industry and how people all over the world eat and live. It's now an established part of our way of life.

**Step 2** **Explain what fast-food is.**
Give examples of fast-food restaurants. Say how eating habits have changed in the last fifty years.
Talk about the fast-food industry.
▶ Cultural Background / Sound File
Talk about the consequences of fast-food consumption.
▶ Text File 1
What are the pros and cons of fast food?

**Step 3** Talk about the influence of food company advertising and say what can be done to limit its impact.
▶ Text File 2

**Step 4** Give examples of people who are trying to change people's eating habits. Say why and how they decided to act. ▶ Video File / Sound File / Text File 1

**Step 5** **Conclude.**
Say if your feelings towards fast food have changed. Give your opinion about the various initiatives you have studied in this unit and answer the question that started your presentation: "Does change always mean progress?"

**• Train yourself**
Follow the steps above and speak for five minutes. If possible, add personal comments. Record yourself and listen to your presentation to improve it.

**• Get ready for a conversation**
Listen to the recording of your presentation and prepare yourself to justify, develop, and exemplify what you have said.

unit 4

# Silicon Valley



To access our audio resources, use our Flashcodes or go to our website: www.ressources.hachette-education.com/boardingpass/1re/units/unit4.html

## "The idea of progress"

***Is Silicon Valley making the world a better place?***

# CULTURAL BACKGROUND

# THE EPICENTER OF TECHNOLOGIES

## 1 What Do You Know About... Silicon Valley?

1. Which Silicon Valley companies do you know?
2. Complete: Silicon Valley is located in ... near .... It is home to hundreds of ....
3. Match the companies' names on the left to their functions on the right.

| | |
|---|---|
| 1. eBay | a. makes satellites and studies the solar system. |
| 2. Yahoo | b. provides consumer-to-consumer sales services. |
| 3. Apple | c. is a video-sharing website. |
| 4. NASA | d. is a search engine. |
| 5. YouTube | e. designs and sells computers, cellphones, music players etc. |

**Wordbox**

- CEO: *PDG*
- **co**mpany: *société*
- **fou**nder: *fondateur*
- **hea**dquarters: *siège (d'une société)*
- **o**ffice: *bureau*

## 2 Silicon Valley, a State of Mind

1 Track 46

1. Explain the "Silicon Valley mentality".
2. What kind of companies can be found in Silicon Valley?
3. Give the reasons that encourage young people to build start-ups.
4. What is the speaker's opinion about the Silicon Valley state of mind? Do you agree?

## 3 In Silicon Valley, Innovation Is Everything

Silicon Valley used to be an agricultural area. In 1951, Stanford University established a "research park", a place where companies could build facilities and conduct research in cooperation with the university.

A pioneer of Silicon Valley, William Shockley, won the Nobel Prize in 1956 for co-inventing the transistor. Then came many other companies that specialized in advanced electronic and information technologies. This continued into the 1980s with such companies as Atari, Apple Computer, etc. Products that were made included memory and logic chips, microprocessors, and custom-made circuits—that are essential to important segments of US industry: computers, telecommunication systems, automobiles, and military contractors.

This has continued. Silicon Valley is characterized by specific ingredients: brilliant scientists, high-risk businesses, rapid success or failure, job mobility, and informal behavior.

1. Draw a timeline of the evolution of Silicon Valley.
2. What was the first invention created in Silicon Valley?
3. Pick out the characteristics of Silicon Valley people and companies.
4. Find the English equivalents for these words: *zone, installations* (§1); *puces* (§2); *échec, comportement* (§3).

## 4 Did You Know?

In April 2014, the American TV channel HBO (*Game of Thrones*, *the Sopranos*, etc.) aired the first episode of a new series called *Silicon Valley*. It follows the lives of five software developers who try to develop a new software platform that will change the world, while living together in Silicon Valley.

Would you like to watch this series? Why or why not?

**Action!**

### Give a presentation on a Silicon Valley-based company

Search the Internet for information about a Silicon Valley-based company. Then make a presentation along these lines: date of creation – founder – purpose or functions – target audience.

# A DAY WITH GOOGLE GLASS

Drew Olanoff, from TechCrunch, is talking about Google Glass today.

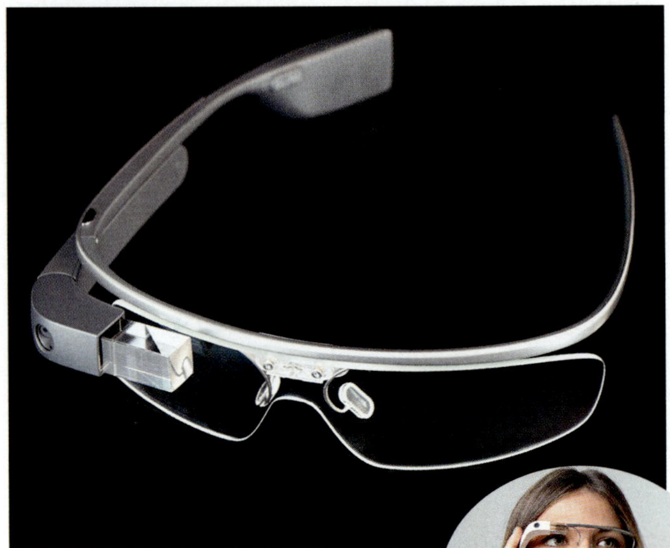

## TRAIN YOUR EARS

1. Listen and repeat. Mind the stress. 1 Track 47
computer • field of vision • direction • reply • transcribes • automatically • interesting • world-changing
2. Listen to the words from the Wordbox and repeat. 1 Track 48

### Wordbox

Nouns
- bust: *fiasco*
- device: *appareil*
- headlines: *gros titres*

Adjective
- handy: *utile*

Verbs
- be redundant: *faire double emploi*
- swipe (the screen): *balayer (l'écran)*

## Before you watch

1. Look at the picture and say what you know—or can guess—about the device.

## Now watch

B1+ A2+ Use the question sheet in your eWorkbook.

2. Discuss what you have understood.

## Recap

3. Find out information about what the journalist uses the device for; pick out its various functions.
4. Explain how these functions can be performed.
5. Say how the journalist feels about Google Glass.

## React

6. Look at the comments below and explain the pros and cons of using this device.

- Soon we'll turn into zombies, waiting for Google to give us orders!! As cool as it looks at first glance, it will have immense negative effects.
- Why would we want to buy something a smartphone can do?!? A smartphone is much cheaper.
- This is pretty cool. I don't understand why so many people are upset. 🙂
- I look stupid with glasses. I want Google contacts!
- Another device so people don't have to get out of the house. Google Glasses promote anti-social behavior.
- Imagine how many traffic accidents the email notifications could cause… ☹
- A true hands-free experience! Instead of staring at your smartphone screen, you can stare at your environment.

7. Would you like to wear these glasses?

**Sum up the document in French.**

## Action!

### Write an article about Google Glass

As a journalist for the *San Francisco Chronicle*, you attended a presentation on Google Glass. Write an article: describe the functions of Google Glass; then give your opinion about this invention.

SOUND FILE

# DELIVERY DRONES

**Online retailer Amazon might one day use drones. BBC reporter Nigel Casterman reports.**

## TRAIN YOUR EARS

1. **Read out loud; then listen and repeat.** Track 49
vehicle • interest • via • commercial • minute • camera • service • surveillance • method • military

2. **Match the words with their phonetic transcriptions and read them out loud. Then listen to the recording and check your pronunciation.** Track 50
customer • purpose • wasteful • package • founder • safety • used • retailer
['pækɪʤ] • ['faʊndə] • ['ri:teɪlə] • ['ju:zd] • ['pɜ:pəs] • ['seɪftɪ] • ['kʌstəmə] • ['weɪstfʊl]

3. **Read out loud; then listen and check the pronunciation of the *-ed* ending.** Track 51
considered • announced • posted • unmanned • proved • used • expressed • resolved

## Before you listen

1. Read the introduction and explain what the device in the photo is and what it is used for.
2. Imagine the reasons why Amazon wants to get into the drone business.

## Now listen

B1+ A2+ Use the question sheet in your eWorkbook. Tracks 52 to 55

3. Listen to the document and take down notes.

## Recap

4. Classify your notes:
   - what Amazon wants to do with drones;
   - the different uses of drones;
   - the advantages and disadvantages of drones.

## React

5. Do you think using delivery drones is a reasonable idea?

**Sum up the document in French.**

## Action!

**Give a two-minute talk about delivery drones**

You have two minutes to convince people about the benefits or dangers of delivery drones.

# TEXT FILE 1

## Before you read

1. Considering the title and the pictures, guess what the text may be about.
2. Imagine why these young people decided to "start young".

## Now read

B1+ A2+ Use the question sheet in your eWorkbook.

3. Read the text and check your guesses.

## Work on Words

1. **Guess the meanings of these words that belong to the lexical field of physical activities and sports.** hustling (to class), hitting (the books), acing (tests) (l. 2-3), diving (l. 14)
2. **Use context clues to guess what "instead" means** (l. 6 and 14).
3. **Guess the difference between the English words "experiment" and "experience".**
4. **What is the word "bankrolling" made up of?** (l. 28) Considering the sentence that comes after it, guess what "bankrolling" means.
5. **Give a verb and a noun that belong to the same family as "applicants"** (l. 32).

> Grammar La comparaison See p. 80

## Recap

4. Talk about:
   – Eden Full: who she is, what she did, why, etc.;
   – the experiment: initiator, purpose, offer, rules, etc.;
   – the common point between Eden, Steve Jobs and Bill Gates.

## React

5. In your opinion, what does Peter Thiel want to prove with this initiative?
6. What do you think of Thiel's experiment? If you were Eden, would you take the offer?
7. Is starting young the key to success?

## Sum up

1. **Listen to our recorded summary.** Track 57
2. **Use the words below to write your own summary of the text.**
   - Eden Full – dropped – Princeton – offer
   - offered – grant – project – solar panel
   - Peter Thiel – cofounder – Facebook
   - intention – encourage – innovative
   - applicants – selected – pitch – assembly – investors

# Starting Young

Track 56

Eden Full should be back at Princeton by now. She should be hustling to class, hitting the books, acing tests. [...] She isn't doing any of that. Instead, Ms. Full has done something extraordinary for a Princetonian: she has dropped out. It wasn't the exorbitant cost of college (nearly $55,000 a year). She says she simply received a better offer [...].

Ms. Full, 20, is part of one of the most unusual experiments in higher education today. It rewards smart young people for not going to college and, instead, diving into the real world of science, technology and business.

The idea isn't nuts. After all, Bill Gates and Steve Jobs dropped out, and they did O.K.

Of course, their kind of success is rare, degree or no degree. Mr. Gates and Mr. Jobs changed the world. Ms. Full wants to, as well. She has built a low-cost solar panel and is starting to test it in Africa. [...]

The experiment was the idea of Peter A. Thiel, 44, a billionaire, who gambled on a company that eventually became PayPal, the giant of online payments. More recently, he got in early on a little start-up called Facebook. Since 2010, he has been bankrolling people under the age of 20 who want to find the next big thing. His offer is this: $50,000 a year for two years, few questions asked—just no college! [...]

Candidates must be under 20 when they apply. The final step is straight out of Silicon Valley: applicants get two and a half minutes to pitch their ideas to would-be mentors, most of them successful entrepreneurs.

Caitlin Kelly, *The New York Times*, September 15th, 2012.

### Wordbox

Nouns
- degree: *diplôme*
- higher education: *études supérieures*

Verb
- gamble: *miser*

Action!

## Act out the conversation between Eden and her parents

In threes or pairs, imagine the conversation between Eden and her parents when she told them she wanted to drop out of college. Then act out your dialogue.

## TEXT FILE 2

# The New Zuckerbergs

Track 58

**Is Silicon Valley Wasting Its Talent On Foolish Ideas?**

If you want to become the new Mark Zuckerberg, you try your luck in Silicon Valley, burrowing into some startup or incubator. Right now, it seems there are more talented people in Silicon Valley and neighboring San Francisco than ever. [...]

Silicon Valley has the most tech talent in the world. The area is bursting with potential, full of people who grew up with the Internet and are willing to take risks. There are great developers, salespeople, and marketers with access to major money and unprecedented knowledge. Yet the majority of projects founded by Silicon Valley talent are social, real-time, location-based iPhone apps or services. They might add a new flavor to our life, but often only for a moment. We don't need another website to crowd-source restaurant reviews [and an app to add more filters to our photos].

We have lots of problems worth tackling and solving. [...] We consume far too much energy and too many resources. The healthcare system is a wreck. We're running out of parking spots, hotel rooms, and affordable housing. Even in the cash-flush Valley, homelessness is rampant.

Some of these issues have been tackled in recent years, with the advent of the sharing economy and fundraising platforms where everyday individuals can fund brilliant projects. [...] We need to harness the talent making services to create meaningful projects that actually help someone. Why not dream bigger and create our own legacy by building something that really matters?

Kasper Hulthin, fastcompany.com, June 24th, 2013.

1. Judging from the pictures and the title, imagine what you are going to read.
2. Read the article and explain:
   - the qualities and talents that Silicon Valley people have (§1 and 2);
   - why these talents are wasted, according to the author;
   - the meaning of this sentence: "They might add a new flavor to our life, but often only for a moment." (l. 14-15);
   - what the author considers as priority problems (§3);
   - what a "meaningful project" is (l. 26-27).

**Now discuss the links between this text and the text on p. 77.**

3. Referring to the two texts, give your own answer to the question in the subtitle of text 2.
4. Compare the contents of the two texts: topics, actions, opinions, etc.


Grammar L'expression de la quantité See p. 80


**Action!**

**Present an app of your choice**

Think of an app you find particularly useful. Make a short presentation for the class.

# HOW TO PITCH A PROJECT

Good morning! My name's Cyrus and I'm the CEO and cofounder of ZocDoc.

About six months ago I had a really bad ear infection. I needed to see an ear specialist. I logged into my insurance company's website to find a doctor. There were 191 practitioners! I called some of the numbers listed but they didn't actually work. When I finally got one that worked, it took four days to get an appointment. I decided I had to do something.

I quit my job to found ZocDoc. ZocDoc is an online way to book doctor and dentist appointments. You enter the zip code where you are to find out which doctors are immediately available in the neighborhood.

With this app, all users need to do to make an appointment is to click on a time, go through a simple check out process, and they can get an appointment confirmed immediately. And this works 24 hours a day.

**Action!**

**Prepare a pitch to present a new invention.**

1. **Observe the model.**
   a. Say what the function of each paragraph is.
   b. Say how Cyrus manages to be convincing.
   TICE c. Watch a video presenting a pitch on the Internet. You may enter the words "good + pitch + video" on your browser. Concentrate on the speaker's attitude and say what makes a good pitch.

2. **Prepare your pitch.**
   TICE a. Invent a new product or go to https://impactchallenge.withgoogle.com/bayarea2014 to select the best invention.
   b. Decide on what information you will use in your pitch.

3. **Write your speech.**
   a. Use the model above to write the text of your speech (four paragraphs).
   b. Practise reading your speech out loud to sound as convincing as possible and look confident.

# LANGUAGE WORKSHOP

GRAMMAR

## La comparaison (Text File 1 p. 76)

Précis grammatical p. 188

a. Drones are faster, more eco-friendly, and less wasteful than trucks.
b. Eden Full received a better offer.
c. Applicants must be as convincing as possible.
d. Eden was luckier than other candidates.
e. Silicon Valley is home to the biggest tech companies in the world.
f. It is one of the most unusual experiments in higher education today.

### Rappelez-vous

1. Pour comparer deux éléments, on utilise un ... . Pour comparer un élément à l'ensemble de sa catégorie, on utilise un ... .
2. Dîtes comment on forme un comparatif (supériorité, égalité, infériorité) et un superlatif.
3. Quels comparatifs et superlatifs irréguliers connaissez-vous ?

### Allez plus loin

1. Repérez les comparatifs dans les phrases *a* à *d*.
2. Dites en quoi les exemples *e* et *f* sont différents des exemples *a*, *b* et *c*.

### Exercises

1. **Give the comparatives (+, -, or =) or the superlatives (+++) of the following adjectives.**
talented (+); useful (=); new (+); bad (+); interesting (–); safe (+); handy (+); easy (+++)

2. **Translate into English.**
a. Ici, Google est la société la plus connue.
b. Le dernier iPhone est plus fin que les précédents et il a un plus grand écran.
c. Uber a été élue l'application la plus utile.
d. Il est plus dangereux de faire atterrir le drone que d'utiliser un parachute.
e. Les idées développées dans la Silicon Valley ne sont pas aussi révolutionnaires qu'elles pourraient l'être.

3. **Compare the following nouns.**
a. iPhone 5 / iPhone 6 (*thin-large*)
b. Smartwatch / smartphone (*useful*)
c. Google Glass / smartphone (*handy*)
d. Drones / trucks (*fast*)
e. Drones / delivery man (*reliable*)

## L'expression de la quantité (Text File 2 p. 78)

Précis grammatical p. 211

a. We have lots of problems worth tackling.
b. We use too much energy and too many resources.
c. Some of these issues have been tackled.
d. Few apps are very meaningful.

### Rappelez-vous

1. Faites la liste des quantifieurs que vous connaissez.
2. Classez-les de la plus grande à la plus petite quantité.

### Allez plus loin

1. Relevez les quantifieurs dans les exemples *a* à *d*.
2. Quels sont ceux qui fonctionnent avec des noms dénombrables ? avec des noms indénombrables ?

### Exercise

1. **Fill in the blanks with *much, many, little, few,* or *a few*.**
a. ... people rush to the Apple stores when a new iPhone is released.
b. To spend so ... money for an electronic device is just crazy!
c. In ... years' time, drones will deliver pizzas.
d. ... people know that Steve Jobs created the first Apple computer in a garage.

2. **Which words or phrases cannot be used in these sentences?**
a. *Few / Little* devices today are not connected to the Internet.
b. Before starting on a new project, scientists determine *how much / how many* funding is available.
c. *Much / Many / A lot of* companies want to get in the drone business.
d. *Many / Few* innovative ideas were born in Silicon Valley.

## GRAMMAR GAME

### Comparing game

**Sit in a circle. One student makes a sentence containing a comparison. The next student has to find a new comparison with the last object or person mentioned.**

Ex.: A bike is more eco-friendly than a car. / A car is heavier than a table. / A table...
If a player misses their cue or uses a noun or adjective that has been used before, he/she is out.

## Exercises

**1. Pick the odd word out. Give a reason for your choice.**
a. an engineer – a scientist – an applicant
b. a laptop – a tablet – a personal computer
c. inventive – affordable – creative
d. innovate – invest – fund

**2. Classify the words below under the following headings: tech devices - innovation – investment**
laptop; revolutionize; scientist; techie; tablet; innovate; fund; entrepreneur; USB stick; discover; recruit; inventive; run a company; design; wearable; CEO.

**3. Complete the crossword using the Word bank.**

**Across**
2. a small portable computer
4. having an ability to think of new ideas
6. someone who works in science
9. completely new and different
10. someone who knows a lot about computers

**Down**
1. to find new people to join a company
3. inexpensive
5. to make a drawing or a plan of something that will be built
7. to make something better
8. a large school where you can study after high school in the US

## Word bank

### Nouns
- applicant: *candidat*
- college (US): *université*
- computer scientist: *informaticien(ne)*
- data: *données*
- degree: *diplôme*
- discovery: *découverte*
- engineer: *ingénieur*
- entrepreneur: *entrepreneur*
- funding: *financement*
- improvement: *amélioration*
- laptop: *ordinateur portable*
- personal computer: *PC*
- scientist: *scientifique*
- software program: *logiciel*
- staff: *personnel*
- tablet: *tablette*
- techie/geek: *fondu d'informatique*
- touch screen: *écran tactile*
- USB stick: *clé USB*

### Verbs
- apply for: *poser sa candidature pour*
- design: *concevoir/dessiner*
- discover: *découvrir*
- fund: *financer*
- improve: *améliorer*
- innovate: *innover*
- invent: *inventer*
- invest in: *investir dans*
- pitch an idea to someone: *présenter une idée à qqn*
- produce: *produire*
- recruit/hire: *recruter*
- revolutionize: *révolutionner*
- solve a problem: *résoudre un problème*
- start/run a company: *fonder/diriger une société*

### Adjectives
- affordable: *abordable*
- compatible with: *compatible avec*
- creative: *créatif*
- handy: *pratique*
- high-tech: *haute-technologie*
- innovative: *innovateur*
- inventive: *inventif*
- revolutionary: *révolutionnaire*
- resourceful: *ingénieux (personne)*
- talented: *talentueux*

# COMPRENDRE UN DOCUMENT ORAL

## An interview with entrepreneur Eden Full

Eden Full and her Sunsaluter

### Étape 1
### Préparer l'écoute

Anticipez le contenu du document oral : observez le titre – et l'image, s'il y en a une – et rappelez-vous ce que vous savez déjà du sujet.

**À vous !**

**Que pouvez-vous deviner du document que vous allez écouter ? Notez quelques idées et faites une liste de mots que vous vous attendez à entendre.**

### Étape 2
### Écouter une première fois 1 Track 59

Identifiez le type de document (discours, interview, débat, reportage…), le sens global et le nombre d'intervenants.

**À vous !**

**Combien y a-t-il d'intervenants ? Quelles informations avez-vous repérées ? Faites une présentation rapide, orale ou écrite, du document en anglais.**

### Étape 3
### Écouter à nouveau et prendre des notes 1 Track 59

Repérez les mots accentués et prenez-les en notes. Rappelez-vous que les mots porteurs de sens sont généralement plus accentués que les autres et mis en relief.

**À vous !**

**Notez les mots accentués. Comparez votre liste avec celle de votre voisin(e). Écoutez à nouveau le document pour vérifier.**

### Étape 4
### Classer et créer des liens

Classez et mettez en relation les éléments que vous avez relevés. C'est ainsi que vous pouvez reconstruire le sens de ce que vous entendez. N'oubliez pas que vous pouvez vous aider de l'attitude des intervenants (rires, hésitations...).

**À vous !**

**Tirez parti des mots que vous avez relevés et classés : utilisez-les pour faire des phrases simples mais complètes à l'oral ou à l'écrit.**

### Étape 5
### Reconstruire le sens

Il est normal de ne pas comprendre tous les mots utilisés dans le document – mais vous en avez compris suffisamment pour savoir de quoi il est question. Vous pouvez donc faire un compte – rendu de ce que vous avez compris.

**À vous !**

**Écoutez le document autant de fois que nécessaire pour répondre aux questions suivantes.** 1 Track 59

a. Que savez-vous d'Eden Full ?
b. Qu'est-ce que le Sunsaluter d'Eden ?
c. Que dit-elle de son voyage ?
d. Qui est David Colt ? Que pense-t-il du projet d'Eden ?
e. Que pense Eden de David Colt ?

**Rédigez, en français, un compte-rendu de ce que vous avez compris (une idée par paragraphe).**

# Your Project

## Pitch your invention or app to Silicon Valley investors

**Organize a competition to select the best project of the class.**

- **Work in groups of two or three.**

### Step 1

Invent a new product or app—or choose one from the Internet. For ideas, you can type "best apps" + 2015 (or another year). You can also go to the site:
TICE www.tomsguide.com/t/apps
Determine its precise purpose and functions.
Get ready to sell your idea: make sure you can answer the question "why would people want to buy this thing?" and prepare a drawing, a Word document, or PowerPoint slide on your invention. Action! p. 74

### Step 2

Each group prepares a pitch to present their product or app and gets ready to answer questions to defend their idea.
Writing WORKSHOP p. 79 Action! p. 78

### Step 3

Prepare the award ceremony with the class: decide on the categories (the best presentation, the most useful app, the weirdest app, etc), the time given to each group to present their project, the awards given, etc.

### Step 4

Each group gives a pitch in front of the class, trying to be as convincing as possible.
Tips:
– include a visual document;
– practise before giving your talk;
– talk to the audience and keep eye contact, do not read;
– show that you believe in what you are saying;
– speak slowly and clearly.
Each group discusses and chooses the app they prefer. Then they explain their choice to the class.

*The class votes for the best invention in each category. The winners are awarded their prize.*

TechCrunch Disrupt is an event where technology startups are competing in front of investors and simultaneously launching their products and services. Even if you don't win, media coverage* is huge and just being there guarantees you a stand-out* position.

# TechCrunch Disrupt— the Startup Place to Be

### Speakers and Ideas

This three-day event is more than just a parade of startups, or as they call it, Startup Battlefield. It is packed-full with speeches from entrepreneurs like Astro Teller, or CEOs like Yahoo's Marissa Mayer. The speakers give talks about their experiences and tell the stories of their companies.

### Hacking* Competition

There is also a 24-hour "hackathon" where hackers try to build something in one day. Many interesting and/or funny ideas are born there, and perhaps some of them will evolve into full-fledged* startups.

### Startup Battlefield

The most exciting part of the event is Startup Battlefield. From the hundreds of startups that apply, six are picked for the finals and present their companies to a panel of judges made of innovators and investors. In the latest edition of TechCrunch Disrupt, Alfred, a Boston-based company, came on top and received the $50,000 grand prize.

Hrvoje Hrsto, domain.me, May 9th, 2014.

*media coverage: *couverture médiatique*
*stand-out: *qui sort du lot*
*hacking: *(ici) programmation*
*full-fledged: *accompli*

# Apple, Google, Samsung, and Health Apps

For decades, medical technology firms have searched for ways to let diabetics check blood sugar easily, with scant* success. Now, the world's largest mobile technology firms are getting in on the act.

Apple Inc, Samsung Electronics Co, and Google Inc, searching for applications that could turn wearable technology like smartwatches and bracelets [...] into must-have items, have all set their sites on monitoring* blood sugar [...].

These firms are variously hiring* medical scientists and engineers, developing glucose-measuring features in future wearable devices, the sources said. [...]

Diabetes afflicts 29 million Americans [...]. Many diabetics prick* their fingers as much as ten times daily in order to check levels of a type of sugar called glucose.

Non-invasive technology could take many forms. Electricity or ultrasound could pull glucose through the skin for measurement, for instance, or a light could be shined through the skin so that a spectroscope could measure for indications of glucose. [...]

Silicon Valley is already opening its vast wallet.

Christina Farr, www.reuters.com, June 23rd, 2014.

*scant: *peu de*
*monitor: *surveiller*
*hire: *recruter*
*prick: *piquer*

# Healthcare Technology: 3D-Printing

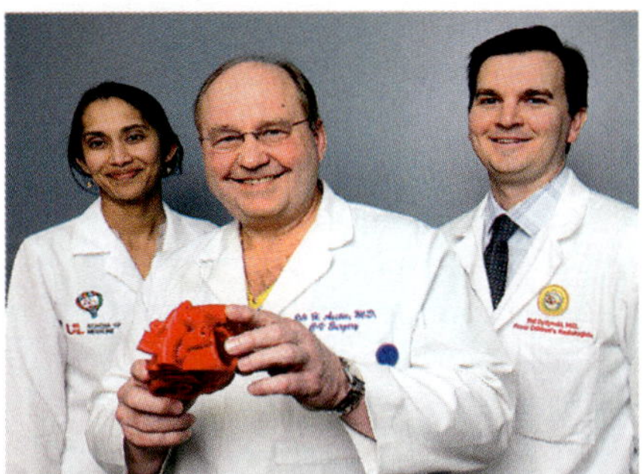
A 3D-printed human heart

Imagine printing* a human liver* or a kidney*? One day this will be possible. With a desperate global shortage* of organs for transplant, the medical industry is pouring* resources into developing technologies that will make this a reality.

"Eighteen people die every day in the US waiting for a transplant," says Michael Renard, executive vice president for commercial operations at San Diego-based Organovo, one of the companies that is leading the way in tissue engineering. [...]

Like other forms of 3D-printing, living tissue is printed layer* by layer. First a layer of cells* is laid down by the printer, followed by a layer of hydrogel [...]; then the process repeats. The cells fuse, and the hydrogel is removed to create a piece of material made entirely of human cells. [...]

Alongside human tissue, 3D printing is being used to develop body parts. In February, Cornell University in Ithaca, New York, announced it had used 3D printing to create an artificial ear* for treating those who'd lost part of an ear to cancer or an accident. [...]

The technology is similarly revolutionizing prosthetics*. The manufacturer Bespoke Innovations produces Fairings, a 3D-printed covering that can be personalized and worn around the existing prosthetic.

www.dezeen.com, May 19th, 2013.

Fairing Prosthetic by Bespoke Innovation

*print: *imprimer*
*liver: *foie*
*kidney: *rein*
*shortage: *pénurie*
*pour: *(ici) investir*
*layer: *couche*
*cell: *cellule*
*ear: *oreille*
*prosthetics: *prothèses*

1. Read the article(s) and, in small groups, prepare a report in French about what you read.
2. Search the Internet for information and make a short presentation for the class:
   – Explain why an event like Techcrunch Disrupt is important.
   – Find other examples of technologies that are changing healthcare.

COMPREHENSION

## How To Fix the Gender Gap in Technology

The United States has produced viable female presidential candidates, women athletes who command millions of dollars in endorsements*, and the first female Nobel economist. Yet there is still no female equivalent of a Steve Jobs, Bill Gates, or Mark Zuckerberg. Women continue to lag behind* men in computer science. Even among the younger generation of tech companies, including Facebook, Google, and Twitter, fewer than 10 percent of all computer programmers are women [...].

Over the past 10 years, three times as many jobs have been created in STEM fields—science, technology, engineering, and math – than in non-STEM fields, and STEM workers have been far less likely to experience unemployment. [...]

Economists expect those trends to continue over the coming decade. And if American women can't step up to meet the growing demand, our foreign competitors will. Brazil, India, and Malaysia are among the rising powers that have much more successfully prepared girls to enter computer science. [...]

So what can schools do to encourage girls in this direction?

In Pajaro Valley, CA, researcher Jill Denner launched a program that teaches low-income Latina girls and boys, in gender-segregated classrooms, to create their own computer games.

Laura Reasoner Jones, a computer teacher at McNair Elementary School in Fairfax County, VA, launched the GEMS club: Girls Excelling in Math and Science. The club is an afterschool program that gets girls busy building rockets, studying strawberry DNA*, and programming their own computer games using free web-based tools [...].

Jasmine Gao, 18, participated in an afterschool program called the Technovation Challenge, hosted at Google's New York headquarters, and realized her interest in gaming could translate into a career.

Run by a nonprofit called Iridescent Learning, Technovation teaches teams of low-income girls programming and business skills by asking them to develop a real mobile web app and then "pitch" it to a team of judges. Jasmine's team developed "Trending", an app that shows shoppers fashion trends and directs them to nearby stores or online retailers that carry a specific shoe or skirt. [...]

Jasmine is now studying finance and computer information systems at Baruch College and hopes to someday launch her own tech business. "I had this preconception that it was mostly geeky men who did programming and it was extremely math and science heavy," Jasmine said. "But it's actually easy. And the opportunities presented through it are enormous."

Dana Goldstein, slate.com, June 7th, 2012.

*endorsement: *publicité*
*lag behind: *rester à la traîne*
*likely to: *susceptible de*
*DNA: *ADN*

**Questions Doc**

1. Choose and write down the right answer.
This article deals with:
– the unemployment rate of women in the US;
– the under-representation of women in technology;
– women who play video games.

2. Right or wrong? Justify your answer by quoting from the text.
**a.** The number of women computer programmers in the US is low.
**b.** Jobs relating to science and technology are hard to find.
**c.** Women CEOs are rare in large tech corporations.
**d.** Some countries have given girls more opportunities to study technology.

3. Choose and write down the right answer(s).
Various programs have been launched across the country to:
– encourage girls' interest in technology;
– prove that girls are better at science than boys;
– help women to write successful CVs and find jobs;
– help fight gender stereotypes in technology.

4. What programs initiated across the US are mentioned in the article? For each program, give:
– the name;
– the initiator;
– the place;
– the target audience;
– the activities.

5. What did Jasmine Gao create during the program she participated in?

6. Choose the right adjective to complete the following sentence. Then justify your answer by quoting from the text.
*bored with – dissatisfied with – unhappy about – excited about.*
Now Jasmine Gao is ... computer science.

## EXPRESSION

**Choose one of the following subjects.**

**A. Write a speech**

You are working for a big tech company but you feel that there are not enough women working with you. You plan on encouraging high school girls to study science and technology. Write the speech you are going to give.

**B. Write an interview**

As a journalist, you have interviewed a successful woman working in the technology sector. She told you about her current job, her studies, and her career choices. Write out the interview.

# "Oral"

## COMPREHENSION

**"Innovation Is Built on Failure"**

www.marketplace.org/topics/wealth-poverty/starting-over-startup-when-it-time-stop

*(00:21 to 02:01)*

1. Listen to the document three times and take down notes.
2. Then write a report on it, in French.

## EXPRESSION

### "The idea of progress"

***Is Silicon Valley making the world a better place?***

• **Prepare your presentation in note form**

Step 1 **Introduce the notion of progress in Silicon Valley.**

Make a presentation of Silicon Valley. "In Silicon Valley, innovation is everything..." Cultural Background

Step 2 **Explain what innovation is.**

Give examples of new devices invented in Silicon Valley. Say what impact they have on our lives.
Video File / Sound File / Text File 2 / Technology Corner

Talk about the pros and cons of new technologies.
Text File 2

Step 3 **Talk about tech innovators.**

Give examples of people/companies who are trying to keep innovation going. Say why and how they decided to act. Video File / Sound File / Text File 1 / Technology Corner

Step 4 **Talk about the purpose of Silicon Valley.**

State the problems that could be solved thanks to Silicon Valley. Text File 2 / Technology Corner

Step 5 **Conclude.**

Give your opinion about the various devices and initiatives you have studied in this unit. Answer the question: "Is Silicon Valley making the world a better place?"
Say what you expect from Silicon Valley in the next ten years.

• **Train yourself**

Follow the steps above and speak for five minutes. If possible, add personal comments. Record yourself and listen to your presentation to improve it.

• **Get ready for a conversation**

Listen to the recording of your presentation and prepare yourself to justify, develop, and exemplify what you have said.

# unit 5 A Nation of Gunfighters



To access our audio resources, use our Flashcodes or go to our website: www.ressources.hachette-education.com/boardingpass/1re/units/unit5.html

## "Places and forms of power"

***Why do Americans love guns and what is the social cost of gun ownership?***

*Non-violence*, bronze sculpture by Carl Fredrik Reuterswärd in 1987, United Nations Headquarters, New York.

CULTURAL BACKGROUND

# GUN VIOLENCE IN THE USA

## 1 What Do You Know About ... Basic Gun Facts?

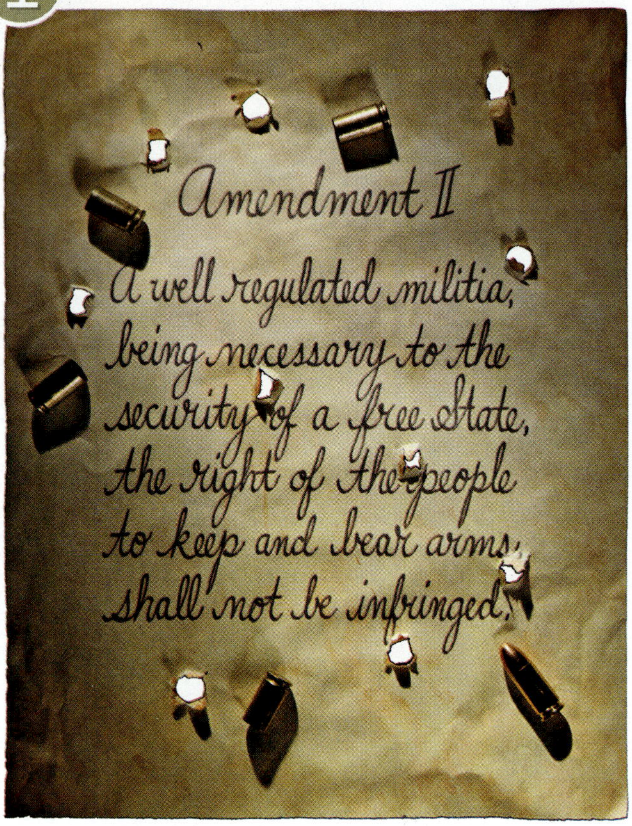


1. Say what the picture shows. Complete: This is the Second Amendment to the …
2. Identify the main clause and the supporting argument.
3. Explain what a "militia" is.
4. Fill in the blanks with the right figures: 100,000 – 20 times – one million – 30,000
   The firearms homicide rate in the US is … higher than in other rich countries. On average, more than … people are shot each year and … of them die. More than … people in the US have been killed with a gun since 1968, when Dr. Martin Luther King, Jr. and Robert F. Kennedy were assassinated.

## 2 A Very Powerful Lobby

2 Track 01

**Listen to the recording and report about the National Rifle Association of America (NRA):**
- definition;
- what they want;
- what they provide;
- their arguments;
- what they do to counterbalance their position;
- their mode of action.

## 3 An Old Wild West Tradition

America's frontier tradition is an important reason for Americans' attachment to their guns: when American pioneers moved west to transform the wilderness into a "civilized" region, they had to face danger—everywhere: from the Indians, from wild beasts, and from bandits. They had to defend themselves. Courage and strength, traditional American ideals, were necessary for the survival of America.

These ideals are still very present in modern-day America. Today, almost 50% of households in America have guns, and it is easy to buy—or steal—guns anywhere. Yet, gun use causes injuries, homicides, suicides, and domestic violence. Victims include children playing with loaded weapons, teenagers walking unsafe streets, women in abusive relationships, and adults defending their homes.

People use guns for all sorts of trivial reasons. For example, a 12-year-old boy recently shot his mother following a row over his household chores. Or a man killed his neighbor because he found his dog annoying.

1. Comment on the picture and the frontier tradition it illustrates.
2. What are the traditional American ideals quoted?
3. State the consequences of guns being everywhere.
4. Pick out the two examples of gun use for trivial reasons.
5. Give the equivalents: *espace sauvage – force – survie* (§1); *foyer – blessures – chargées* (§2); *corvée* (§3).

## 4 Gun Crime Statistics

Comment on the poster:
– say what the statistics show;
– explain the goal of the campaign.

**Action!**

### Make a two-minute presentation about guns in America

Make a presentation on guns in the US. Use information from the documents on these pages. Try not to stop talking for one minute. Ask your friends to time you.

VIDEO FILE

# LOOPHOLES IN THE GUN LAW

## TRAIN YOUR EARS

1. **Listen and repeat. Mind the stress.** 2 Track 02
Colorado • politicians • munition • magazines • firearms • emotion • constitution • amendment • infringed • massacre • purchased • conservative • indicator • nationwide

2. **Check the meaning of these words; then listen and repeat.** 2 Track 03
reminder • Capitol • striking • munition magazines • background checks • inflict • harm • firearms • tool • costly • infringed • afford • massacre • scarred • requires • purchased

## Before you watch

1. Look at the cartoon and choose the best equivalent for the title of the video:
– Pro-gun activists have found ways to legally sell guns in spite of the law.
– Pro-gun activists have killed the politicians who voted for the gun laws.
– Nobody can buy guns in the US anymore.
2. Imagine you make a TV report on the topic. Who would you interview? What would their arguments be?

## Wordbox

**Nouns**
- background checks: *vérifications*
- bill: *article de loi*
- harm: *mal, douleur*
- law: *loi*
- loophole: *échappatoire*
- munition magazine: *chargeur*
- reminder: *rappel*
- tool: *outil*
- trainers: *baskets*

**Verbs**
- bear: *porter*
- digest: *digérer*
- infringed: *enfreindre*
- purchase: *acheter*
- require: *avoir besoin de*

**Adjectives**
- costly: *onéreux, cher*
- scarred: *meurtri*
- striking: *surprenant*

**Expressions**
- for the sake of: *pour l'amour de*
- nationwide: *dans tout le pays*

## Now watch

B1+ A2+ Use the question sheet in your eWorkbook.

3. Take notes and sum up what you have understood.

## Recap

4. Explain what has happened in Colorado.
5. Develop the pro-gun and the anti-gun arguments.
6. Explain why the situation in Colorado is particularly interesting.

## React

7. What would you have voted? Why?

**Sum up the document in French.**

## Action!

### Write an article entitled "Is America Changing?"

Instead of broadcasting his TV report, Greg Milon, a Sky News reporter, decides to write an article about the situation in Colorado, entitled "Is America changing"? Write the article.

SOUND FILE

# ALARMING SURGE IN URBAN VIOLENCE

In our studio today, Taryn W. Brill is hosting a radio talk show.

**TRAIN YOUR EARS**

1. Read these words out loud. Then listen and repeat. 2 Track 04
homicide • epidemic • ravaging • crisis • violence • carnage • criminal • combination • factors • solicit • theory • vacant
2. Listen and repeat. Mind the stress. 2 Track 05
3. Look up these words in the dictionary; then listen and repeat. 2 Track 06
probation • practitioner • dropouts • dilapidated • layoff

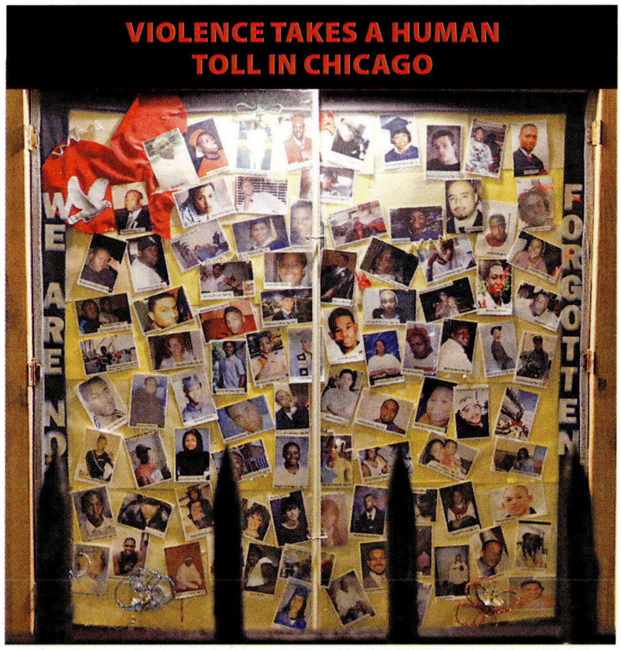


The faces of Chicago's victims.

## Before you listen

1. Judging from the photo, the title, and the introduction, say what you expect to hear.

## Now listen

B1+ A2+ Use the question sheet in your eWorkbook. 2 Track 07

2. Listen to the document and take down notes.

## Recap

3. Talk about:
– the issue (facts observed, questions);
– John Paitakes, the expert who is being interviewed;
– the expert's findings.

## React

4. Compare what you heard with some situations in France.

Sum up the document in French.

### Wordbox

Nouns
- dr**o**pout: *décrocheur*
- guest: *invité*
- lay**off**: *licenciement*
- prob**a**tion, par**o**le: *liberté conditionelle*
- surge: *montée*

Verb
- take a toll: *causer des pertes*

Adjective
- vacant: *vide*

### Action! Illustrate the surge of violence in American cities

Copy the diagram below and fill it in with the causes of violence in American cities.

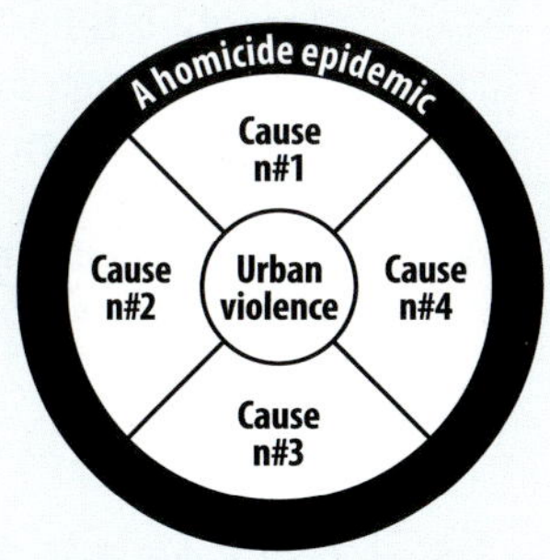

# TEXT FILE 1

## Before you read

1. Look at the little girl in the photo on the right-hand page: what is your impression?
2. Considering the title, make guesses about the content of the text: who, feelings, what, etc.

## Now read

B1+ A2+ Use the question sheet in your eWorkbook.

3. Read the text and check your guesses.

## Work on Words

1. Considering that "bully" means *harceleur*, guess the reason why Mr. Allen carried a gun at school and the meaning of the word "deterrent" (l. 20).
2. Judging by what comes before and after this sentence, what can it mean? "She gave him the dressing down of a lifetime." (l. 23)
3. Judging by what Mr. Allen says in the next sentence, what did he feel? "Mr. Allen said he remained plagued by guilt." (l. 28)
4. **Translate these compound nouns into French:** emergency room technician – sock drawer – metal detectors

> Grammar *For, since, ago* See p. 98

## Recap

4. Pick out information about:
   – Mr. Allen: his age, his job, where he lives, where he went to school;
   – his years at school: what he had in his school bag; what for; how he got it; his friends' reactions; his feelings at that time;
   – what happened later in his school, the consequences.

## React

5. Explain why Mr. Allen says, "My mother saved my life." (l. 24).
6. Describe his evolution about guns and explain the title of the text.
7. Imagine you were in Mr. Allen's class, what would you do?

## Wordbox

**Nouns**
- bully: *brute*
- guilt: *culpabilité*
- gun: *pistolet*
- knapsack: *sac à dos*
- peer: *camarade*

**Verbs**
- galvanize: *pousser à agir*
- shoot: *tirer*

**Adjectives**
- foul: *ignoble*
- plagued: *assailli*

## Sum up

1. **Listen to our recorded summary.** 2 Track 09
2. **Use the words below to write your own summary of the text.**
   - Mr. Allen – high school – gun – knapsack
   - bully deterrent – friends – guns
   - fortunately – mother – gun – forbade
   - later – student – shot – school
   - today – guilty – told – authorities
   - picture – girl – shot – theatre – take action

# "I Could Have Saved Lives!"

Track 08

Several years ago, Mr. Allen, 46, an emergency room technician, was held up at gunpoint in Brooklyn in the middle of the day by three teenagers. [...]

But it took seeing a portrait of Veronica Moser-Sullivan, 6, the youngest victim of the movie-theater shooting in Aurora, CO, [...] eating an ice-cream cone with a child's joyful abandon to galvanize him into action.

[He showed] the little girl's picture, which he carried with him. [...]

[Mr. Allen] admitted that he had not always been against guns. For years, Mr. Allen said, he carried a gun every day. To high school. The gun, which he had bought on the street for $150, went to class, along with his pencils and notebooks, at Thomas Jefferson High School in Brooklyn—his bully deterrent, he said. He was hardly the only one who had a firearm, he said. Those were the days before metal detectors at high school doors, he added, and he carried the weapon until his mother found it in his sock drawer. She gave him the dressing down of a lifetime, he said. The gun was gone. "My mother saved my life."

In 1992, after Mr. Allen graduated, a 15-year-old, Khalil Sumpter, fatally shot Tyrone Sinkler, 16, and Ian Moore, 17, in the second-floor hallway of his high school. [...]

Mr. Allen said he remained plagued by guilt that he never told the authorities about what some of his peers had carried in their knapsacks. "I felt I could have saved those lives, if they had known we all had guns at school," he said.

Sarah Maslin Nir, *The New York Times*, January 21st, 2013.

Action!

**Make a speech to convince students not to have guns**

Mr. Allen visits Thomas Jefferson High School. He delivers a speech in front of the students to convince them not to have guns. Act out his role: write the speech. Then record yourself.

## TEXT FILE 2

# First Day at School

Track 10

"Are you excited?" she said. "First day of second grade!" The little girl kicked her feet against the back of the seat.

"Are you nervous?" her mother asked. "It's OK if you are. School can be scary sometimes but you have some great teachers and they're going to make sure that you're safe and have a lot of fun."

The little girl pressed her face against the glass. [...]

"You're going to draw," she said. "And run and play."

Two guards stood like statues on either side of the doors. The car lurched forward and the woman rolled down her window.

"Yes," she said. "Jenny Ryan. Second grade. Mrs. Gitting's class." She handed the woman an ID* and waited for the attendant to check her name against the computer. [...]

The attendant scanned the computer screen and then leaned back as a photo printed out behind her. She placed the photo into a yellow lanyard* then placed it on a clipboard and stuck it out the window.

"Better safe than sorry," the attendant said. "You can pull up there to the right and let her out at the drop off zone. Make sure she's wearing this lanyard when you let her go. They won't let her in without it."

There was an officer standing on the curb. [...] The sunlight sparkled over the metal of his gun and the little girl marveled at the sight.

"He has a gun," the girl said. "Are there bad guys here?" [...]

"No, no, sweetie," she said. "He's just here to make sure the bad guys stay away."

Dan Evon, *Fire With Fire*, December 20th, 2012.

*ID: *carte d'identité*
*lanyard: *cordon*

1. Look at the picture and react.
2. Read the text and talk about:
   - the two main characters and the situation (relationships, age, place, special occasion, etc.);
   - the little girl's feeling and the way her mother tries to reassure her;
   - what the girl sees through the car window and the impression these details make;
   - the security measures taken by the school.
3. What conclusion can you make about the type of society these two characters live in?
4. Comment on the dialogue in l. 31 to 33.

**Now discuss the links between this text and the text on p. 95.**

5. Focus on the sources of these texts and compare.
6. What are the common points and differences between Thomas Jefferson High School and Jenny's new school?
7. To what extent do you think text 2 is total fiction?

**Grammar** Les prépositions de lieu et particules
See p. 98

### Action! Write school safety rules

In pairs, write a list of rules and regulations that could be posted at the entrance of Jenny's school.

# HOW TO WRITE AN ESSAY

**Action!**

**Write a 150-word essay on the following topic: "Should private citizens be allowed to legally own guns?"**

Technical progress is a key to happiness. Man has made breakthroughs in so many fields, thanks to technical progress that he can be proud of his achievements. Medicine is the case that comes to mind first, yet electricity, mass-production, or computers are also real assets.

However, it is true that technical progress is not without drawbacks. Mad-cow disease is an example of the negative effects of increasing the production of meat. Furthermore, the industrial revolution, which was made possible by the progress of technologies, has resulted in a world full of pollution. On top of that, global warming, which is one of the consequences of this pollution, will probably result in more natural catastrophes.

All things considered, many discoveries can have positive aspects. Yet, past and recent events show that the quality of life is often put at risk by blind technical progress, so, I believe we should encourage it but add a moral dimension to it.

**1. Observe the model.**

a. Identify the topic.

b. Say what the role of each paragraph is.

c. In each paragraph, identify the following elements:

- §1: general argument – development – examples;
- §2: linking word – argument 1 – example – linking word – argument 2;
- §3: linking word – opinion.

d. Say what the value of each link word is.

**2. Prepare your arguments.**

a. Write an introduction to present your topic.

b. Think of arguments in favour of and against gun control. Develop each argument with an example or an explanation. Write these elements in note form in a chart like the one below.

| **For gun control** | |
|---|---|
| Argument 1: … | Example or explanation: … |
| Argument 2: … | Example or explanation: … |
| **Against gun control** | |
| Argument 1: … | Example or explanation: … |
| Argument 2: … | Example or explanation: … |

c. Use the model above to write your conclusion.

**3. Write your essay.**

a. Use your notes to write up your essay.

b. Use linking words to make your organization clear.

GRAMMAR

## For, since, ago (Text File 1 p. 94)

Précis grammatical p. 192

a. Several years ago, Mr. Allen was held up at gunpoint by three teenagers.
b. There has been a metal detector in this school since 2003.
c. He has been carrying a gun for years.
d. For years, he carried a gun every day.

### Rappelez-vous

- *Ago* s'utilise avec le ... (forme verbale). Il signifie ... .
- *Since* marque ... . Il s'utilise avec ... et se traduit par ... .
- *For* indique ... . Il peut s'utiliser avec ... et se traduit alors par ... . Il peut aussi s'utiliser avec ... et se traduit alors par ... .

### Allez plus loin

1. Traduisez les phrases *a* à *d*.
2. Expliquez la différence entre les phrases *c* et *d*.

### Exercises

**1. Which word can come before these phrases: *for* or *since*?**

a. ... three days
b. ... Monday
c. ... he was young
d. ... twenty minutes
e. ... all his life
f. ... 2005
g. ... a very long time
h. ... she was born
i. ... Christmas
j. ... 10 years

**2. Put the verbs into the correct form.**

a. He ... about the Aurora shooting a few years ago. (*read*)
b. Since December 2012, there ... at least 91 school shootings in America. (*be*)
c. My father ... a student in this school for more than ten years. (*be*)
d. He ... for three years for owning a gun without a permit. (*be jailed*)
e. He ... a gun for nearly two decades now. (*own*)

## Les prépositions de lieu et particules (Text File 2 p. 96)

Précis grammatical p. 203

a. The woman rolled **down** her window.
b. You can let her **out at** the drop-off zone.
c. The little girl walked **to** the door.
d. They won't let her **in without** it.
e. Finally, she walked **into** the classroom.

### Rappelez-vous

- Faites la liste des prépositions de lieu que vous connaissez.
- Classez ces prépositions : celles qui indiquent une position et celles qui indiquent un mouvement.

### Allez plus loin

1. Identifiez la fonction des mots en gras dans les exemples *a* à *e* : servent-ils à introduire un complément (ce sont des prépositions) ou à transformer le sens d'un verbe (ce sont des particules) ?
2. Traduisez les phrases *a*, *d* et *e*. Que remarquez-vous ?

### Exercises

**1. Fill in the blanks with a preposition.**

HENRY: Hello, James, is my wife ... home?
JAMES: Yes, sir.
HENRY: Good. Can you bring her ... the phone?
JAMES: Your wife is ... the bathroom with the plumber, Sir.
HENRY: My wife's ... the bathroom with her boyfriend! James, go ... my bedroom, and find the box ... my bed. There's a gun ... it. Take it ... , go ... the bathroom and shoot my wife. *(Two gun shots)*
HENRY: Well done, James! What did you do with the gun?
JAMES: I put it ... the swimming pool ... the back garden, Sir.
HENRY: But we haven't got a swimming pool, James!
JAMES: Oh, I see. Well, then, you've got the wrong number, I'm afraid, Sir.

**2. Translate into French.**

a. She swam across the river.
b. She immediately ran off.
c. They ran down the stairs.
d. They drive along the river.
e. I cycled through the city.

## GRAMMAR GAME

### Find the hidden objects

**Look at the picture (eWorkbook).**
You have exactly three minutes to find as many objects from the following list as possible and write a sentence to locate it.
*Ex.: The mask is on the wall, on the top, in the middle.*
Then, in groups, compare your answers.

The winner is the student who has found the most objects.
*violin – banana – shield – moon – earth – Eiffel tower – shoe – bottle – glass – ashtray – dollar – lipstick – scarf – ring – pistol – tea-pot – statue – rainbow – hat – rose – bowstie – heart – spade – necklace – T-shirt – knife – handbag – tentacles – gift – ghost – no-smoking sign – magnet*

## Exercises

**1. Pick out the words that make the second sentence mean the same as the first one.**

a. They broke the window to enter my house.
→ They ... my house.

b. This area is very dangerous.
→ This area is not ... at all.

c. He said he would kill me if I didn't do what he wanted.
→ He ... me.

d. He did not look like someone who would kill people.
→ He didn't look like a ... .

e. Nobody saw what happened.
→ There were no ... .

f. A man took out a gun and fired at the boy.
→ A man took out a gun and ... the boy.

g. A woman was hurt.
→ A woman was ... .

**2. Pick out the two verbs in the word bank that can complete the sentence below. Then give other verbs of your own.**

You can ... a gun.

**3. Pick out the nouns referring to people and classify them from the most dangerous to the inoffensive.**

**4. Give the nouns corresponding to these verbs with their French translation (some are similar to the verbs!):** *injure – load – defend – fear – fight – threaten*

## Word bank

### Nouns

- **bul**let: *balle*
- **cri**minal record: *casier judiciaire*
- fear: *peur*
- **fi**rearm: *arme à feu*
- gun: *pistolet, revolver*
- gun **li**cense: *permis de port d'armes*
- law: *loi*
- **mur**der(er): *meurtre (meurtrier)*
- **out**law: *hors-la-loi*
- rifle: *fusil*
- **ro**bber: *voleur*
- **ro**bbery: *cambriolage*
- **shoo**ting: *fusillade*
- stray **bul**let: *balle perdue*
- threat: *menace*
- thug: *voyou*
- **wea**pon: *arme*
- **wit**ness: *témoin*

### Verbs

- **ad**vocate: *préconiser*
- **a**ssault: *agresser*
- ban: *interdire*
- be a**fraid**: *avoir peur*
- be kept in **cus**tody: *être placé en garde à vue*
- break into: *entrer par effraction dans*
- break the law: *enfreindre la loi*
- de**fend**: *défendre*
- fear: *craindre*
- fight: *se battre*
- file a **law**suit: *faire un procès*
- **in**jure: *blesser*
- load: *charger*
- own: *posséder*
- pre**vent** (from): *empêcher (de)*
- **sen**tence: *condamner*
- shoot: *tirer (arme à feu)*
- **threa**ten: *menacer*

### Adjectives

- **bu**llet-proof: *pare-balle*
- **cau**tious: *prudent*
- **fa**tal: *mortel*
- **gui**lty: *coupable*
- **in**jured: *blessé*
- safe: *sûr*
- safe and sound: *sain et sauf*
- tough: *dur, sévère*
- un**har**med: *indemne*

SKILLS TRAINING

# PRONONCER ET ENTENDRE LES VOYELLES

**On distingue les voyelles dites « longues » ou « tendues », que l'on reconnaît par le signe [:] qui suit leur symbole, et les autres voyelles, dites « brèves » ou « non tendues ».**

## 1 Le son de *sit* [ɪ]

Plus à l'avant que le son français de « site » ; il est plus court et moins tendu, et se rapproche du [e]. Les lèvres s'entrouvrent à peine.

**Écoutez et répétez.** 2 Track 11

*I think he is guilty. – The little girl kicked her feet. – He is a little bit of a hit.*

## 2 Le son de *tea* [iː]

Beaucoup plus à l'arrière que le son de « type », et plus tendu. Les lèvres fournissent un effort et s'étirent vers les oreilles (comme lorsque l'on prononce *cheese*…).

**Écoutez et répétez.** 2 Track 12

*There were thirteen teenage girls in the street. – It was easy for the police.*

## 3 Le son de *bed* [e]

Proche du son français de « bête » ou « belle », mais un peu plus bref.

**Écoutez et répétez.** 2 Track 13

*He'll be defended by his friend. – He felt depressed. – He was held up at gunpoint.*

## 4 Le son de *cat* [æ]

Prononcez « a » en pensant à « è » – un peu comme quand vous êtes vraiment dégoûté !

**Écoutez et répétez.** 2 Track 14

*It was a fantastic match. – It happened on Saturday. – I'm bad at maths.*

## 5 Le son de *bar* [ɑː]

Très en arrière, dans le fond de la gorge. Entre le « a » et le « oh » que vous prononcez quand vous êtes choqué.

**Écoutez et répétez.** 2 Track 15

*They <u>are</u> fans of fire arms – This is Barbara's car. – The classroom was dark.*

## 6 Le son de *bush* [ʊ]

Moins tendu, plus en avant et plus bref que le son de « boule ».

**Écoutez et répétez.** 2 Track 16

*He put up a good fight. – I took a full view. – They stood in the wood.*

## 7 Le son de *moon* [uː]

Plus en arrière que le son de « boule ». Les lèvres se tirent en avant comme quand on est surpris.

**Écoutez et répétez.** 2 Track 17

It was proof. – Don't be rude. – It's a rule.

## 8 Le son de *cut* [ʌ]

Au milieu de la bouche ; beaucoup moins tendu que le son de « rue », entre celui de *kit* et celui de *cot*.

**Écoutez et répétez.** 2 Track 18

*They are getting tough on drugs. – They were stuck in the mud. – He loved his younger brother.*

## 9 Le son de *pot* [ɒ]

Court, très détendu, plus ouvert que le « o » français, un peu comme quand on prononce « bof ».

**Écoutez et répétez.** 2 Track 19

*They followed the cops. – Obviously, he's got a job.*

## 10 Le son de *door* [ɔː]

Très en arrière, très profond dans la gorge, comme lorsque, vraiment choqué, vous prononcez « oh ».

**Écoutez et répétez.** 2 Track 20

*He'll talk about the law. – There are four doors. – It's a fault.*

## 11 Le son de *bird* [ɜː]

Très ouvert, assez proche du mot « cœur ».

**Écoutez et répétez.** 2 Track 21

*This is dirty work. – Don't be nervous, Sir. – It's an emergency.*

## 12 Le son de *again* [ə]

Cette voyelle neutre n'existe que dans les syllabes inaccentuées des mots de plusieurs syllabes. Elle est très fréquente pour la forme faible des mots grammaticaux.

**Écoutez et répétez.** 2 Track 22

*The president evoked dozens of problems. – I met Officer Purden.*

Your Project

# Organize a talk show

**In groups, organize a talk show: "Should guns be controlled?"**

- **Work in groups of three or five.**

## Step 1

In each group there is (are):
- a talk show host;
- one (or two) member(s) of a pro-gun group Action! p. 92;
- one (or two) member(s) of an anti-gun group Action! p. 95.

## Step 2

Prepare your show. Writing WORKSHOP p. 97

The talk show hosts work together and brainstorm to find a name for the show.

They decide on how they will introduce the topic, and prepare the questions they will ask their guests.

The members of the pro-gun groups search the web to find arguments to prepare the show. Then they share the arguments they have found.

The members of anti-gun groups search the web to find arguments to prepare the show. Then they share the arguments they have found. These sites could be useful:

TICE

www.csgv.org
www.nyagv.org
www.nra.org
www.nationalgunrights.org
www.talkshows.about.com/od/morningshows/a/howtobeatalkshowhost.htm
www.mo-am.com/2011/04/07/10-tips-to-become-a-tv-presenter

## Step 3

Carry on with the talk shows.

The host introduces the topic of the show and the guests Action! p. 91.

The guests answer the host's questions, develop their arguments, and rebut their opponents' arguments.

The hosts moderate and encourage debate between the guests.

*Record the talk shows.*
*It is a good idea to make a TV talk show: shoot the shows, then select the most interesting parts and add music.*
*Present the shows to the class.*

# ART HISTORY CORNER

# Gunfighters IN THE ARTS

## Painting

Many painters have been inspired by the colorful history of the 19th century Wild West. Life was hard and danger was everywhere. Sheriffs, outlaws, peaceful ranchers, cowboys, bandits... they all needed guns, and they knew how to handle them. People did not hesitate to use their arms against animals and humans who got in their way.

*Gunfight at OK Corral*, Harry Bishop, 1968

*Target Practice*, Tom Lovell, 1986

Many people died violently and the average age of death was about 35. Gunfights were facts of everyday life and have often been portrayed.

Women also learnt how to shoot, and they used their arms without hesitation.

▸ **Frederic Remington** (1861–1909) specialized in depictions of life in the Old American West. In the painting below, cowboys are shooting at Indian Apaches who are behind them.

*A Dash for the Timber*, Frederic Remington, 1889

## Music

When cowboys and pioneers had finished their day's work, families gathered, and they would sing, or play music, and dance. Some made rhythm instruments out of dried gourds and blocks of wood. Usually there was at least one fiddler*. If there were no musicians, the people would make their own music, chanting, singing, clapping*, and stamping their feet.

These songs and ballads are generally anonymous and many versions existed. In many are mentioned arms and gunfights.

*fiddler: *violoniste*
*clap: *applaudir*

▸ ***The Cowboy*** (anonymous)

*Oh, a man there lives on the Western plains,*
*With a ton of fight and an ounce of brains,*
*Who herds the cows as he robs the trains*
*And goes by the name of cowboy.*

▸ ***Billy the Kid*** (anonymous) — TICE Search on Youtube

Contemporary singers still refer to the image of the cowboy in modern songs.

▸ ***Bad Guys Always Die*** (Eminem) — TICE Search on Youtube

▸ ***Wild Wild West*** (Stevie Wonder/Will Smith) — TICE Search on Youtube

## Literature

Western fiction is a genre of literature set in the American Old West frontier usually in the period from the late 18th to the late 19th century. The genre peaked around the early 1960s, largely due to the popularity of western TV shows such as *Bonanza*.

**James Fenimore Cooper** (1789-1851)
He wrote the most famous frontier novels, set in the Appalachian Mountains and areas west of there. *The Prairie* is certainly the most representative of his works.

**Louis L'Amour** (1908-1988)
He was a prolific and hugely popular writer of mostly western novels and short stories. His first western novel, *Hondo* (1953), gained him instant success.

**Western comics**
They were very popular, particularly from the late 1940s until 1970s. They carried the written accounts of legendary Old West gunslingers: Wyatt Earp, Doc Holliday, Wild Bill Hickok, Buffalo Bill, Bat Masterson, etc. Notable Western comics included *Rawhide Kid*, *Two-Gun Kid*, and *Marvel Wild Western*.

**21st century western fiction**
The genre has seen a revival with the publication of monthly western fiction series such as *The Trailsman*, *Slocum*, *Longarm and The Gunsmith*.

## Movies and TV series

Western movies are an indelible part of America's heritage. They portray a world of bold and courageous men, strong women, fast horses… and faster guns. The traditional western hero does not speak much; he fears nothing; he solves problems with his gun. Real gunfighters did not shoot to disarm or to impress their opponents but to kill them.
In popular western television shows like *Bonanza*, *The Big Valley*, *Have Gun–Will Travel*, and *Rawhide*, gunfights are routine events.
*Gunsmoke* (1955-1975) was the longest-running western TV series ever; a formal Hollywood gunfight takes place during the show's opening credits*.

*credits: *génériques*

***The Magnificent Seven***
(John Sturges, 1960)
The movie follows a group of seven American gunfighters who band together to defend an oppressed Mexican village. It is one of the most iconic movies of all times.

Best line: "It's only a matter of knowing how to shoot a gun. Nothing big about that."

***The Man Who Shot Liberty Valance***
(John Ford, 1962)
One of the great western classics. It questioned the role of myth in forging the legends of the West.

***The Outlaw Josey Wales***
(Clint Eastwood, 1976)
An ex-confederate soldier returns home after the war to find his family murdered by a group of unionists. Refusing to surrender, he sets off on a path of revenge.

Best line: "Dyin' ain't much of a living, boy."

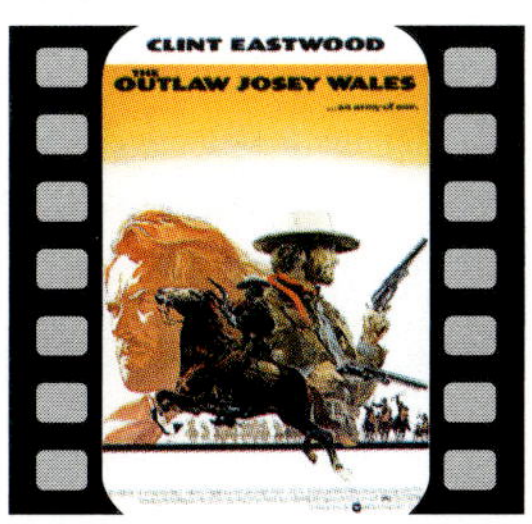


***Unforgiven***
(Clint Eastwood, 1992)
Retired Old West gunslinger Will Munny takes on one last job, with the help of his old partner and a young man.

Best line: "Hell of a thing, killing a man. You take away all he's got and all he's ever gonna have."

***The Homesman***
(Tommy Lee Jones, 2014)
Three women who have been driven mad by pioneer life are to be transported across the country by covered wagon.

***The Hateful Eight***
(Quentin Tarantino, 2015)
A few years after the Civil War, Jack Ruth intends to bring Daisy Domergue to justice, in the town of Red Rock. During a blizzard, they seek refuge in a stagecoach stopover on a mountain pass.

- Choose one of the works of art presented on this page. Search the Internet and prepare a presentation (slideshow, poster, or podcast) for the class.

## COMPREHENSION

### 1 They Are Glorifying Gun Culture and Violence!

At a meeting in the Town Hall of South London's Brixton neighborhood, community leaders voiced grief* and rage over the murder of two teenage girls in Birmingham. "The horrendous barbarity of this crime... left me feeling quite sick," said Chairman Lee Jasper, an adviser to London Mayor. At a Whitehall summit called by Home Secretary David Blunkett, politicians, bureaucrats and police officers expressed grave concern over the latest crime statistics.

That both meetings, which took place last week, were about gun crimes, is a rude shock for many Britons, shaking their smug* self-image as a relatively gun-free society, far removed from those trigger-happy cowboys across the Atlantic. The Birmingham carnage—two girls and two boys were injured in the cross-fire between two turf-warring gangs—was supposed to happen in places like Los Angeles or New York, not in British cities. [...] But the Jan. 2 shootings and the gun-crime statistics don't surprise those who live in Britain's inner cities, where drug gangs, particularly Jamaican dealers, protect their multimillion pound profits with weapons.

Although Britain's inner cities are not nearly as violent as America's, the combination of guns, drugs, and gang culture makes for a volatile atmosphere. One young Londoner says many of her friends have stopped going to parties because even a spilled drink can lead to a shooting. Police say some inner-city youths use guns as fashion accessories. [...]

[There were calls] for stronger actions against gangs. But Culture Secretary, Kim Howells, suggested that rap groups, in particular London's band So Solid Crew, were at least partly to blame. Three of the 30-member band have been arrested on separate gun charges. "Idiots like the So Solid Crew are glorifying gun culture and violence," Howells fumed. Home Secretary David Blunkett suggested holding talks with music industry executives about "what is and what isn't acceptable" in song lyrics. The officials discussed more substantive proposals, [...] including tough measures against guns, greater protection for witnesses, and an amnesty for those who turn in illegal weapons. Blunkett promised to ban carrying replica weapons and air guns in public places, and to raise the allowable age for owning an air gun from 14 to 17. He also announced a new minimum five-year sentence for illegal possession of a gun, which he said, "will send a clear message that serious, violent offending will invariably be dealt with in the strongest manner."

*Time*, January 12th, 2003.

*grief: *tristesse*
*smug: *rassurant*

### Questions Doc. 1

1. Give the following information: type of document; source.
2. The main topic of the document is:
   - Violence and gun-bearing in America.
   - Murders of teenagers in Birmingham.
   - Violence and gun-bearing in Britain.
   - Gang-related crime.
3. Here are the key ideas of the text. Put them in the order they appear.
   - The causes of violence in inner cities.
   - The measures suggested to fight the problem.
   - A radical position about the issue.
   - The nation's concern about recent killings.
4. Find the equivalents of the following words in the text: meeting (§1); explosive (§3); managers – arms (§4).
5. True or false? Give the correct answer and justify by quoting the text.
   a. Gangs carry out their drug-dealing activities in Britain, but the killers come from Jamaica.
   b. Parties are a safe place.
   c. Rap groups such as the So Solid Crew are partly responsible for gun violence.
   d. David Blunkett thinks more severe controls should be applied to song lyrics.
6. List the measures proposed by David Blunkett.

## 2 Stricter Gun Laws Alone Won't Stop America's Urban Violence

Andover, Mass. — When my students told me that they hated guns, I was surprised. That's because my students are criminals incarcerated at Suffolk County House of Correction, a medium security prison in Boston where I teach creative writing. [...] They all said that they wished they'd never laid their hands on one.

But many of them will pick one up the minute they're back on the street. Not because of the gun. Because of the street. [...]

[T]here's been a huge push for gun control—not just to protect children in suburban schools from mass shootings but to minimize the more frequent gun violence that dominates our urban streets. But, as I've learned from my students, getting guns off the streets or out of the hands of criminals won't by itself address the problem of gun violence in poor urban communities. America needs to address the underlying circumstances that lead people such as my students to gun violence.

Peggy Rambach, *The Christian Science Monitor*, February 21st, 2013.

### Questions Doc. 2

1. Give information about the students Peggy Rambach teaches.
2. Is Peggy Rambach optimistic about her students' future? Answer and justify by quoting the text.
3. What solution is supported by most people?
4. What solution does Peggy Rambach believe in?

### Questions Docs 1 and 2

1. What topic is common to the two documents?
2. Compare the solutions offered by David Blunkett and the solutions offered by Peggy Rambach.

## EXPRESSION

**Choose one of the following subjects.**

**A. Explain and comment**

Explain and comment on this anonymous reaction after Blunkett's announcement: "Five years is too mild a punishment, give them life! If they carry a gun, they mean to kill."

**B. Give your point of view**

Would you say that rap music encourages violence? Justify your point of view.

# "Oral"

## COMPREHENSION

**US Gun Debate:**
**Obama Unveils Gun Control Proposals**

www.bbc.com/news/world-us-canada-21049942

*(0'00 to 1'50)*

1. Watch the video three times and take down notes.
2. Then write a report on it, in French.

## EXPRESSION

### "Places and forms of power"

***Why do Americans love guns and what is the social cost of gun ownership?***

• **Prepare your presentation in note form**

**Step 1 Introduce the notion.**

"In America, the gun has come to be a symbol of power." Talk about the Second Amendment, the number of gun owners, etc.

**Step 2 Explain why Americans love their guns so much.**

Say what you know about the culture of the old West. Talk about the National Rifle Association (NRA).
▶ Cultural Background

**Step 3 Talk about the violence linked to gun ownership.**

Give examples of events that have been in the news. Mention causes of urban violence. ▶ Cultural Background / Text File 1 / Text File 2

**Step 4 Talk about possible solutions against urban violence.**

Talk about gun control and measures like gun detection. ▶ Video File / Sound File / Text File 2

**Step 5 Conclude.**

Talk about your own feelings about gun ownership.

• **Train yourself**

Follow the steps above and speak for five minutes. If possible, add personal comments. Record yourself and listen to your presentation to improve it.

• **Get ready for a conversation**

Listen to the recording of your presentation and prepare yourself to justify, develop, and exemplify what you have said.

# unit 6 Big Brother Is Watching Us



To access our audio resources, use our Flashcodes or go to our website: www.ressources.hachette-education.com/boardingpass/1re/units/unit6.html

## "Places and forms of power"

***Is pervasive surveillance in our daily lives a danger or a benefit?***

# CULTURAL BACKGROUND

# SPY BRITAIN

## 1 What Do You Know About... CCTV in Britain?

1. What does "CCTV" mean? Choose the right words.
   - ☐ Careful ☐ Closed ☐ Curious
   - ☐ Circuit ☐ Circular ☐ Camera
   - ☐ Television
2. Explain the difference between CCTV and regular TV.
3. When do you think CCTV cameras were invented?
   ☐ in the 1920s ☐ in the 1940s ☐ in the 1990s ☐ in the 2000s
4. When do you think CCTV cameras became very common?
   ☐ in the 1920s ☐ in the 1940s ☐ in the 1990s ☐ in the 2000s

## 2 Who Is Big Brother?

2 Track 23

1. What is the French equivalent of the Big Brother TV show?
2. Who created the character of Big Brother? What is the title of his novel?
3. What is the society described in the novel like?
4. What is the role of Big Brother? Say why screens have been installed everywhere.
5. Explain what people are encouraged to do.
6. Nowadays, what is the name "Big Brother" associated with?

## 3 Surveillance by Numbers in the UK

With only 1% of the world's population, the UK has 20% of its CCTV cameras. There are 6 million CCTV cameras—about one for every 14 people—making the UK one of the most watched places on earth. The average citizen in the UK is caught on CCTV cameras 300 times a day.

An estimated £500 million of public money has been spent on installing cameras in the last decade.

About 70,255 cameras are publicly controlled but there are 70 times more cameras operated by private businesses for the protection of property, crime detection, or safety.

A big concern is the lack of regulation governing the use of private CCTV cameras. More and more homeowners are setting up CCTV systems on their properties. This gives rise to a growing number of complaints from people whose neighbours use private surveillance systems.

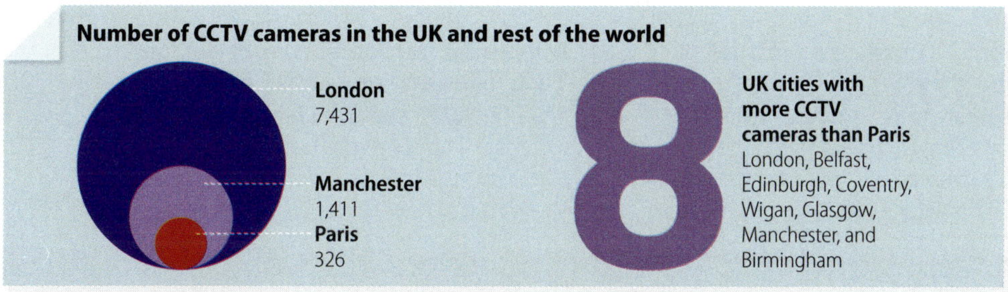


1. Read the numbers out loud and say what each of them corresponds to.
2. Pick out the key sentence in the last paragraph to sum up its contents.

## 4 CCTV Cameras Are Everywhere!

1. Find the equivalents for these French words: *surveiller – magasins – voleur à l'étalage – améliorer – comportement – preuve – bouchons.*
2. Group the different functions of CCTV cameras into categories. Give a title to these categories.

**In stores**, they monitor shoplifters—and also the actions of employees.

**On public transport**, they watch vandals and help to improve safety.

**In banks**, they look for fraud gangs.

**On road sides**, they monitor traffic and detect traffic jams.

**In public places**, like streets, stations, car parks, and public parks, they track unacceptable behaviour and provide evidence in the event of a crime.

Action!

### Make a presentation about Big Brother in today's world

**Work in small groups.**

Using information from the documents, make a short presentation to the class. It should include the character of Big Brother in Orwell's novel and the functions of surveillance devices.

VIDEO FILE

# BEHAVIORAL TARGETING

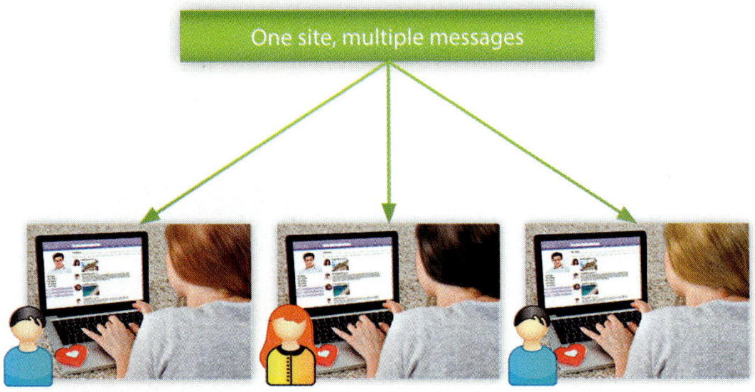

## TRAIN YOUR EARS

1. **Listen to these pairs of words. Translate them and practise pronouncing them.** 2 Track 24
advert/advertiser • interest/interesting • monitor/monitoring • behavior/behavioral • unique/uniquely • target/targeting • potential/potentially • consumer/consumed • excited/excitingly • tracks/tracking • browse/browsing

2. **Read these transparent words out loud. Then listen and repeat.** 2 Track 25
activity • site • server • identifies • interest • simple • consume • incredibly • transparent • benefit • relaxed • commerce • evolving • direction

## Before you watch

1. Look at the pictures and guess the meaning of "behavioral targeting".
2. Explain why advertisers could be interested in it.

## Now watch

B1+ A2+ Use the question sheet in your eWorkbook.

3. Discuss what you have understood.

## Wordbox

Nouns
- behavior: *comportement*
- benefit: *profit*
- file: *fichier*
- step: *étape*

Verbs
- be eager to: *avoir très envie de*
- browse: *parcourir*
- monitor: *surveiller*
- register: *enregistrer*
- shape: *mettre en forme*
- target: *cibler*
- track: *suivre à la trace*
- trade: *commercialiser*

Adverb
- accurately: *précisément*

## Recap

4. Explain what "behavioral targeting" is and how it works.
5. Sum up the different points of view presented in the video.

## React

6. Has your opinion about behavioral marketing changed? Why or why not?

**Sum up the document in French.**

## Action! Discuss your experience as a "targeted consumer"

Think of the ad you have seen on your Facebook profile (or any other site). In pairs, discuss your experience: try to figure out how you have been targeted and say how you feel about it.

# SOUND FILE

## THE END OF PRIVACY?

### TRAIN YOUR EARS

1. **Listen and repeat. Mind the stress. What conclusion can you draw?** 2 Track 26
innovation • information • orientation • creation • location

2. **Read these transparent words out loud. Then listen and repeat.** 2 Track 27
electronic • innovations • personal • internet • person • service • entire • possible • religion • society • surveillance

3. **Listen and concentrate on the pronunciation of the letter *a*; then repeat.** 2 Track 28
gadgets • large • page • social • named • tracking • damage • care • dominate • privacy • data • access • same • all • probably • individual

### Wordbox

Nouns
- concern: *préoccupation*
- floodgates: *vannes*
- soul: *âme*

Verbs
- apply: *s'appliquer*
- care: *se soucier*
- infringe on: *empiéter*
- mine: *exploiter*
- track: *suivre à la trace*

Adjective
- overwhelming: *accablant*

Adverb
- unwittingly: *involontairement*

### Before you listen

1. Look at the pictures and the title of the document. What do you think they illustrate?
2. How would you feel if you were in this family's place? Why?

### Now listen

B1+

A2+ Use the question sheet in your eWorkbook.

3. Listen to the document and take notes. 2 Tracks 29 to 32

### Recap

4. Explain what has become easy thanks to the development of electronic gadgets.
5. Talk about Steve Rambam: who he is and what he thinks.
6. Say how the general public feels.

### React

7. Do you personally feel worried about infringement on your privacy? Give examples.

**Sum up the document in French.**

### Action!

**Warn your friends about what they post on social networks**

Work in pairs. Make a podcast for the school radio to warn your friends about what they should be aware of when they post something on social networks.

# TEXT FILE 1

## Before you read

1. What do the companies illustrated have in common?
2. Link your answer to the title of the text.
3. Considering the picture on the right-hand page, imagine what the situation is.

## Now read

B1+ A2+ Use the question sheet in your eWorkbook.

4. Read the text and check your guesses.

## Recap

5. Find details about:
   – the situation: names and role of each character, who initiated the conference and why;
   – the Circle: what it is, what their motto is;
   – the new device: what it is, what happens when you wear it, how it works.
6. Concentrate on Olivia Santos' speech: list the arguments she uses to promote the new device and the way she presents it.

## React

7. Would you say this device is 100% science fiction? Would you be ready to wear it? Why or why not?
8. Do you think total transparency is necessary to real democracy? Why or why not?

## Work on Words

1. **List the words that belong to the lexical field of the situation:** a meeting.
2. **Give French words that belong to the same families as the following words. Then choose the right synonyms in the list below.**
   - advocate (l.6) – representative (l.9) – citizens (l.13) – applause (l.17) – audience (l.34)
   - inhabitants – ovation – public – congresswoman – encourage
3. **Judging by the rest of the sentence, guess what the phrase "be available"** (l. 26 and 32) **means.**

> Grammar Le *present perfect* See p. 116

### Wordbox

Nouns
- applause: *applaudissements*
- CEO (Chief executive officer): *PDG*
- constituent: *électeur*
- lens: *lentille*
- motto: *devise*
- representative: *député*

Verbs
- advocate: *défendre*
- broadcast: *diffuser*
- nod: *acquiescer*

### Sum up

1. **Listen to our recorded summary.** 2 Track 34
2. **Use the words below to write your own summary of the text.**
   - representative – the Circle – info-tech
   - invented – device
   - wear – recorded – broadcast
   - move – word – available
   - the Circle – citizens – know – leaders
   - democracy – transparency
   - Olivia – wear – constituents – everything

# This Is the Ultimate Transparency

Track 33

*A vast info-tech enterprise—the Circle—has amalgamated the functions of Microsoft, Google, Apple, YouTube, Facebook and Twitter. Tom Stenton, the company's CEO, is conducting a meeting.*

Stenton walked to the center of the stage. "As you know," [he said,] "transparency is something we advocate here at the Circle. I am happy to say that there's a woman who is taking all this very seriously. [...] Let me introduce Olivia Santos, Representative from District 14."

Representative Santos moved to the front of the stage. [...]

"That's right, Tom. I'm as concerned as you are about the need for citizens to know what their leaders are doing. I mean, it is your right, is it not? It's your right to know how they spend their days. Who they are meeting with. Who they are talking to." There was a smattering of applause. Santos smiled, nodded and continued.

"We've all wanted and expected transparency from our elected leaders, but the technology wasn't there to make it fully possible. But now it is. I intend to show how democracy can and should be: entirely open, entirely transparent. Starting today, I will be wearing this new device that the Circle people have invented. My every meeting, movement, my every word, will be available to all my constituents and to the world."[...] Santos held the lens to her lips and kissed it.

Stenton turned to Santos.

"So you're saying that every conversation, every meeting, every part of your day will be broadcast?"

"Yes. It will all be available on my Circle page. Every moment till I sleep."

The audience applauded again, and Stenton indulged them, and then asked for quiet.

Dave Eggers, *The Circle*, Knopf/McSweeney's, 2013.

Action!

## Advertise a product

The Circle has decided to launch an advertising campaign to promote their new device. In small groups, prepare an ad to promote it (poster, TV, or radio spot).

# TEXT FILE 2

## Orwell's Satire Has Become Reality!

Track 35

Let's examine an average day for Mr. Average in a hypothetically average city. Mr. Average wakes up and, over breakfast, switches on the television for the morning news: Cable, satellite, and all digital viewing patterns are monitored by the ever-present media corporations for financial and marketing purposes [...].

If Mr. Average checks his email or cell phone, his activities are monitored by Microsoft, his ISP*, his cell phone company, not to mention the various agencies charged with protecting national security. The cell phone with built-in GSM capabilities which Mr. Average is likely to carry to work has the capability to accurately triangulate its position [...].

The journey to work, whether by automobile, bus, plane or train is closely monitored by an ever growing plantation of CCTV traffic-cameras, recording our journeys, from departure to destination. A growing trend within the automotive industry is to fit new models with tracking devices. If Mr. Average is employed in an office, shop, or virtually any workplace, his movements will be monitored by in-house CCTV cameras. Those who use computers in the workplace invite the attentions of the previously mentioned surveillance giants and most probably their own employers logging their every keystroke. A lunch-break off-premises means further CCTV surveillance from other buildings en route not to mention the ever present cameras used to monitor crime in suburban and commercial districts.

Mr. Average's journey home will be just as much under electronic surveillance as his original journey to work and that's without factoring in Google Earth and Google Street View which are now available to the general public at the click of a mouse [...].

Mr. Average's time is never going to be solely his own ever again.

Alex McGuigan, www.irishredstar.wordpress.com, August 2nd, 2013.

*ISP: Internet service provider

1. Judging from the title, what do you think the text is going to be about?
2. Read the text and say what you have understood.
3. Check the meaning of "average" in a dictionary. Who is Mr. Average?
4. List the devices used by Mr. Average each day. What is their common point?
5. What kind of information is monitored? What for? Who is interested in this information?
6. Comment on the point of view of the author of the article.
7. Do you agree that Orwell's satire has become reality? Why or why not?

**Now discuss the links between this text and the text on p. 113.**

8. Compare the two texts. What is their common message?
9. Explain how the message is conveyed in each text. Which do you think is the most effective?

Grammar Les propositions relatives See p. 116

Action!

**Deliver a speech about the dangers of electronic surveillance**

Prepare a speech about the dangers of electronic surveillance. Then deliver it. Record yourself.

# HOW TO PREPARE FOR A DEBATE

**Speaker 1**

Of course, animals can be studied in the wild–but they can be studied more closely, more rigorously, and over a longer period of time in captivity.

Zoos support scientific research in three ways: they fund field research, employ scientists and make inaccessible animals available for study. For example, a recent study of gorillas in British zoos found that happiness can extend their life expectancy by up to 11 years. This study would not have been possible in the wild. That finding can now be used to help in the conservation of gorillas worldwide. Furthermore, the money raised by zoos can also be spent on animal conservation projects.

**Action!**

**Get ready to participate in a debate on the following topic: "Should CCTV be allowed in schools?" Work in pairs.**

**Speaker 2**

Zoos do not permit longer or more fruitful scientific research. Behavioral research is of little interest when animals are observed in an unnatural habitat.

Environments cause reactions—so no-one can be sure that what is found in a captive environment will be true in natural habitat.

The gorilla study carried out last year is only relevant to captive populations—and only to the zoos concerned. Research into animals may be valuable but it does not need to happen in the context of captivity. Animals should be left in their natural surroundings and not used as tools for public entertainment.

1. **Observe the model.**
   a. Identify the resolution debated. Who is the affirmative speaker and who is the negative speaker?
   b. Concentrate on speaker 1's statement. Pick out the sentence that states his/her position and introduces the topic.
   c. Note down each speaker's arguments and identify the examples or explanations.
2. **Prepare your arguments.**
   a. Decide on the team you want to represent.
   b. Research your topic. Consider the impact of the resolution (social, economical, ethical, practical, environmental impact) and choose one argument.
   c. Support your argument with reasons and elaborate on them. Refer to your experience, what you have heard or read, well-known data, research, or statistics.
   d. Prepare your notes; they must be brief and well organized. Write a few keywords, and use arrows and colors to help you follow your demonstration.
   e. Try to anticipate your opponents' points, and what you will answer.
3. **Practise delivering your speech.**
   In pairs, practise delivering your speech. Remember the following points:
   – eye contact: look at your audience while you speak and use hand gestures to be convincing;
   – voice: speak slowly and clearly; vary your tone to sound interesting and convincing;
   – notes: did you manage to use them adequately? Remember that listening to someone reading a paper is awfully boring.

# LANGUAGE WORKSHOP

GRAMMAR

## Le *present perfect* (Text File 1 p. 112)

Précis grammatical p.196

a. We've all wanted and expected transparency from our elected leaders.
b. But the technology wasn't there to make it fully possible.
c. Now it is available.
d. I will be wearing the device that the Circle people have invented.

### Rappelez-vous

1. Dites ce qui différencie le *present perfect* du passé.
2. Dites comment on met un verbe au *present perfect*.

### Allez plus loin

3. Identifiez les formes verbales dans les exemples *a* à *d*.
4. Justifiez le choix de chacune de ces formes en les opposant.

### Exercises

**1. Which sentences contain a verb in the present perfect?**
a. Stenton had invited Santos.
b. Olivia Santos has been elected.
c. She has been speaking for half an hour.
d. So, you're saying that all your conversations will be recorded.
e. We have always advocated transparency.
f. The audience were waiting for her.

**2. Put the verbs into the *present perfect*.**
a. He + go
b. They + leave
c. We + be listening
d. She + be invited

**3. Which of these words or phrases cannot be used with a *present perfect*?**
always – when I was a child – since 2010 – sometimes – often – last summer – at that time – yet

## Les propositions relatives (Text File 2 p. 114)

Précis grammatical p. 210

a. The cell phone which Mr. Average is carrying to work has the capability to triangulate its position.
b. Those who use computers in the workplace invite the attention of surveillance giants.
c. Mr. Average will be tracked by Google Street View which is now available to the general public.

### Rappelez-vous

1. Donnez les pronoms relatifs que vous connaissez.
2. Dites ce que vous savez de leur emploi (antécédent humain ou non humain ?).

### Allez plus loin

3. Relevez les relatifs dans les exemples *a* à *d*.
4. Identifiez l'antécédent pour chacun.
5. Quel autre relatif pourrait remplacer celui de la phrase *a* ?
6. Quel est le seul exemple dans lequel le relatif peut être omis ? Trouvez pourquoi.

### Exercises

**1. Choose between *who* or *which* to fill in the blanks.**
a. Mr. Average, ... works in the city centre, lives in the suburb.
b. He is used to his journey to work, ... is very long.
c. On his way, there are lots of CCTV cameras, ... have been installed by private companies.

**2. Link the two sentences with a relative.**
a. The cameras are owned by media corporations. The cameras are very high-tech.
b. My sister has installed a camera in her garden. She lives next door.
c. I can access the Internet thanks to my cell phone. My cell phone has Bluetooth.

## GRAMMAR GAME

### Good and bad experiences

Each student writes three sentences about him/herself on separate sheets of paper, starting with *I have…* (try to think of original experiences you have had). All the papers are collected and put into a box.

Each student picks up three sentences at random and walks in the class to interview his/her classmates to find out who these sentences refer to: *Have you ever…?*
The winner is the student who has first identified the authors of his/her three sentences.

## Exercises

1. **Give the nouns corresponding to these verbs (similar to the verb form or not). Some have two nouns. Translate the nouns.**
rule – investigate – gaze – report – spy – trust – search

2. **Choose the right words to translate the words in bold type.**
a. *Elle porte souvent des **habits** gris.* (habits / clothes)
b. *Cela fait partie de ses **habitudes**.* (habits / clothes)
c. *Dans* 1984, *c'est un **délit** de parler à ses voisins.* (crime / murder)
d. *Il a été poursuivi pour **crime**.* (crime / murder)
e. *Je vais **prévenir** mon frère.* (prevent / warn)
f. *Je voudrais l'**empêcher** de faire des sottises.* (prevent / warn)

3. **Replace the words in bold type with words from the word bank.**
a. The man was **watching** me.
b. I do not **have confidence in** him.
c. Please, **stop** her from entering this street.
d. He was **formally accused of** the murder.

4. **Complete the prompt with as many verbs as you can.**
A spy ...

## Word bank

### Nouns
- caption: *légende (sous une photo)*
- concern: *souci*
- crime: *délit*
- data: *données*
- evidence: *preuve*
- habit: *habitude*
- log: *journal (de bord)*
- nightmare: *cauchemar*
- purpose: *but*
- record: *casier judiciaire*
- strength: *force*

### Verbs
- break the law: *enfreindre la loi*
- gaze at: *regarder fixement*
- infringe on: *empiéter sur*
- investigate: *faire une enquête*
- overhear: *surprendre (une conversation)*
- prevent from: *empêcher de*
- prosecute for: *poursuivre (en justice)*
- report: *signaler*
- rule: *diriger*
- scrutinize: *scruter*
- search: *fouiller*
- spy: *espionner*
- track down: *suivre à la trace*
- trust: *faire confiance à*
- wiretap: *mettre sur écoute*

# SKILLS TRAINING

## Comprendre un texte

# The NSA* Prism Program

The National Security Agency has obtained direct access to the systems of Google, Facebook, Apple, and other US Internet giants, according to a top-secret document.

The NSA access is part of a previously undisclosed program called Prism, which allows officials to collect material including search history, the content of emails, file transfers, and live chats, the document says.

*The Guardian* has verified the authenticity of the document, a 41-slide PowerPoint presentation classified as top-secret.

Although the presentation claims the program is run with the assistance of the companies, all companies denied knowledge of any such program. An Apple spokesman said he had "never heard" of PRISM.

Some of the world's largest Internet brands are claimed to be part of the information-sharing program since its introduction in 2007. Microsoft—which is currently running an advertising campaign with the slogan "Your privacy is our priority"—was the first, in December 2007. It was followed by Yahoo, Google, Facebook, YouTube, Skype, and finally Apple.

*The Guardian*, June 7th, 2013.

*NSA: National Security Agency

### Étape 1 Avant de lire

Anticipez : observez le texte (titre, nature, source, illustration) et ce que vous savez déjà du sujet pour émettre des hypothèses – de qui ou de quoi on va parler, de quel pays il s'agit, ce qu'il s'est passé, etc.

**À vous !**

**Observez le texte ci-dessus. À votre avis, de quoi va-t-il traiter ? Comparez vos hypothèses avec celles de vos camarades.**

### Étape 2 Lisez l'ensemble du texte

Lisez une première fois pour vérifier vos hypothèses.

**À vous !**

**Parcourez le texte. Vos hypothèses sont-elles confirmées ?**

### Étape 3 Relisez le texte

Repérez et classez les éléments que vous avez compris. Vous pouvez prendre des notes ou surligner les éléments importants avec des couleurs différentes : la situation, les noms propres, les champs lexicaux, etc. Dans un article de journal, repérez l'information-clé dans la première phrase de chaque paragraphe.

**À vous !**

**Repérez, dans la première phrase de chaque paragraphe, le sujet, le verbe et les mots-clés. Déduisez l'idée principale du paragraphe.**

§ 1 : Quelle est la révélation du jour ?
§ 2 : Que permet Prism ?
§ 3 : Qu'a fait le journal de cette information ?
§ 4 : Quelle est la position des entreprises?
§ 5 : Quelles sont les entreprises citées ? Comparez avec l'information donnée dans ce paragraphe. Qu'est-ce qui la renforce ? Qu'est-ce qui la contredit ?

### Étape 4 Tirez des conclusions

Servez-vous de ce que vous avez compris. Devinez :
– le sens des mots. Observez leur nature, leur formation, leur ressemblance avec le français, le contexte ;
– les informations implicites.

**À vous !**

**Observez les mots ci-dessous en contexte ; donnez leur nature puis déduisez leur sens.**
undisclosed (l.4), collect (l.5), content (l.6), verified (l.8), classified (l.9), denied (l.13), knowledge (l.13), spokesman (l.14), information-sharing program (l.16).

**Repérez la forme du verbe de la première phrase du texte, et comparez avec l'information donnée dans le paragraphe 3. Quelle est la position du journaliste (croit-il à l'existence de Prism, ou croit-il les entreprises citées ?)**

### Étape 5 Reconstruisez du sens

**À vous !**

**Faites le compte-rendu, en anglais ou en français, de ce que vous venez de lire.**

# Your Project

## Organize a debate

Organize a debate in your school: "Should CCTV be allowed in schools?"

- **The class is divided into two teams:**
  - **– team A, the affirmative team, will defend the motion "CCTV should be allowed in your school";**
  - **– team B, the negative team, will rebut the motion and state: "CCTV should not be allowed in your school".**

### Step 1

Individually, prepare two arguments for the resolution of your team. Action! p. 111 Action! p. 114

### Step 2

The members of each team meet and discuss their arguments. They choose the best two arguments and they prepare two speeches (one for each argument) to defend the chosen arguments.

Each team chooses two speakers who will conduct the debate. Writing WORKSHOP p. 115

### Step 3

In turn, the speakers deliver their speeches, that should not be longer than five minutes.

– *Speech 1*: the first affirmative speaker introduces the topic and states the affirmative team's first argument.

– *Speech 2*: the first negative speaker states the negative team's first argument.

– *Speech 3*: the second affirmative speaker states the negative team's second argument.

– *Speech 4*: the second negative speaker states the negative team's second argument.

### Step 4

The members of each team meet again and prepare rebuttals for each of their opponents' arguments. Writing WORKSHOP p. 115

Each team chooses a speaker.

### Step 5

In turn, the speakers deliver their arguments (not more than five minutes).

– *Speech 5*: the negative team states two rebuttals for the affirmative team's two arguments and summarizes their own two reasons.

– *Speech 6*: the negative team states two rebuttals for the affirmative team's two arguments and summarizes their own two reasons.

*Conduct the debate.*

## TECHNOLOGY CORNER

# An Unblinking Eye in the Sky

*A surveillance system designed by a company based in Dayton, Ohio, can track crimes in real time, as they occur. Here's how this persistent system works, and how it compares with traditional police surveillance methods.*

### Helicopter surveillance

Police helicopters typically are used to respond to emergencies or in the immediate aftermath of crimes. They can carry a variety of imaging equipment, including video and infrared cameras that can spot suspects even at night, but the field of view and ability to record events is limited to the area immediately below. T**he helicopter** can fly as low as 200 feet above the ground and survey the crime scene, looking at a suspect's car on escape routes.

Once police find a **suspicious car**, the helicopter can follow it over long distances, for hours at time and is restricted only by fuel capacity and department jurisdiction.

### Persistent surveillance

The small Quest Kodiak plane flies a constant two-mile circle at an altitude of 8.000 to 10.000 feet. It takes high-resolution aerial images from a bank of 12 cameras every second over the surveilled area. The images are sent to analysts in a command center, often working alongside police.

The planes operate over a **25-square-mile area** for six to eight hours.

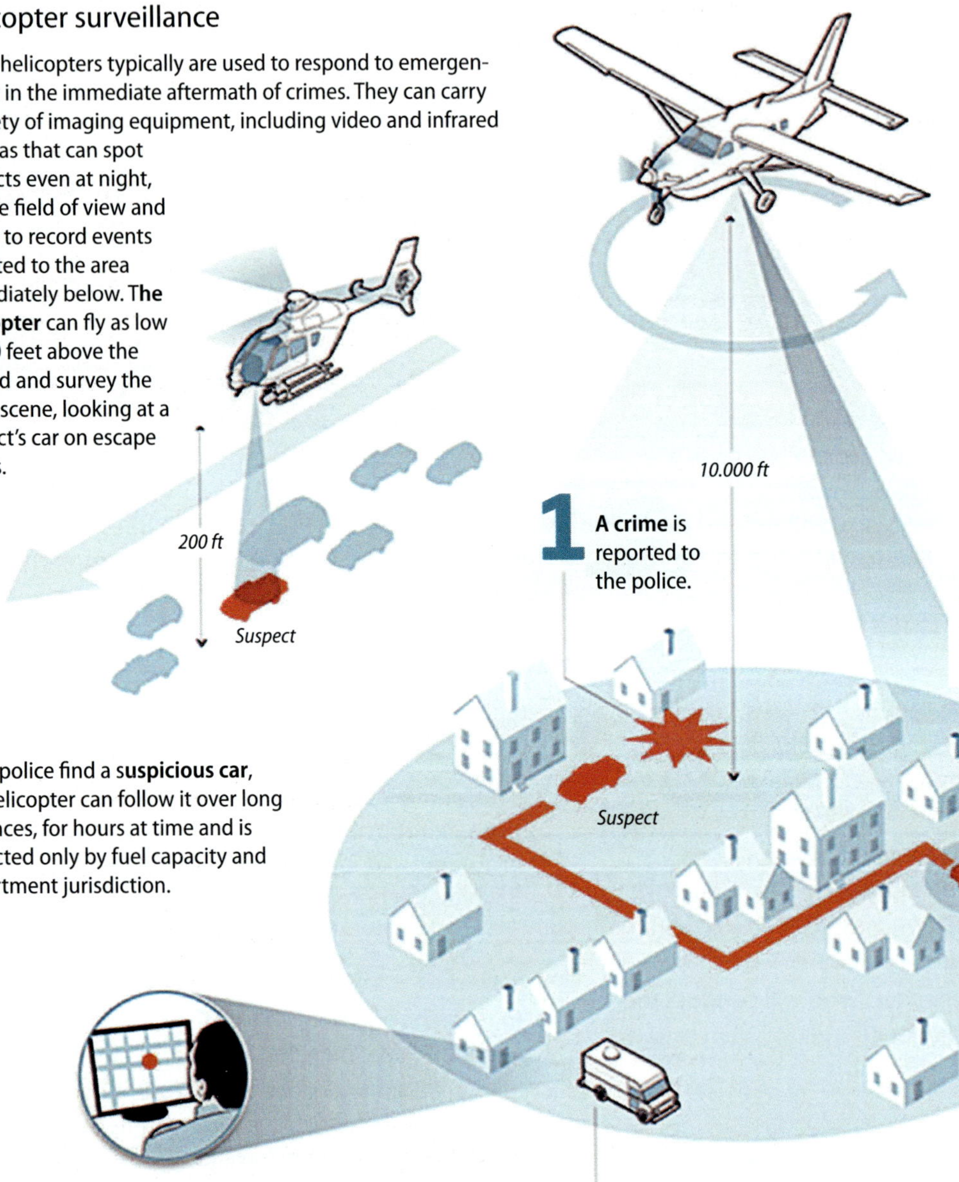


**1** **A crime** is reported to the police.

**2** **Technicians in the command center** analyze images of the area of the crime and attempt to identify people or vehicles that are involved. A person appears in the imagery as a single pixel an can be tracked fo hours, so long as he or she remains outdoors and visible from above. Vehicles, because they are larger and in generally stay outdoors, are even easier to track.

**3** **The analysts the follow the subsequent movements of the suspec**t and share with police, who often are in the command center with company technicians. According to Ross McNutt, the company's president, the technology once helped capture a burglar in Dayton before he got home.

*The Washington Post*, February 5th, 2014.

# Drones

**What are drones good for?**

Drones are awesome. They fly, swim or drive and they can do this on their own. Many models have their own AI* which acts as an autopilot, but they can be remotely controlled by the user. Drone enthusiasts have found many uses for these gadgets, such as aerial photography or aerial surveillance.

**Surveillance drones**

Surveillance drones, or unmanned* aerial systems (UASs), are capable of highly advanced surveillance. Drones already in use can carry various types of equipment including live-feed* video cameras, infrared cameras, heat sensors, and radar. Some military versions can stay in air for hours or days at a time, and their high-tech cameras can scan entire cities, or alternatively, zoom in and read a milk carton from 60,000 feet. They can also carry Wi-Fi crackers* and fake* cell phone towers that can determine your location or intercept your texts and phone calls. Drone manufacturers even admit they are made to carry "less lethal" weapons such as Tasers or rubber bullets.

Drones use in the United States is set to expand rapidly over the next few years: the FAA* estimates as many as 30,000 drones could be flying in US skies by 2020.

As the numbers of entities authorized to fly drones accelerates in the coming years, EFF will continue to push for transparency in the drone authorization process and work to ensure the privacy of all Americans is protected.

www.eff.org, 2014.

*AI: artificial intelligence
*unmanned: *sans équipage*
*live-feed: *flux en direct*
*Wi-Fi crackers: *logiciel destiné à cracker la wifi*
*fake: *truqué* *FAA: Federal Aviation Administration

# New Cloud Technology Turns Smartphones into Surveillance Cameras

ATLANTA, 2014. At ASIS, one of the world's largest security conferences, Smartvue® Corporation announced a new application called Contribute®. This application turns any smartphone, tablet, or smart glasses into portable or wearable surveillance cameras. This innovation allows users to share videos and photos in realtime as events unfold.

Security personnel could use Contribute® to stream live video and upload recorded video directly to security management when approaching a suspect or incident.

http://globenewswire.com.

1. Read the article(s) and, in small groups, prepare a report in French about what you have read.
2. Make a presentation about drones: how they work, what they can do; what you think about the possibilities.

COMPRESSION

## Big Brother Is Watching You

It was a bright cold day in April, and the clocks were striking thirteen. Winston Smith, his chin nuzzled into his breast in an effort to escape the vile wind, slipped quickly through the glass doors of Victory Mansions, though not quickly enough to prevent a swirl of gritty dust from entering along with him.

The hallway smelt of boiled cabbage* and old rag* mats. At one end of it a coloured poster, too large for indoor display, had been tacked to the wall. It depicted simply an enormous face, more than a metre wide: the face of a man of about forty-five, with a heavy black mustache and ruggedly handsome features. Winston made for the stairs. It was no use trying the lift. [...] The flat was seven flights up, and Winston, who was thirty-nine, and had a varicose ulcer above his right ankle, went slowly, resting several times on the way. On each landing, opposite the lift shaft, the poster with the enormous face gazed from the wall. It was one of those pictures which are so contrived that the eyes follow you about when you move. BIG BROTHER IS WATCHING YOU, the caption beneath it ran.

Inside the flat a fruity voice was reading out a list of figures which had something to do with the production of pig-iron*. The Voice came from an oblong metal plaque like a dulled mirror which formed part of the surface of the right-hand wall. Winston turned a switch and the voice sank somewhat, though the words were still distinguishable. The instrument (the telescreen, it was called) could be dimmed, but there was no way of shutting it off completely. He moved over to the window [...].

Outside, even through the shut window pane, the world looked cold. Down in the street little eddies of wind were whirling dust and torn paper into spirals, and though the sun was shining and the sky a harsh blue, there seemed to be no colour in anything except the posters that were plastered everywhere. The black-mustachio'd face gazed down from every commanding corner. There was one on the house front immediately opposite. BIG BROTHER IS WATCHING YOU, the caption said, while the dark eyes looked deep into Winston's own. Down at street level another poster, torn at one corner, flapped fitfully in the wind, alternately covering and uncovering the single word INGSOC. In the far distance a helicopter skimmed down between the roofs, overhead for an instant like a bluebottle*, and darted away again with a curving flight. It was the Police Patrol, snooping into people's windows. The patrols did not matter, however. Only the Thought Police mattered. [...]

The telescreen received and transmitted simultaneously. Any sound that Winston made, above the level of a very low whisper, would be picked up by it; moreover, so long as he remained within the field of vision which the metal plaque commanded, he could be seen as well as heard. You had to live–did live, from habit that became instinct–in the assumption that every sound you made was overheard, and, except in darkness, every movement scrutinized.

George Orwell, *Nineteen Eighty-Four*, Secker & Warburg, 1949.

*cabbage: *choux*
*rag mats: *paillasson*
*pig-iron: fonte
*bluebottle: *mouche bleue*
*snoop: *espionner*

## Questions

1. This text is an extract from:
   ☐ a blog ☐ a diary ☐ a novel ☐ an article
2. What do you know about the main character?
   – Name:
   – Age:
   – Physical condition:
3. Choose the right adjective. Justify with two quotes from the text.
   The city looks: ☐ joyful ☐ desolate ☐ full of energy ☐ overpopulated
4. Find information about the poster:
   – its size;
   – what it depicts;
   – its slogan;
   – the places where it appears;
   – the impression it conveys.
5. Find information about the telescreen:
   – what it is;
   – what its function is.
6. Explain the function or role of:
   – the helicopter (l. 28);
   – the Thought Police (l. 30-31).
7. In one sentence, describe the kind of society Winston lives in.

## EXPRESSION

**Choose one of the following subjects.**

**A. Write Winston's letter**

Winston manages to hide from the telescreen and writes a letter to a friend in a free country to tell him about the world he lives in and how he feels about it. Write this letter.

**B. Write an essay**

To what extent would you say that this novel, which was science fiction, is still relevant today?

# "Oral"

## COMPREHENSION

**Surveillance in Schools**

www.abc.net.au/news/2009-07-23/uk-students-and-teachers-under-surveillance/1364026

*(00:22 to 1:58)*

1. Watch the video three times and take down notes.
2. Then write a report on it, in French.

## EXPRESSION

### "Places and forms of power"

***Is pervasive surveillance in our daily lives a danger or a benefit?***

• **Prepare your presentation in note form**

Step 1 **Introduce the notion of power.**

"Power is the ability to control or influence people or events. Power may be accepted or resisted. Surveillance is a tool for power…"

Step 2 **Explain the title of the unit: Big Brother Is Watching Us.**

Say what you know about Orwell's novel to explain the title. Mention facts about CCTV. ▶ Cultural Background / Sound File / Text File 2

Step 3 **Say how surveillance is implemented in our modern world.**

Give examples of surveillance devices.

▶ Video File / Sound File / Text File 2 / Technology Corner

Step 4 Explain the criticism implied in the fiction documents and talk about their satirical aspect.

▶ Text File 1 / Text File 2

Step 5 **Conclude.**

Talk about your own perception of surveillance.
Do you appreciate its benefits or do you resent its pervasive presence?

• **Train yourself**

Follow the steps above and speak for five minutes.
Add personal comments. Record yourself to improve your presentation.

• **Get ready for a conversation**

Listen to the recording of your presentation and prepare yourself to justify, develop, and exemplify what you have said.

unit 7

# Scotland the Brave

## "Myths and heroes"

***What does it mean to be Scottish? The making of an identity.***



To access our audio resources, use our Flashcodes or go to our website: www.ressources.hachette-education.com/boardingpass/1re/units/unit7.html

CULTURAL BACKGROUND

# A SMALL NATION WITH BIG AMBITIONS

## 1 What Do You Know About... Scotland?

1. **How many islands does Scotland have?**
   a) 7 b) 79 c) 790
2. **What is the capital city of Scotland?**
   a) Glasgow b) Aberdeen c) Edinburgh
3. **What is the name of the famous lake where a monster is said to live?**
   a) Loch Monstro b) Loch Grass c) Loch Ness
4. **What is the name of the highest mountain in Scotland?**
   a) High Peak b) Ben Nevis c) Ben Ness
5. **What is the other name of The Saltire (the flag of Scotland)?**
   a) St. Andrew's Cross b) Tricolour c) Baner Cymru
6. **Which of these inventions are Scottish?**
   a) The telephone by Alexander Graham Bell in 1876
   b) Photography by Louis Daguerre in 1839
   c) The television by John Logie Baird in 1926
7. **What is the population of Scotland?**
   a) 2 million b) 5.2 million c) 18 million

## 2 A Turbulent History

2 Track 36

**Read the questions and then listen to the recording.**

1. List the invaders mentioned. Say what some of them brought to Scotland.
2. Draw a timeline. Note down the dates you hear and then the events that correspond to them.
3. Explain why James had two names: James VI and, later, James I.

## 3 The King who Forged a Nation

Robert the Bruce was Scotland's greatest king. He was crowned in 1306. Scotland was under English occupation. Scots' national resistance had developed into a 30 years' war of independence in which Robert the Bruce played a leading role. He defeated the English army at Bannockburn in 1314.

He was a natural leader. His followers admired him for fighting alongside his men, and sharing their hard life.

Robert the Bruce had always wanted to go on a crusade. When he realized that he was going to die, at age 54, he requested that his heart be taken to the Holy land. So, his followers set off for the crusade with the heart of their leader in a silver casket. They were stopped in Spain but the heart was taken back to Scotland.

Robert the Bruce united and freed a nation that had consisted of diverse groups and tribes. The spirit of pride and independence he created remains strong to this day as is illustrated in the film *Braveheart* (1995).

1. Why was Robert the Bruce respected and admired? (four answers)
2. Explain what "going on a crusade" means.
3. Did Robert really go on a crusade? What did he ask his followers to do?
4. Give the arguments that justify the title.
5. Find the equivalents for these words: *se battre* (§1) – *partisans* ; *partager* (§2) – *cœur* (§3) – *coffret* (§3) – *fierté* (§4).

## 4 A Demand for Autonomy

A demand for autonomy has grown in the last fifty years. Scotland was granted its own parliament in 1999. It has a large autonomy in matters of education, health, and justice. In 2014, a referendum on whether Scotland should be independent or remain in the UK took place. The Scots decided to remain British.

TICE
Search the Internet for information about the referendum that took place in 2014 (leaders, arguments, political ads, etc.).

**Action!**

### Make a presentation about Scottish traditions

Work in small groups. Do research and prepare a short presentation about one of the following folk traditions or heroes:
Bagpipes – Haggis – kilts and tartans – Burns an'a'that! – the Highland games – Bonnie Prince Charlie – Robert Burns.
Then present your topic to the rest of the class.

VIDEO FILE

# GHOSTS TO VISIT

TRAIN YOUR EARS

1. **Listen and repeat.** 2 Track 37
leather • apron • hunt • spookiest • sure • scientists • particular • candle • vault • trivial • Edinburgh • shoemaker

2. **Read these transparent words out loud. Listen to check and repeat.** 2 Track 38
haunted • tunnels • volunteers • paranormal • experiment • experience • reputation • chamber • corpse • choice • report • spirit • judged • moment

## Before you watch

1. In pairs, look at the picture and make a list of words that come to your mind. Share with the class.
2. Watch the opening track and make guesses about what you have seen: place, what is shown in the photos at the beginning, explanation given…

## Now watch

B1+ A2+ Use the question sheet in your eWorkbook.

3. Discuss what you have understood.

## Recap

4. Talk about:
– the event announced in the beginning;
– what sometimes happens in the vault and how it is explained;
– the journalist's experience and her opinion.

## React

5. Would you say the people who claim they have seen a ghost are lucky people, dreamers, stupid people or liars? Discuss your choices in pairs and then with the class.
6. Do you believe in ghosts? Why, or why not?

**Sum up the document in French.**

### Wordbox

**Nouns**
- apron: *tablier*
- cobbler: *cordonnier*
- ghost: *fantôme*
- hunt: *chasse*
- leather: *cuir*
- shoemaker: *cordonnier*
- sighting: *apparition*
- vault: *caveau*

**Adjectives**
- deep: *profond*
- headless: *sans tête*
- spooky: *sinistre*

### Action! Write a sensational short article

As a journalist in charge of an enquiry on Edinburgh's ghosts, you have spent the night in the tunnel mentioned in the video. You have seen something that could be the ghost of the shoemaker. Write a sensational short article about your experience.

SOUND FILE

# SCOTTISH MYTHS AND LEGENDS

TRAIN YOUR EARS

1. Read these words out loud. Then listen and repeat. 2 Track 39
certain • beauty • dramatic • impression • arrival • tradition • emperor • brave • monster • legend

2. Which syllables are stressed? Listen and repeat. 2 Track 40
opinions • complimentary • historian • mystery • experienced • synonymous • tradition • supernatural • resulting • interesting

3. Listen to the recorded words, write them down and repeat. 2 Track 41

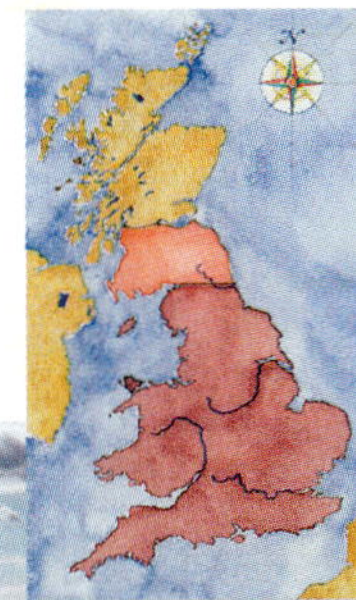

Hadrian's Wall was built in A.D. 122, when England was under Roman rule. It ran from the west coast to the east coast.

## Before you listen

1. Say where Hadrian's Wall is located. Guess why Emperor Hadrian had this wall built.
2. Considering the pictures and the title of the document, say as much as you can about what you are going to hear about.

## Now listen

B1+

A2+ Use the question sheet in your eWorkbook.
2 Tracks 42 to 45

3. Listen to the document and take down notes about what you have understood.

## Recap

4. Talk about:
– the ideas commonly associated to Scotland;
– the origins of Scottish myths and legends.

## React

5. What do the words "Scottish legends" now evoke for you?

**Sum up the document in French.**

## Action!

### Act out a dialogue: "Beware of the wild people of the North!"

Work in pairs. Student A is a young English boy/girl living in the 1st century, not far from the Scottish border. He/she wants to go beyond Hadrian's Wall and see what Scotland looks like. Student B is his/her grandfather/grandmother – who wants to frighten him/her so that he/she won't go.
All students prepare their arguments for five minutes. Then, they act out the dialogue.

# TEXT FILE 1

## Before you read

1. Judging from the photos and the title of the text, what kind of text do you think you are going to read?
2. Imagine: the story, the atmosphere, and the details.

## Now read

B1+ A2+ Use the question sheet in your eWorkbook.

3. Read the text and check your guesses.

## Recap

4. Talk about:
   - the situation;
   - the general atmosphere and the details that created it;
   - Darwin's feelings and what he was afraid of;
   - John Edmonstone's point of view;
   - what happened at the end.

## React

5. Would you say Edmonstone and Darwin were superstitious? Why or why not?
6. What do you think the creature was?
7. Comment on the last sentence of the text.

## Work on Words

1. Find five verbs from the text dealing with sight and translate them into French.
2. Observe the adjectives below. Give the nouns they are derived from and translate them. Then find other adjectives built on the same pattern.
   glassy – monstrous – scientific – ghostly – massive
3. Observe the word "unreliable". Say what it is made of and translate it into French.
4. Find the English equivalents for the following words:
   *apparition – trempé – forme – plonger – ondulation*

> Grammar Les articles See p. 134

## Sum up

1. Listen to our recorded summary. 2 Track 47
2. Use the words below to write your own summary of the text.
   - rowing – storm
   - raining – soaked
   - abrupt noise – terrified
   - monster
   - beach – shape – water
   - creature – dipped back – water
   - looked – loch – see – disappeared
   - sign – remained – never – existed

# Lost on Loch Ness

Track 46

*A Scottish doctor, Charles Darwin, and his friend, John Edmonstone, are rowing on Loch Ness in a terrible storm.*

**June, 1827**

"Can you see what it is?" John Edmonstone asked as he strained at the oars. His eyes were glassy with terror.

"I can't even see the shore," Darwin answered.

Darwin watched for any sign of the monstrous wake they'd first encountered ten minutes ago. He shivered, his clothes soaked through. An abrupt noise split the rain. [...]

"What in God's name was that?" Darwin cried.

"It's the beast, Mr. Darwin. I'm sure of it."

Darwin, of course, had heard the tales of a creature living in the loch, though the rare sightings were always made by the friend of a friend. He knew that such secondhand anecdotes were completely unreliable. Direct observation was the only viable scientific method for documenting new species. [...]

A ghostly edifice appeared in the fading light. Darwin turned to Edmonstone with a smile. "It's the tower of Urquhart Castle."

"Thank the Lord." [...]

"On our visit yesterday, I noticed a small beach where we can pull ashore until this wretched rain subsides."

"With pleasure."

Edmonstone pulled with even greater haste. They were only minutes from reaching shore when the boat rocked again. A massive shape rose from the water. [...]

Darwin looked up and saw a sight he knew he would remember no matter how long he lived. A huge black eye focused on him, reflecting the light of his lantern like a cat's eye. Before the creature dipped back below the water, it hesitated for a moment. Then with a splash, it was gone. [...]

This beast was unknown to science, perhaps unique. [...]

The boat skidded up the beach, and the two men tumbled out onto the rocks. Darwin and Edmonstone paused to catch their breath, peering at the loch to see if any sign of the creature remained. Not even a ripple of water betrayed that it had ever existed.

Boyd Morrison, *The Loch Ness Legacy*, Sphere, 2013.

Urquhart Castle, Loch Ness

### Wordbox

Nouns
- oars: *rames*
- shore: *rivage*
- wake: *sillage*
- ripple: *ondulation*

Verbs
- shiver: *trembler*
- split: *déchirer*

Action!

## Write an article for the local gazette

You are a journalist for the local paper. Write a short article to report on Edmonstone and Darwin's experience.

# April 2014: Is Nessie Back?

Track 48

**April 21st, 2014**

Only last week there was feverish excitement after a satellite image appeared on Apple Maps, apparently showing the creature —but is it a real sighting of the creature or clever marketing?

**Nessie's fan club over the moon**

Members of the Official Loch Ness Monster Fan Club claim they have studied the image seen on Apple's global satellite map application that shows the allegedly 100-foot-long creature. They say if you zoom in on Apple images you can even see the monster's giant flippers.

Andrew Dixon, chief executive of Creative Scotland*, said: "Whatever it is, it's just below the surface, so unless there have been secret submarine trials going on in the loch, the size of the object would make it likely to be Nessie."

Nessie's fan club devotees say they have ruled out all other possibilities for the grainy image, including a floating log or a giant seal.

**Nessie fans, prepare to be disappointed!**

However, a number of sceptics, including deep-sea biologist Andrew Thaler, have suggested that the image is a boat's wake, and that the vessel has been blurred out in keeping with Google and Apple's tendency to delete any personally identifying information.

Chris Matyszczyk, of CNET, even suggests the excitement may be manufactured by Apple, as the image can only be viewed on iPads or iPhones.

**A Monster Marketing Seminar**

Nessie's story has been around since the 6th century, but businesses in the Highlands look at the Loch Ness Monster with great interest. A Monster Marketing Seminar took place in Inverness in May 2014 to consider the importance of the Loch Ness Monster to the region's tourism industry. Nessie attracts around 300,000 visitors a year, bringing local businesses £30m annually.

Adaptated from www.independant.co.uk, April 27th, 2014; www.foxnews.com, April 21st, 2014; www.scotsman.com, April 21st, 2014.

*Creative Scotland is the development body for the arts and creative industries in Scotland.

1. Look at the picture and read the title. What do you expect to read?
2. List the arguments that prove Nessie's existence and the arguments that contradict it.
3. To see the photo that appeared on Apple Map, type "Apple Maps Nessie April 2014" on the Internet.
4. Why would Apple "manufacture the excitement"? (l. 24-25)
5. To what extent is such controversy important for Scotland?

**Now discuss the links between this text and the text on p. 131.**

6. Explain what these two documents illustrate about Nessie's place in Scotland.
7. To what extent is Nessie part of Scottish identity?

Grammar L'expression du doute et de la certitude See p. 134

**Action!**

**Record a radio piece of news**

On April 2014, a satellite image appeared on Apple Maps, apparently showing Monster Nessie. Record the piece of news that was broadcast on Radio Scotland on that day.

# HOW TO MAKE AN EFFECTIVE SLIDESHOW

Action!

**Make a slideshow to promote Scotland.**

Work in small groups.

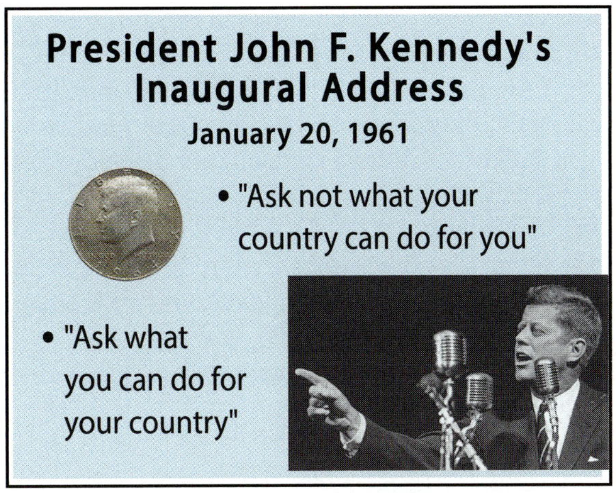

1. **Observe the model.**
   a. Compare the two slides above. Which is the most effective? Why?
   b. Judging from the model, say what makes a slide effective:
   – colors;
   – visuals;
   – layout (*mise en page*);
   – length of text written on the slide;
   – fonts;
   – background.
2. **Prepare your slideshow.**
   a. Watch examples of videos promoting Scotland on the Internet. You may find ideas on the following websites:
   TICE
   www.visitscotland.com
   www.youtube.com/watch?v=6i63UReFH4M
   b. Decide on four or five aspects of Scotland you want to show the type of information you want to pass on, and the number of slides you will make.
   c. Find visuals to illustrate your points.
   d. Decide on the text you will write on each slide.
   e. Prepare a short comment on each point and record it.
3. **Create your slideshow.**
   a. Create your slides. You can use software such as PowerPoint, IrfanView, OpenOffice.org, Impress, etc.
   b. Insert your recording on each slide. You can also add music for more drama and emotion to your speech.

# LANGUAGE WORKSHOP

GRAMMAR

## Les articles (Text File 1 p. 130)

Précis grammatical pp. 183 et 184

a. They were rowing on Ø Loch Ness.
b. It's the beast.
c. Darwin watched for any sign of the monstrous wake they'd first encountered ten minutes ago.
d. The rare sightings were always made by the friend of a friend.
e. The creature dipped back below the water.
f. A ghostly edifice appeared in the fading light.
g. A huge black eye focused on him, reflecting the light of his lantern.
h. This beast was unknown to Ø science.

### Rappelez-vous

Il y a trois articles en anglais : … , … et … .
– L'article … est l'article indéfini … .
– L'article … est l'article défini … .
– On choisit l'article … pour introduire un nom pluriel non déterminé, un nom abstrait ou certains noms comme les noms de lac.

### Allez plus loin

Observez les énoncés *a* à *h* et justifiez le choix des articles soulignés.

### Exercises

**1. Complete with *a/an*, *the*, or *ø*.**

a. Peter O'Connor was walking along … shore of … Loch Ness when he saw … shape on … loch.
b. At first he thought it was … rowing boat.
c. But then he saw … brown object.
d. A few weeks later, … scientific expedition was planned to make … general study of … Loch Ness.
e. … participants used … cameras and … echo sounder mounted on … boat.
f. They saw what appeared to be … monster's back moving through … water.
g. They also saw … object that continuously changed … shape on … surface of … water.
h. … numerous echo soundings were taken.

**2. Translate the following sentences and compare the articles used in English and in French.**

a. L'Écosse fait partie du Royaume-Uni.
b. La musique fait partie de la tradition écossaise.
c. Le docteur O'Brian habite à Dundee.
d. Il joue de la cornemuse tous les samedis dans un bar du centre-ville.
e. La tradition est de boire du whisky en écoutant de la musique.

## L'expression du doute et de la certitude (Text File 2 p. 132)

Précis grammatical pp. 182 et 197

a. Apple's global satellite map application shows an allegedly 100-foot-long creature.
b. A satellite image appeared on Apple Maps, apparently showing the creature.
c. The excitement may be manufactured by Apple.
d. The size of the object makes it likely to be Nessie.
e. There can't be secret submarine trials going on.

### Rappelez-vous

Pour donner son opinion sur la véracité d'un fait, on peut utiliser :
– un auxiliaire modal (donnez-en la liste et classez-les selon le degré de probabilité estimé par le locuteur) ;
– des adverbes tels que … .

### Allez plus loin

Dans les exemples, repérez le point de vue du journaliste et dites quel(s) mot(s) l'indique(nt).

### Exercise

**Translate into English.**

a. C'est probablement vrai. *(deux possibilités)*
b. Il est possible que cette forme soit celle d'un bateau. *(deux possibilités)*
c. Cette forme serait celle de Nessie, le monstre du Loch Ness. *(deux possibilités)*
d. Il n'est pas possible qu'ils aient vu quelque chose au fond de l'eau.
e. Cet homme a peut-être rêvé. *(deux possibilités)*

## GRAMMAR GAME

### Who could it be?

**Work in large groups.**

Each student picks up the name of one member of the group.

Everybody prepares a statement describing this person.
*Ex.: He/she is a wonderful tennis player.*

In turn, each member of the group gives their opinion on who the person could be, using a modal or an adverb.
*Ex.: Jennifer is likely to be a wonderful tennis player because… / Nicolas can't be a wonderful tennis player because…*, etc.

On goes the game until everybody has been identified!

## Exercises

**1. Find synonyms for these words in the word bank.**
bad – macabre – horrible – king – kingdom – sorcerer

**2. Fill in the blanks with words from the list.**
a. Many Scottish castles are said to be inhabited by … ; they are haunted.
b. How do you know if a spirit is good or … ?
c. It was a terrible and … revenge!
d. I have made a promise. I will not break my … .
e. Robert the Bruce … the English army at Bannockburn.

**3. Make a mind map.**
Copy the mind map below on a sheet of paper and fill it in with as many words or phrases as possible.

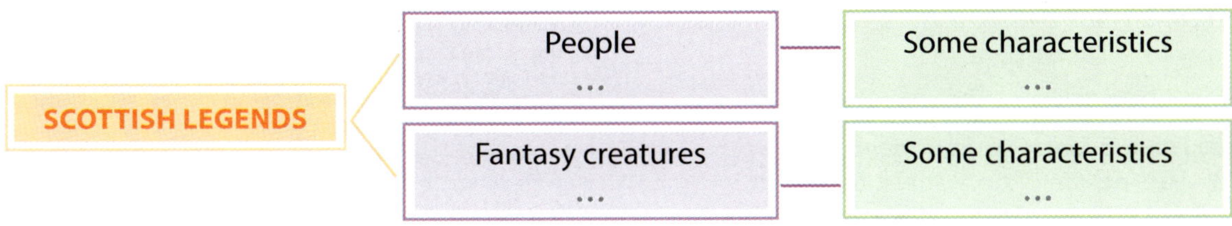


## Word bank

### Nouns
- conspiracy: *conspiration*
- creature, beast, monster: *monstre*
- devil: *diable*
- event: *événement*
- fairy: *fée*
- fairy tale: *conte de fée*
- follower: *partisan*
- ghost: *fantôme*
- giant: *géant*
- goblin: *lutin*
- king/queen: *roi/reine*
- mist: *brume*
- oath/vow: *serment/vœu*
- realm, kingdom: *royaume*
- revenge: *vengeance*
- sorcerer/witch: *sorcier/sorcière*
- tale: *conte*
- sovereign: *souverain(e)*
- warrior: *guerrier*
- wizard: *magicien*
- wrath, great anger: *fureur*

### Verbs
- believe: *croire*
- defeat: *vaincre*
- defend: *défendre*
- fight for: *se battre pour*
- ooze: *suinter*
- shiver: *trembler*

### Adjectives
- blood-thirsty: *assoiffé de sang*
- courageous, brave: *courageux*
- evil: *mauvais, mal*
- fierce: *féroce*
- frightful, awe-inspiring: *terrifiant*
- ghastly: *horrible*
- ghostly: *fantomatique*
- grisly: *macabre*
- haunted: *hanté*
- malevolent/benevolent: *malveillant/bienveillant*
- wretched: *misérable*

# SKILLS TRAINING

# Utiliser le dictionnaire

**Cette page s'applique aussi bien aux dictionnaires papier qu'aux dictionnaires en ligne : reverso.net, larousse.fr, wordreference.com, etc.**

A

**cool** /ku:l/

A *n* 1 (coldness) fraîcheur *f*; 2 ○(calm) sang-froid *m*; **to keep one's ~** (stay calm) garder son sang-froid; (not get angry) ne pas s'énerver; **to lose one's ~** (get angry) s'énerver; (panic) perdre son sang-froid — C

B *adj* 1 [*day, drink, water, weather*] frais/fraîche; [*dress*] léger/-ère; [*colour*] froid; **it's ~ today** il fait frais aujourd'hui; **to feel ~** [*surface, wine*] être frais/fraîche; **I feel ~er now** j'ai moins chaud maintenant; **it's getting ~, let's go in** il commence à faire frais, rentrons; 2 (calm) [*approach, handling*] calme; **to stay ~** garder son sang-froid; **to keep a ~ head** garder la tête froide; **keep ~!** reste calme; 3 (unemotional) [*manner*] détaché; [*logic*] froid; 4 (unfriendly) froid; **to be ~ with** *ou* **towards sb** être froid avec qn; 5 (casual) décontracté, cool○; **he's a ~ customer** il n'a pas froid aux yeux; 6 (for emphasis) **a ~ million dollars** la coquette somme d'un million de dollars○; 7 ○(sophisticated) branché○; **he thinks it's ~ to smoke** il pense que ça fait bien de fumer; **it's not ~** ça fait nul○; 8 ○US (great) super○! — E

C *vtr* 1 (lower the temperature of) refroidir [*soup, pan*]; rafraîchir [*wine, room*]; **to ~ one's hands** se rafraîchir les mains; 2 fig calmer [*anger, ardour*]

(B)

D — Phrasal verbs

■ **cool down**: ▸ **~ down** [*engine, water*] refroidir; fig [*person, situation*] se calmer; ▸ **~ [sth] down** refroidir [*mixture*]; rafr…chir [*wine*]; ▸ **~ [sb] dow…** rafraîchir; fig

Grand dictionnaire Anglais Hachette Oxford

## La phonétique (A)

Faites particulièrement attention aux signes vocaliques et à l'accent de mot. Certains dictionnaires en ligne vous donnent accès à l'écoute du mot.

**1** **Prononcez les mots transcrits ci-dessous en respectant la place de l'accent.**
[pɪ'dɛstrɪən] ['maʊntɪn] [ə'raɪvəl] [ˌsaɪən'tɪfɪk]

## Les catégories grammaticales (B)

Avant de rechercher un mot, demandez-vous à quelle catégorie grammaticale il appartient.

**2** **Devinez – ou cherchez – la signification de ces abréviations que l'on rencontre couramment.**
C – ¢ – conj – GB – i.e. – pp – refl – s.o. – sth – US – vi – vtr

**3** **Pour traduire les mots en gras, nous avons trouvé le mot donné dans le dictionnaire. Cherchez l'erreur !**
a. Darwin watched for any sign of the monstrous **wake** they'd first encountered. (wake = *réveiller*)
b. An abrupt noise **split** the rain. (split = *fente*)
c. The beauty of Scotland will shine and create a **lasting** impression. (last = *dernier*)

**4** **Cherchez le mot *well*, et donnez sa traduction selon la catégorie grammaticale demandée.**
a. Adverbe – b. Adjectif – c. Verbe (*well up*) – d. Exclamatif – e. Nom

## Les domaines d'emploi (C)

En français comme en anglais, beaucoup de mots on plusieurs sens selon leur domaine d'emploi – qui vous sont souvent indiqués avec des abréviations.

**5** **Devinez ce que signifient les abréviations suivantes dans la partie français-anglais.**
zool – jur – litt – culin – mil – fig – fin – usu – bot – med
Réponses (livre du prof)
zoologie – juridique – littéraire – culinaire – militaire – figuré – financier – usuel – botanique – médecine

**6** **Trouvez la traduction du mot « cours ».**
a. Ceci ne va pas changer le **cours** des choses.
b. Au **cours** de l'année, j'ai lu trois livres sur l'Ecosse.
c. Ce **cours** d'eau s'appelle The Thane.
d. J'ai un **cours** d'anglais à 10 heures.
e. Le **cours** de la livre est élevé.
f. Il fait ses études dans un **cours** privé.

## Les verbes à particule ou préposition (D)

Certains verbes « caméléons » prennent un sens différent de leur sens premier s'ils sont accompagnés d'une particule adverbiale ou d'une préposition.
Ex.: go *aller* ; go on *continuer*

**7** **Cherchez les verbes en gras dans votre dictionnaire. Donnez leur sens premier puis trouvez ce qu'ils signifient dans l'exemple.**
a. Darwin and Edmonton **kept** on rowing until they arrived at the shore.
b. They **were looking** at the Castle.
c. They **looked** for any sign of the creature.
d. Some tourism professionals **are looking** into turning Loch Ness into a theme park.
e. On their way home, they **ran** into an old man who said he had seen Nessie.
f. Sceptics say the story **was made** up.

## Les exemples (E)

**8** **Rectifiez l'erreur dans chaque traduction.**
a. Cela dépend du temps. *It depends of the weather.*
b. La température est fraiche. *The temperature is fresh.*
c. She broke the law. *Elle a cassé la loi.*
d. He picked me up. *Il m'a choisi(e).*

# Plan a school trip to Scotland

## Prepare a five-day trip to Scotland for your class.

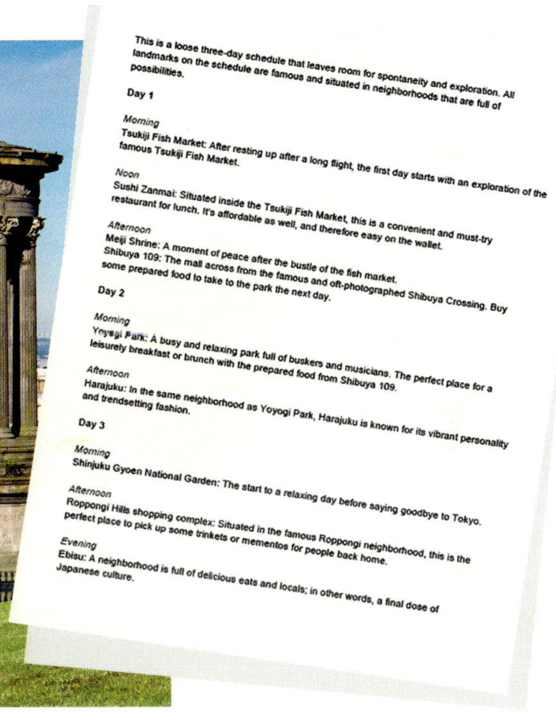

This is a loose three-day schedule that leaves room for spontaneity and exploration. All landmarks on the schedule are famous and situated in neighborhoods that are full of possibilities.

**Day 1**

*Morning*

Tsukiji Fish Market: After resting up after a long flight, the first day starts with an exploration of the famous Tsukiji Fish Market.

*Noon*

Sushi Zanmai: Situated inside the Tsukiji Fish Market, this is a convenient and must-try restaurant for lunch. It's affordable as well, and therefore easy on the wallet.

*Afternoon*

Meiji Shrine: A moment of peace after the bustle of the fish market.
Shibuya 109: The mall across from the famous and oft-photographed Shibuya Crossing. Buy some prepared food to take to the park the next day.

**Day 2**

*Morning*

Yoyogi Park: A busy and relaxing park full of buskers and musicians. The perfect place for a leisurely breakfast or brunch with the prepared food from Shibuya 109.

*Afternoon*

Harajuku: In the same neighborhood as Yoyogi Park, Harajuku is known for its vibrant personality and trendsetting fashion.

**Day 3**

*Morning*

Shinjuku Gyoen National Garden: The start to a relaxing day before saying goodbye to Tokyo.

*Afternoon*

Roppongi Hills shopping complex: Situated in the famous Roppongi neighborhood, this is the perfect place to pick up some trinkets or mementos for people back home.

*Evening*

Ebisu: A neighborhood is full of delicious eats and locals; in other words, a final dose of Japanese culture.

- **Divide the class into groups.**

### Step 1

Make a list of things and places you'd like to see. Locate them on a map and then select your destinations and the visits you want to make.

You may visit the following websites to find ideas.

TICE
www.lonelyplanet.com/search?q=scotland
www.visitscotland.com/holidays/plan-your-trip
www.explorescotland.net/holiday-in-scotland
www.scotlandwelcomesyou.com/scotland-travel-information

### Step 2

Organize your visits: decide on the visits you will make each day. Do not plan too many visits! Leave time for exploration and unexpected events.

Prepare arguments to justify the choices you have made.

### Step 3

Budget the amount of money you plan to spend on transportation, lodging, food, and visits. You can find everything on the Internet.

- **Transportation:**
  – from home to your destination (and back!): plane, boat, bus…
  – from one place to another: bus, train, on foot…
- **Lodging:** hotels, youth hostels, Bed and Breakfast places…
- **Food:** restaurant, cooking, snacks…
- **Visits:** admission fees.

### Step 4

Make a slideshow to present your project to the class.

Writing WORKSHOP p. 133

ART HISTORY CORNER

# SCOTLAND IN THE ARTS

**Artists, writers, and poets all contributed to the emergence of Scotland's strong national identity, and are part of our modern notion of Scotland and Scottishness.**

## Painting

The Scottish landscape, with its dramatic mountain wildernesses, has been a source of inspiration for native artists for centuries. But art in Scotland has not developed in isolation: artists have been in close contact with European art, especially in France and Italy.

Samuel John Peploe, *The Yellow Dress*, 1908-9.

Horatio McCulloch, *Loch Lomond*, 1861.

Francis Campbell Boileau, *Iona, The East Bay*, 1928.

## Music

### The bagpipe

Scotland's national instrument, the iconic bagpipe, is still hugely popular. The sound of the bagpipe can be heard everywhere, parading through Scottish towns and cities. Plenty of events around Scotland showcase bagpipes, in particular the annual piping festival Piping Live! and the World Pipe Band Championships in Glasgow, and the Edinburgh Millitary Tattoo. The bagpipe even has a museum in Glasgow, the National Piping Centre.

With its bagpipe music, ***Flower of Scotland*** is frequently sung at special occasions and sporting events. Written in 1967 by Roy Williamson of the folk group The Corries, it refers to the victory of the Scots at the Battle of Bannockburn in 1314.

**Flower of Scotland**

*O Flower of Scotland*
*When will we see*
*Your like again,*
*That fought and died for*
*Your wee bit hill and glen,*
*And stood against him*
*Proud Edward's army*
*And sent him homeward*
*Tae think again*
*The Bonny Earl of Murray*
*Ye Highlands, and ye Lawlands,*
*Oh where have you been?*
*They have slain the Earl of Murray,*
*And they layd him on the green.*

**Rock bands**

Scottish music isn't all about the bagpipes and popular music. The country is home to a number of internationally-renowned bands like the famous rock bands Simple Minds or Franz Ferdinand, both originating from Glasgow.

## Literature

The influence of Scottish history and dramatic landscape can be seen throughout Scottish literature and poetry. Many Scottish writers are internationally renowned writers.

**Robert Burns (1759–1796)**
The national poet of Scotland is celebrated worldwide. His works contain many traditional folk songs.

***Auld Lang Syne***
Should auld acquaintance be forgot,
and never brought to mind?
Should auld acquaintance be forgot,
and days of auld lang syne?

**Sir Walter Scott (1771–1832)**
Many of his works remain classics, with titles such as *Ivanhoe*, the tale of a knight who comes home from crusade to find he's been disinherited, *Rob Roy* or *Waverley*.

**Robert Louis Stevenson (1850–1894)**
Born in 1850, in Edinburgh, Scotland, Robert Louis Stevenson became a literary celebrity during his life when works such as *Treasure Island*, *Kidnapped*, and *Strange Case of Dr. Jekyll and Mr. Hyde* were released.

**John Buchan (1875–1940)**
His adventure novel, *The Thirty-Nine Steps*, was one of the earliest spy stories and formed the basis for a number of film adaptations, notably by Alfred Hitchcock.

**Muriel Spark (1918–2006)**
Her best-known novel, *The Prime of Miss Jean Brodie*, is set in 1930s Edinburgh. Miss Brodie is a teacher who gives her six ten-year-old girl students an education that will make them an elite group.

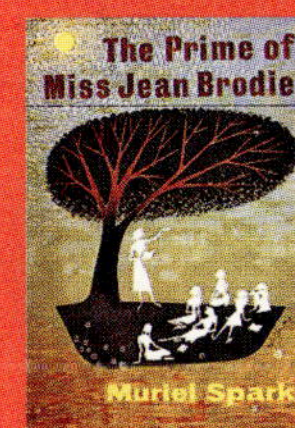


## Movies

With its spectacular scenery of mountains and lochs and the richness of its history and tradition, Scotland has been a favorite setting for many film directors.

***Local Hero*** (Bill Forsyth, 1983)
A Houston business man, "Mac", persuades the residents of a fictional coastal Scottish village to sell their village to his American oil company. The film captures the spirit of a small, Scottish coastal village.

***Highlander*** (Russell Mulcahy, 1986)
This British-American action fantasy film stars Christopher Lambert and Sean Connery. The film depicts an ages-old battle in the 16th century, between immortal warriors.

***Braveheart*** (Mel Gibson, 1995)
This epic historical medieval war drama film portrays William Wallace, a 13th-century Scottish warrior who led the Scots in the First War of Scottish Independence against King Edward I of England.

***Trainspotting*** (Danny Boyle, 1996)
The story takes place in 1980s Leith, an economically deprived district of Edinburgh. It stars Ewan McGregor as an Edinburgh drug addict attempting to turn his back on the city's drug scene. It paints a far less idyllic view of Scotland than many of the movies on this list.

***Sweet Sixteen*** (Ken Loach, 2002)
Ken Loach gives an honest approach to Scotland's social ills, depicting typical juvenile delinquent Liam and his strained attempts at creating a better life for himself and his mother.

***Skyfall*** (Sam Mendes, 2012)
James Bond is Scottish! The James Bond series went to Scotland for a climactic sequence set in the spy's ancestral home, Skyfall.

- Get into groups and choose one of the arts presented on this page. Each member of the group searches the Internet to select a piece of art they find particularly relevant and makes a presentation (slideshow, poster, or podcast) for the class.

## COMPREHENSION

### 1 The Ghosts of Mary King's Close

There are few places better situated to debating paranormal phenomena than Mary King's Close in Edinburgh. The close was inhabited during the 16th and 17th centuries before the plague ravaged families living in the tightly packed tenement buildings.

The celebrity of the close's supernatural resident is Annie, a ghostly pre-teen who (so the story goes) scared the daylights out of a Japanese psychic in 1992. This lady had been unimpressed by the tour until she arrived at one of the many small rooms. There she was suddenly struck by an overwhelming feeling of sickness, hunger, and cold and, when she tried to leave, felt the ghastly tug of a ghostly hand on her leg.

It is believed that [poor Annie] had been left to die by her family. Since then, people from round the world have come to "Annie's room". Many have told tour guides of seeing impressions of the spirit in the room.

The tour itself is a wonderful experience and well-orchestrated by the operators, Continuum. Authentically dressed guides lead visitors out of the sunshine downstairs into the murky past through vaults and alleyways that form the remnants of 17th-century Edinburgh. A growing list of people who believe they've seen spirits here has led to a number of experiments being conducted in the close. Ryan O'Neill from Scottish Paranormal, a group of amateur enthusiasts of the supernatural, captured "very faint white or transparent spheres" when photographing the recreated workshop. [...]

The close is not short of scientists looking into paranormal activity. In April 2001, [...] Dr. Caroline Watt of Edinburgh University [...] had her own experience of ghosts in Mary King's Close [...].

"I was in a part of the close where no one else was supposed to be," she says. "I heard footsteps and the sound of rustling clothing. I was annoyed because I thought it was someone intruding on our experiment, but when I asked the tour guides I found out there was no one there."

www.scotsman.com, July 26th, 2005.

## Questions Doc. 1

1. What is Mary King's Close?
2. Explain why this place is a perfect setting for a ghost story.
3. Say what you have learnt about Annie.
4. List the evidence reported of the ghost's existence.
5. Explain why the tour is said to be "well-orchestrated" (l. 14).
6. Would you say the journalist believes in the existence of ghosts? Why or why not?

## EXPRESSION

**Choose one of the following subjects.**

**A. Write a dialogue**
After the tour in Mary King's Close, a ghost believer and a skeptic discuss. Write the dialogue.

**B. Give your opinion**
Do you believe in paranormal phenomena? Why or why not?

# "Oral"

## COMPREHENSION

**Scotland Vote "No" to Independence**

www.youtube.com/watch?v=nKJ7ppAFhhQ

1. Watch the video three times and take down notes.
2. Then write a report on it, in French.

## EXPRESSION

### "Myths and heroes"

***What does it mean to be Scottish? The making of an identity***

• **Prepare your presentation in note form**

**Step 1** **Introduce the notion: "the Scottish identity".**
Example: What does it mean to be Scottish? National identity is generally constructed by a shared history, language, culture, and ethnic origin. What makes a Scotsman today?

**Step 2** **A shared history**
Talk about the people that invaded and influenced Scottish society.
▶ Cultural Background / Sound File
Talk about the heroes that forged the Scottish identity.
▶ Cultural Background
Show how the Scots' opposition to Britain contributed to a nationalistic feeling.
▶ Cultural Background / Sound File

**Step 3** **A shared culture**
Give examples of some characteristics: landscapes, myths and legends, language, traditions.
Explain why Scottish people are attached to these aspects of their culture.
▶ Sound File / Text File 1 / Text File 2

**Step 4** **The Scots today**
Explain how Scotland has become part of a larger nation: the United Kingdom.
▶ Cultural Background
Show that, although the Scots have decided to remain in the UK, they still preserve their identity.
▶ Text File 2/ Written Exam

**Step 5** **Conclude.**
Say what your idea of Scotland was before you worked on this unit and whether it has changed or not. Answer the question you asked in your introduction: what does it mean to have a national identity?

• **Train yourself**

Follow the steps above and speak for five minutes. If possible, add personal comments. Record yourself and listen to your presentation to improve it.

• **Get ready for a conversation**

Listen to the recording of your presentation and prepare yourself to justify, develop, and exemplify what you have said.

# unit 8 Slaves Who Dared

"Myths and heroes"
*How did some extraordinary people manage to survive and fight slavery?*



To access our audio resources, use our Flashcodes or go to our website: www.ressources.hachette-education.com/boardingpass/1re/units/unit8.html

Patricia Bruitle,
*Hope at Sunrise*, 2007.

CULTURAL BACKGROUND

# AN OVERVIEW OF SLAVERY IN AMERICA

## 1 What Do You Know About... Slavery?

**In pairs, decide whether the following statements are true or false.**

| | True | False |
|---|---|---|
| 1. The Europeans invented slavery. | ☐ | ☐ |
| 2. The Egyptians, the Greeks, the Romans, and African nations used conquered people as slaves. | ☐ | ☐ |
| 3. A black slave trade started with the discovery of the Americas by Europeans in 1493. | ☐ | ☐ |
| 4. Two to three million people were deported. | ☐ | ☐ |
| 5. Many millions died on slave ships or in wars and raids. | ☐ | ☐ |
| 6. Slaves were used to exploit land, and gold and silver mines. | ☐ | ☐ |
| 7. In the 19th century, slavery was legal all over the USA. | ☐ | ☐ |
| 8. New York State was a free state and Georgia was a slave state. | ☐ | ☐ |
| 9. Slavery was declared illegal in Britain in 1833, in France in 1848, and in the USA in 1865. | ☐ | ☐ |
| 10. It is President Kennedy who issued a proclamation liberating all slaves. | ☐ | ☐ |

## 2 Runaway Slaves

2 Track 49

1. Listen and put these titles into the right order:
   - The Underground Railroad
   - Statistics about Slaves Who Gained Their Freedom
   - Slaves' Living Conditions
2. Give the reasons why slaves tried to run away.
3. Say what happened when runaway slaves were captured.
4. Give a definition for the Underground Railroad.
5. Say what these words refer to: stations; stockholders; conductors.
6. Pick out the four numbers in the last sentence and say what they correspond to.

### Wordbox

Nouns
- network: *réseau*
- railroad: *ligne de chemin de fer*
- stockholder: *actionnaire*

Verbs
- tear apart: *séparer*
- whip: *fouetter*

Adjective
- underground: *souterrain*

## 3 The Triangle Trade

In the 17th century, ships left British ports like Liverpool and Bristol (or French ports like Nantes or Bordeaux) for Africa, full of firearms, gunpowder, metals, alcohol, cotton goods, knives, and mirrors—things that African chiefs appreciated. These goods were exchanged for slaves—who had been captured in local tribal wars.

By the 1760s, British ships were carrying about 50,000 slaves a year across the Atlantic; this journey was called "the Middle Passage". Slaves who had survived the journey were sold to plantation owners in the West Indies or the southern colonies of America (Virginia, the Carolinas, Georgia), where they spent the rest of their lives working on cotton, tobacco, sugar cane, and coffee plantations.

The slave-produced goods were shipped back to Britain, where they were manufactured or refined and then either sold locally or re-exported at a vast profit. The slave trade brought in huge amounts of money to Britain.

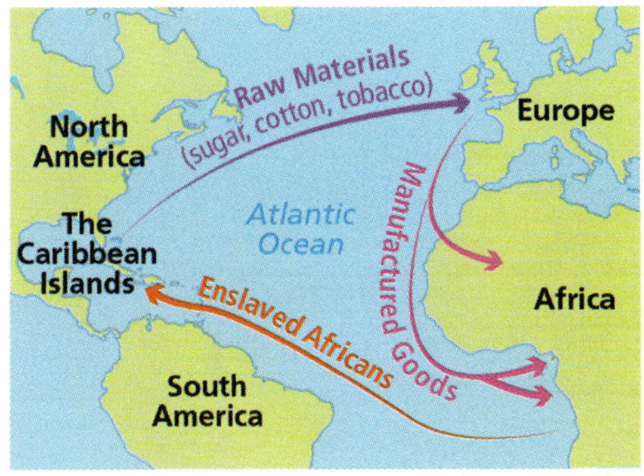


1. Pick out the three important steps in the slave trade. Say what the ships transported on each step.
2. Find the equivalents of these words: *armes à feu, poudre à canon* (§1) ; *voyage* (§2) ; *sommes* (§3).

## 4 A Harrowing Voyage

The journey took 6 to 8 weeks. The slaves were packed tightly on-board slave ships. Often they were chained down. Conditions were terrible. Families were separated. The food and the water were often contaminated. Many slaves died or threw themselves overboard to avoid captivity.

1. Say what the living conditions on slave ships were like.
2. Guess what the title means.

**Action!**

### Prepare a quiz about slavery

Work in groups. Each group prepares a ten-question quiz about slavery.
Groups then exchange quizzes and try to answer as many questions as possible.

VIDEO FILE

# THE LEGACY OF SLAVERY

Steve McQueen, *Twelve Years a Slave*, 2013.

Large numbers of slaves were purchased to work on cotton plantations.

## Before you watch

1. Talk about the life of slaves on cotton plantations.
2. What do you think Americans may feel about movies that deal with slavery?
3. Explain the title of the document.

## Now watch

B1+ A2+ Use the question sheet in your eWorkbook.

4. Take notes and sum up what you have understood.

## Recap

5. Explain what the impact of films about slavery has been in America and the changes that have occurred.
6. Say what the key question about slavery legacy is.
7. List the different opinions that are presented in the document and explain these people's arguments.

## React

8. Would you be interested in seeing a movie about slavery or not? Why?

**Sum up the document in French.**

## TRAIN YOUR EARS

1. **Match the following words with their French translation. Then listen and repeat.** 2 Track 50

avoided • debt • doubt • era • forward • issue • owe • reflect • reignite • searing • skirted

*brûlant • contourné • dette • devoir • doute • en avant • évité • ère • rallumer • réfléchir • problème*

2. **Read these transparent words out loud; then listen and repeat.** 2 Track 51

actors • producers • cameras • question • discussion • plantation • historians • neglected • descendant • politician • reflect • mention • debt • doubt

## Wordbox

Nouns
- graves: *tombes*
- issue: *sujet*
- legacy: *legs, héritage*
- owners: *propriétaires*
- spot: *tache*
- sins: *péchés, fautes*

Verbs
- abuse: *maltraiter*
- reignite: *rallumer*
- remain: *demeurer*
- skirt: *contourner*

Adjectives
- painful: *douloureux*
- prominent: *éminent*
- searing: *brûlant*

Adverb
- forward: *vers l'avant*

## Action! Present a movie

In groups, search the web to select a movie dealing with slavery and prepare a presentation. Give your presentation to the class.

# WHEN SLAVES ARRIVED IN THE AMERICAS

**Abolition campaigner and former slave Olaudah Equiano describes his arrival on the island of Barbados.**

A Slave Auction

The slaves were brought in early so that buyers who desired to inspect them might enjoy that privilege. The negroes were examined with as little consideration as if they had been brutes; the buyers pulling their mouths open to see their teeth, pinching their limbs to find how muscular they were, etc.

*The New-York Tribune*, 1859

## TRAIN YOUR EARS

1. **Read these transparent words. Then listen to check and repeat.** 2 Track 52
merchants • planters • separate • examined • conducted • signal • confined • scruple • initial • instruments • torture • creatures • intolerable
2. **Listen to the words from the Wordbox and repeat them. Mind the stress.** 2 Track 53
3. a. **Pronounce the words below. Note down their stress pattern (Ooo, oOoo, etc.). Listen to check.** 2 Track 54
separate • examined • attentively • conducted • immediately • together • relations • separated • initial • occasion • instruments • despair • preferred

## Before you listen

1. Judging from the introduction, the picture, and the caption, guess what you are going to hear.
2. Find out where the island of Barbados is.

## Now listen

B1+ A2+ Use the question sheet in your eWorkbook. 2 Tracks 55 to 58

3. Listen to the document and take notes.

## Wordbox

**Nouns**
- **auc**tion: *vente aux enchères*
- bone: *os*
- **cus**tody: *garde*
- **i**ron: *fer*
- load: *charge*
- **par**cel: *paquet*

**Verb**
- rush: *se précipiter*

**Adjective**
- **bran**ded: *marqué au fer*

## Recap

4. Talk about:
– what happened to the slaves when they arrived in America;
– how the slave sales took place and what the consequences were;
– the slaves' conditions;
– Olaudah's feelings.

## React

5. What does the fact that many slaves were branded with their master's name show?
6. What was the consequence on the slaves of the treatment they had?

**Sum up the document in French.**

## Action!

### Record a testimony

Olaudah Equiano wants to leave a recording to his grandchildren to tell them about his condition when he was a slave. Work in pairs to prepare his presentation in note form. Record yourself.

# TEXT FILE 1

## Before you read

1. Look at the picture on this page. Then close your book and recap what you know about Solomon Northup.
2. Find out on the Internet where Saratoga is located. Was it in a free state or a slave state?
3. Look at the picture on the right-hand page. Imagine what the situation is.

## Now read

B1+ A2+ Use the question sheet in your eWorkbook.

4. Read the text and check your guesses.

## Recap

5. Talk about the situation and the two characters' relationships.
6. Explain why two places—a city, Saratoga; and a state, Georgia—are mentioned and what the two men disagree on.
7. Talk about the two characters' feelings.
8. Explain what Radburn's role is.
9. Find in the text a definition for "the paddle and the cat o' nine tails".

## React

10. Say what the phrase "human stable" (l. 24) implies.
11. Say what you think of Northup's personality (quote from the text to justify).

### Wordbox

Nouns
- hell: *enfer*
- lie: *mensonge*
- stable: *écurie*
- whip: *fouet*

Verbs
- hush: *faire taire*
- yield: *céder*

Adjective
- foul: *ignoble*

## Work on Words

1. **Complete the lexical field of speech** with verbs from paragraph 1: say, ...
2. **Which verb echoes the verb "hush"** (l. 20) in the next sentence?
3. Find four adverbs with a -ly ending. Translate them. Then make similar adverbs with these adjectives: free – brutal. Translate them.

## Sum up

1. **Listen to our recorded summary.** 2 Track 60
2. **Use the words below to write your own summary of the text.**
   - Northup – plantation – convince – Burch – free
   - Burch – had bought – Northup – property
   - Northup – agree – Burch – angry – ordered – employee – whips
   - Northup – beaten – maintained – position
   - courageous

> Grammar **Le passif** See p. 152

# Twelve Years a Slave

Track 59

"Well, my boy, how do you feel now?" said Burch. I replied that I was sick, and inquired the cause of my imprisonment. He answered that I was his slave—that he had bought me. I asserted, aloud and boldly, that I was a free man—a resident of Saratoga, where I had a wife and children, and that my name was Northup. I complained bitterly of the strange treatment I had received. He denied that I was free, and declared that I came from Georgia. Again and again I asserted I was no man's slave, and insisted upon his taking off my chains at once. He tried to hush me but I would not be silent. Finding he could not quiet me, he flew into a towering passion. [...]

**Burch, the slave owner, and Solomon Northup.**

During this time Radburn was standing silently by. His business was to oversee this human [...] stable, receiving slaves, feeding, and whipping them. Turning to him, Burch ordered the paddle and cat o' nine tails to be brought in. He disappeared, and in a few moments returned with these instruments of torture. [...]

As soon as these formidable whips appeared, I was seized by both of them, and roughly divested of my clothing. With the paddle, Burch commenced beating me. Blow after blow was inflicted upon my naked body. When his unrelenting arm grew tired, he stopped and asked if I still insisted I was a free man. I did insist upon it, and then the blows were renewed, faster and more energetic. Still I would not yield. All his brutal blows could not force from my lips the foul lie that I was a slave.

My sufferings I can compare to nothing else than the burning agonies of hell!

**Solomon Northup, 1853**

*Twelve Years a Slave.* Narrative of Solomon Northup, a citizen of New York, kidnapped in Washington City in 1841 and rescued in 1853, from a cotton plantation near the red river in Louisiana.

Action!

## Make a presentation about Solomon Northup

Search the Internet for information about what happened in the life of Solomon Northup after he got to freedom in 1853. Then make an oral presentation of his biography.

# Crossing The River: a Kentucky Slave Narrative

Track 61

*A first-hand account of a slave who secretly transported other slaves across the river from Kentucky, where he was enslaved, to Ohio, a free state.*

"I just knew there was a lot of slaves wantin' to get free, and I had to help 'em."

"I was born on a plantation that belonged to Mr. Jack Tabb in Mason County, Kentucky. Mr. Tabb was a pretty good man. He used to beat us, sure; but not nearly so much as others did. He was kinda funny sometimes; he used to have a special slave who didn't have nothin' to do but teach the rest of us how to read and write, and figure.

Mr. Tabb was always good to me. He used to let me go around in the day and night. T'is how I came to be the one who carried runaway slaves over the river. I made three and four trips a month.

I never got anything from a single one of the people I carried over the river to freedom. I didn't want anything. I could have been free any night myself, but I figured I wasn't gettin' along so bad so I would stay on at Mr. Tabb's place and help the others get free. I did it for four years.

Mr. Tabb was different from the other owners. For every slave who came through his place, he had a good word, and something to eat. He helped us a lot.

One night, in 1863, I carried across about twelve people on the same night. Somebody must have seen us and they set out after me. I had to run away from Mr. Tabb's plantation and live in the woods.

I saw that I could never do any more good in Mason County, so I decided to take my freedom, too."

From an interview with Arnold Gragston, conducted in 1937.

1. Read the title and the subtitle. Say what you understand about the author and imagine what you are going to read.
2. Read the text and recap:
   – say as much as possible about Arnold Gragston and about Mr. Tabb;
   – explain how Gragston became an Underground Railroad conductor;
   – say what Gragston stopped doing. Why?
3. Say what l. 30-31 reveal about Gragston and comment.

**Now discuss the links between this text and the text on p. 149.**

4. Compare Mr. Tabb with Mr. Burch.

Grammar *Used to* + V / *be used to* + V-*ing*
See p.152

Action!

## Write an article about Kentucky runaway slaves

As a journalist for *The Ohio Journal*, write an article about slaves from Kentucky who escaped to freedom.

# HOW TO MAKE A HISTORICAL PANEL

**Action!**
**Make a panel presenting Olaudah Equiano.**
Work in pairs.

## Thurgood Marshall

**Thurgood Marshall was a courageous civil rights lawyer who lived in a period when racial segregation was legal. Marshall realized that the best ways to bring about change was through the legal system. Between 1938 and 1961, he presented more than thirty civil rights cases before the US Supreme Court.**

**He went on to become the first African-American Supreme Court Justice in American history.**

**Thurgood Marshall**
"We will only attain freedom if we learn to appreciate what is different and muster the courage to discover what is fundamentally the same."

**BROWN v. BOARD OF EDUCATION OF TOPEKA**
This was his most important case (1954), which ended segregation in public schools. Marshall challenged the doctrine, pointing out that "separate but equal" was just a myth disguising racism. He argued that if all students were indeed equal, then why was it necessary to separate them? The Supreme Court agreed, and Black children were allowed to attend white schools.

**SEGREGATED SCHOOLS**
By law, black and white students had to attend separate public schools. As long as schools were "separate but equal"—providing equal education for all races—segregation was considered fair.
In reality, segregated schools were unequal: white schools were far more privileged than black schools, which were poor and overcrowded…

**1. Observe the model.**

a. Say what type of information is displayed in each part of the panel.

b. True or false? Discuss to justify your answers.
– The panel should present as much information as possible.
– Presenting the general historical context is important.
– Explaining the impact the character presented has had is useless as people can guess it from the information presented.

**2. Prepare your panel.**

a. Read the following biography of Olaudah Equiano and select the information you will use.

Olaudah Equiano was born in Nigeria in 1745. Aged 11, he was kidnapped by native slave-holders and sold to European slave traders. He ended up in Virginia where he was bought by a sailor in the Royal Navy. He followed his master in Britain's Seven Years War with France. In England, he gained a basic education. Then he was sold to Captain Doran in the Caribbean. Doran helped Equiano to purchase his freedom. Equiano became Doran's business partner but slaveholders attempted to kidnap him and return him to slavery. Feeling unsafe, he returned to Britain. There, he met people who supported the abolition of the slave trade. His friends encouraged him to write a book about his life. Later, Equiano devoted his life to campaigning against slavery. In 1792, he married an English girl. They had two daughters. He died in 1797 in London.

b. Search the Internet to find visuals and additional information.

TICE
www.bbc.co.uk/history/historic_figures/equiano_olaudah.shtml
www.biography.com/people/olaudah-equiano-39207
http://en.wikipedia.org/wiki/Olaudah_Equiano

**3. Make your panel.**

a. Write short paragraphs to present the points you want to highlight about Olaudah Equiano.

b. Organize your paragraphs on your panel and add pictures to illustrate them.

GRAMMAR

## Le passif (Text File 1 p. 148)

Précis grammatical p. 201

a. Northup was sold into slavery in 1841.
b. He had been kidnapped by a slave trader.
c. Burch said that he had bought me.
d. Blows were inflicted upon my naked body.

**Rappelez-vous**

- Définissez ce qu'est une voix passive.
- Dites comment on met un verbe à la voix passive. Donnez un exemple.

**Allez plus loin**

1. Repérez les groupes verbaux au passif dans les exemples *a* à *d*.
2. Repérez un complément d'agent. Dites par quoi il est introduit.
3. Identifiez l'énoncé qui n'est pas au passif. Mettez-le à la voix passive. Expliquez pourquoi la voix active a été préférée dans cet énoncé.
4. Mettez les autres énoncés à la voix active (vous devrez inventer un sujet).
5. Transformez l'exemple *d* pour faire référence à l'avenir.

**Exercises**

1. **Put these sentences into the passive voice.**
   a. Slave owners separated families.
   b. They used to beat slaves very often.
   c. They gave slaves permission to go to church on Sundays.
   d. Slaves were occasionally allowed to learn to read and write.
2. **Translate into English using the verb "catch".**
   a. Il fut capturé.
   b. Il sera capturé.
   c. Ils sont souvent capturés.
   d. Il se peut qu'il soit capturé.
3. **Make complete passive sentences.**
   a. Slavery – abolish – 1865
   b. Northup – be – enslave – 12 years – when he – rescue – in 1853
   c. In the 21st century – some people – sell – as slaves
   d. I hope – slavery – abolish – in all countries in the next 10 years.

## *Used to* + V / *be used to* + V-ing (Text File 2 p. 150)

Précis grammatical p. 213

a. Mr. Tabb used to let me go around in the day and night.
b. Many slaves were used to being beaten.

**Rappelez-vous**

- Comparez *used to* dans les deux énoncés : forme et valeur.
- Traduisez les énoncés en français.

**Allez plus loin**

Il ne faut pas confondre :
– *used to* + V, qui est une forme grammaticale renvoyant au ...
– *be used to*, qui est ... et signifie soit ... , soit ... .

**Exercises**

1. **Complete with "used to" or "be used to" in the right form.**
   a. Gragston ... carry runaway slaves across the river.
   b. Mr. Tabb ... treat his slaves correctly.
   c. Many slaves ... being submissive, so not many of them revolted.
   d. Gragston ... be treated correctly, so he did not run away.
2. **Translate into English.**
   a. Il avait des esclaves, mais ensuite il les a libérés.
   b. Les planteurs avaient l'habitude d'être servis.
   c. Avant d'être kidnappé, Solomon Northup n'avait pas l'habitude d'être frappé.

## GRAMMAR GAME

### Make a "sentence competition"

**Work in groups of five or six, and sit in circles.**

Each student chooses two slips of paper from the teacher (a grammar category and a verb), and writes a sentence in the passive voice using the verb in the right form and adding as many details as possible.

# VOCABULARY

## Exercises

**1. Rephrase these sentences using the prompts and words from the word bank.**

1. The masters took advantage of their slaves.
→ The slaves were … .

2. The slaves were chained together by their hands and feet.
→ They were … .

3. In 1862 President Lincoln issued a proclamation liberating all slaves.
→ President Lincoln promised the slaves would be … .

4. The slaves were not allowed to say what they thought.
→ They didn't have … .

**2. Give the corresponding nouns referring to people.**

Ex.: slavery → slave

slave trade • slave ownership • recruitment • running away • abolish

**3. Complete this interview of a slave descendant.**

1. What was it like for your ancestors to work in the … … ?
→ It was hard working in them. Their backs hurt at the end of the day from bending over so much.

2. How did the slave owners … … the runaways?
→ They went after them with dogs.

3. When did the Confederate armies … ?
→ In 1865. That was the end of the war.

4. How long was your grandfather … … … ?
→ Oh, for about 30 years of his life.

5. What did he do when he … his … ?
→ Not much. He was so worn out from slavery that he died soon afterwards.

## Word bank

**Nouns**

- abolitionist: *abolitionniste*
- auction: *vente aux enchères*
- cotton fields: *plantations*
- emancipation: *affranchissement*
- enforce human rights: *faire respecter les droits de l'homme*
- freedom of speech: *liberté de parole*
- fugitive: *fugitif*
- observance of human rights: *respect des droits de l'homme*
- revolt: *révolte*
- runaway: *fugitif*
- ship: *bateau*
- slave owner: *propriétaire d'esclave*
- slave trader: *trafiquant d'esclaves*
- slavery: *esclavage*

**Verbs**

- abolish: *abolir*
- be enslaved: *être asservi*
- be exploited: *être exploité*
- be in shackles: *être enchaîné*
- deny someone's rights: *nier les droits de quelqu'un*
- hunt down: *pourchasser*
- hold in bondage: *tenir en esclavage*
- oppress: *opprimer*
- recover one's rights: *recouvrer ses droits*
- recruit: *recruter*
- surrender: *se rendre*
- trade in slaves: *faire la traite des esclaves*
- set free: *libérer*
- suffer: *souffrir*
- whip: *fouetter*

## SKILLS TRAINING

# Enrichir son style à l'écrit

### Améliorez votre vocabulaire

Utilisez un vocabulaire riche et varié. Évitez les mots passe-partout comme *good*, *be*, *have*, etc.
Par exemple, vous pouvez remplacer *good* par des mots comme *excellent*, *exceptional*, *great*, *marvelous*, *wonderful*, *pleasing*, *super*, *enchanting*, etc.

**1 Remplacez les mots en gras en choisissant un équivalent dans la liste.**
*It was a* ***nice*** *day. I had decided* ***to go away*** *from the plantation. I felt* ***happy*** *and started running. And my master* ***arrived****. I tried to hide behind a* ***big*** *tree. "Solomon, come here," he* ***said****. He had seen me and he was* ***displeased****.* ***And*** *I was whipped and* ***put*** *in a dark room for 3 days.*

- *run away, escape, flee, run off*
- *turn up, appear*
- *pleasant, agreeable, enjoyable*
- *enraged, furious, angry*
- *enormous, huge, giant*
- *jailed, locked up*
- *glad, cheerful, joyful*
- *then, suddenly, so, consequently*
- *shout, yell, ordered*

### Enrichissez vos phrases

On peut introduire un grand nombre d'informations dans une phrase enrichie.

**4 Observez un modèle.**

a. Observez cette « phrase noyau » – qui présente le film *Beloved*. Donnez la fonction grammaticale des mots.

*This movie focuses on the experience of a slave.*

b. À chaque étape, repérez les éléments que nous avons ajoutés et donnez leur fonction grammaticale. Dites quelles informations supplémentaires sont données.
- *This movie focuses on the experience of a black woman slave, named Sethe.*
- *This movie focuses on the experience of a black woman slave, named Sethe, who escaped to Ohio from a Kentucky plantation in 1856.*
- *Based on the Pulitzer prize-winning novel by Toni Morrison, this movie focuses on the experience of a black woman slave, named Sethe, who escaped to Ohio from a Kentucky plantation in 1856.*

**5 Présentez un film de votre choix.**
Suivez les étapes, comme dans le modèle (exercice 4), pour compléter cette amorce et ajouter des informations.
*This movie focuses on/depicts/relates/explores…*

### Reliez vos phrases

Évitez une succession de phrases simples. Pensez à les relier en utilisant des subordonnées ou des connecteurs logiques.
**Observez ces deux phrases complexes.**
- *I had one brother, William, who was two years younger than myself — a bright, affectionate child.*
- *My parents lived in a comfortable home, and, though we were all slaves, I always felt protected.*

**2 Reliez les deux phrases avec un relatif.**

a. *Black people were transported from Africa to America. Black people had been captured in tribal wars.*
b. *White children were more privileged than black schools. Black schools were poor and overcrowded.*
c. *The issue of slavery has been avoided for too long. The issue now appears in movies.*

**3 Trouvez plusieurs manières de relier les deux phrases.**

a. *I was unhappy. I decided to run away.*
b. *The weather was very bad. I could not cross the river.*
c. *Mr. Tabb is a rather nice man. Some people hate him.*

### Corrigez-vous

Prenez le temps de vous corriger.

**6 Corrigez les 7 erreurs.**
Types d'erreurs (dans l'ordre) : possessif – relatif – temps – ordre des mots – pronom – relatif – préposition.
*When Fred left for work that morning, her wife said "Promise me you will not cross the river, Fred". Fred agreed but he thought: "I know which I am doing!"*
*When he arrives at the cotton field, he saw his friend, Mary. She was carrying a bag very big. "I must help her," Fred thought, and he walked towards her. He did not have time to see the plantation manager which immediately came with his whip. Fred was taken back at the plantation.*

# Your Project

## Set up an exhibition

Set up an exhibition entitled "Slaves Who Dared" in your school.

### Step 1

Divide the class into three groups.
Each group chooses one of the following topics: 1, 2, or 3.

**1. General background:**
- Slave trade
- The Underground Railroad
- The abolition of slavery

**2. Slaves who made history:**
- Henry "Box" Brown
- Joseph Cinque
- Sojourner Truth
- Harriet Tubman
- Nat Turner
- Frederick Douglass

**3. Whites who helped:**
- Levi Coffin
- Prudence Crandall
- Harriet Beecher Stowe
- John Brown

### Step 2

**Groups divide the work between themselves.**
Search the Internet to find information about your theme. Select the information you find most relevant and find pictures to illustrate it. Action! p. 145 Action! p. 147 Action! p. 150

TICE

You may rely on the following websites:
- www.class.uh.edu/gl/abol3.htm
- www.dummies.com/how-to/content/key-abolitionists-leading-the-antislavery-movement.html
- http://abolition.e2bn.org/people.html
- http://education-portal.com/academy/lesson/abolitionist-movement-important-figures-in-the-fight-to-end-slavery.html#lesson
- www.nationalgeographic.com/railroad/index.html
- www.civilwar.com
- www.gilderlehrman.org/history-by-era/slavery-and-anti-slavery/resources/facts-about-slave-trade-and-slavery

### Step 3

Prepare your historical panels: write short paragraphs to present the historical events or characters you have chosen. Illustrate your paragraphs with visual documents. The groups organize their panels.

Writing WORKSHOP p. 151

*Display your class's exhibition in the school so that your schoolmates can learn more about slavery and US abolitionist heroes.*

ART HISTORY CORNER

# SLAVERY IN THE ARTS

## Painting

In the 17th and 18th century, high-class Europeans liked to have slaves represented in their portraits to show off their wealth and social status.

Slavery has also been an inspiration for artists. Some depicted slaves in their everyday occupations; others – who were abolitionists – denounced the slaves' conditions and depicted them being bonded, whipped and auctioned.

## Music

When African slaves were brought to America, they came along with their singing traditions. Their emotional and physical sufferings made the bonds among them very strong. It is in songs that this powerful sense of community and culture was expressed and that their emotions were conveyed. These songs are divided into several categories: spiritual, work or recreational songs.

**Negro spirituals** Slaves were devoutly religious. They sang religious songs a cappella, only accompanied by handclapping* and foot stamping*.

- ***Go down, Moses*** — TICE Search on Youtube

**Work songs** – They were sung in the fields, and provided rhythm for repetitive chores. Singing helped workers to synchronize their efforts.

- ***Hammer song*** — TICE Search on Youtube

*handclapping: *applaudissements*
*foot stamping: *piétinements*

**Other purposes**
Songs had other purposes as well. They might serve to communicate. In some instances, song lyrics conveyed secret messages planning rebellions or disseminating information among slaves. For example, those who were planning to escape would pass songs from one group to another so that everybody knew. Other songs were socio-political protests. Slaves used many objects to communicate these messages: drums, spoons, plates, tools, and of course their own voices.

Slave songs were very important as they helped the slaves remember their history.

***Oh freedom***
*Oh, freedom, oh, freedom,*
*Oh freedom over me.*
*And before I'd be a slave*
*I'd be buried in my grave*
*And go home to my Lord and be free.*

## Literature

The slave narratives – some are accounts of former slaves; others are novels – describe the slaves' conditions and had an impact on the American public. Some have been adapted into movies (see below).

▸ ***Uncle Tom's Cabin*** (Harriet Beecher Stowe, 1852)
It was the bestselling novel in the 19th century, and though it depicted a somewhat stereotypical picture of black slaves, it inspired the abolitionist struggle.

▸ ***Incidents in the Life of a Slave Girl*** (Harriet Jacobs, 1861)
This autobiographical account chronicles the odyssey of Harriet Jacobs who escaped from a life of servitude in North Carolina to liberty and reunion with her children in the North.

▸ ***The Confessions of Nat Turner*** (William Styron, 1992)
Styron wrote the story of a 1831 revolt, led by a remarkable Negro preacher named Nat Turner, an educated slave.

▸ ***A Long Way from Home*** (Connie Briscoe, 2000)
The author explores the lives of three generations of African-Americans living at Montpelier plantation in Virginia – and their relationships with their white masters.

▸ ***A Mercy*** (Toni Morrison, 2008)
This novel is set in America around 1690. Slave labour sustains farming and trade. A mother prefers to cast off* her daughter in order to save her.

*cast off: *se débarrasser de*

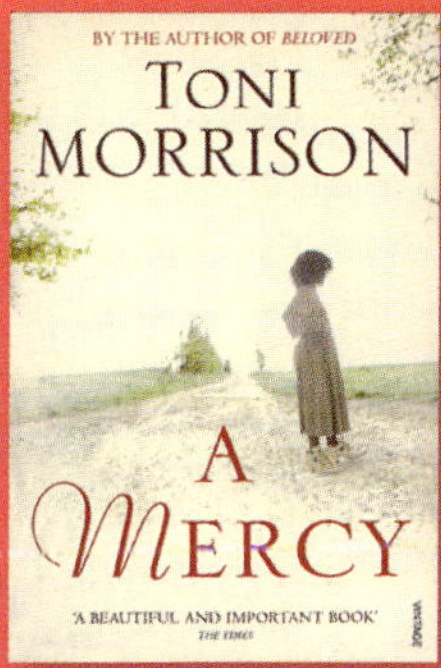


## Movies

Hollywood has long been reticent to tackle the subject of slavery – but, in recent years, several movies have attracted the attention of the audience to the horrible reality of slavery.

▸ *Gone with the Wind*
(Victor Fleming, 1939)
One of the first American movies, it depicted slaves as happy, jovial and in really demeaning stereotypes.

▸ *Roots* (A TV mini-series, 1977)
This popular TV series related the dramatic plight of slaves and probably changed Americans' perception of their own history. It was based on the best–selling novel by Alex Haley Jr. The movie depicts Haley's ancestral line from slavery to freedom.

▸ *Amistad* (Steven Spielberg, 1997)
It presents the transatlantic slave trade; it looks at the Middle Passage, the journey on a slave ship across the Atlantic Ocean. Countless millions of Africans died on this long, torturous journey from illness, starvation, and brutality. Much of the story involves a court-room drama about the free man who led the 1839 revolt.

▸ *Beloved* (Jonathan Demme, 1998)
Based on the Pulitzer prize-winning novel by Toni Morrison, this movie focuses on the experience of a black woman slave, named Sethe, who escaped to Ohio from a Kentucky plantation in 1856. When slave hunters find her in Ohio, she kills her daughter and attempts to kill her other children to prevent them from going back to Kentucky as slaves.

▸ *Django Unchained*
(Quentin Tarantino, 2012)
This movie is loosely based on the life of Bass Reeves, the first African American federal Marshall in the United States. Django is an escaped slave who works to purchase his wife's freedom.

- Get into groups and choose one of the arts presented on this page. Each member of the group searches the Internet to select a piece of art they find particularly relevant and makes a presentation (slideshow, poster or podcast) for the class.

COMPREHENSION

## My Ancestors Were Slave Owners

I was not brought up by anybody in particular that I know of. I had no training, no cultivation. The birds of the air, or beasts of the field are not freer from moral culture than I was. No one seemed to care for me till I was able to work, and then it was Hannah do this and Hannah do that, but I never complained as I found a sort of pleasure and something to divert my thoughts in employment. [...]

The busiest life has its leisure moments; it was so with mine. I had from the first an instinctive desire for knowledge and the means of mental improvement. Though neglected and a slave, I felt the immortal longings in me. In the absence of books and teachers and schools I determined to learn if not in a regular, approved, and scientific way. I was aware that this plan would meet with opposition, perhaps with punishment. My master never permitted his slaves to be taught. Education in his view tended to enlarge and expand their ideas; made them less subservient to their superiors, and besides that its blessings were destined to be conferred exclusively on the higher and nobler race. Indeed though he was generally easy and good-tempered, there was nothing liberal or democratic in his nature. Slaves were slaves to him, and nothing more. Practically he regarded them not as men and women, but in the same light as horses or other domestic animals. He supplied their necessities of food and clothing from motives of policy, but [di]scounted the ideas of equality and fraternity as preposterous and absurd. Of course I had nothing to expect from him, yet "where there's a will there's a way."

I was employed about the house, consequently my labors were much easier than those of the field servants, and I enjoyed intervals of repose and rest unknown to them. Then, too, I was a mere child and some hours of each day were allotted to play. On such occasions, and while the other children of the house were amusing themselves I would quietly steal away from their company to ponder over the pages of some old book or newspaper that chance had thrown in [my] way. Though I knew not the meaning of a single letter, and had not the means of finding out I loved to look at them and think that some day I should probably understand them all.

My dream was destined to be realized. One day while sitting on a little bank, beneath the shade of some large trees, at a short distance from my playmates, an aged woman approached me. She was white, and looked venerable with her grey hair smoothly put back beneath a plain sun bonnet, and I recollected having seen her once or twice at my master's house whither she came to sell salves and ointments, and hearing it remarked that she was the wife of a sand-digger and very poor. She smiled benevolently and inquired why I concealed my book, and with child-like artlessness I told her all. How earnestly I desired knowledge, how our Master interdicted it, and how I was trying to teach myself. She stood for a few moments apparently buried in deep thought, but I interpreted her looks and actions favorably, and an idea struck me that perhaps she could read, and would become my teacher. She seemed to understand my wish before I expressed it.

"Child," she said ", [...] I will dispense to you such knowledge as I possess. Come to me each day. I will teach you to read in the hope and trust that you will thereby be made better in this world and that to come." Her demeanor like her words was very grave and solemn.

"Where do you live?" I inquired.

"In the little cottage just around the foot of the hill" she replied.

"I will come: Oh how eagerly, how joyfully," I answered "but if master finds it out his anger will be terrible; and then I have no means of paying you."

She smiled quietly, bade me fear nothing, and went her way. [...]

The next day and the next I went out to gather blackberries, and took advantage of the fine opportunity to visit my worthy instructress and receive my first lesson. [...]

"Hannah, my dear, you are welcome" she said coming forward and extending her hand. "I rejoice to see you. I am, or rather was a northern woman, and consequently have no prejudices against your birth, or race, or condition [...].

I had heard of the North where the people were all free, and where the colored race had so many and such true friends.

Hannah Crafts, *The Bondwoman's Narrative*,
Henry Louis Gates, Jr., 2002.

*conceal: *cacher*

## Questions

1. Sum up the text in a few words: The narrator is … . She tells about … .
2. Quote the words that give you information about Hannah.
   Her family: …
   Her looks: …
   Her daily life: …
   Her dream: …
3. Quote the sentence which sums up the relationship between the master and his slaves.
4. The text is made up of two parts. What words mark a change in the story?
5. Give information about the person Hannah met.
   Her colour and origin: …
   Her position towards slavery: …
   What she did for Hannah: …
6. Considering Hannah's story, explain what she means by "where there's a will there's a way." (l. 31)

## EXPRESSION

**Choose one of the following subjects.**

A. Imagine you are the old woman who taught Hannah to read. She writes a diary page about her meeting with Hannah and about her relationship with the little girl.

B. Mr. Wheeler, Hannah's master, has found out that Hannah has been taught to read. He calls the child. Write the conversation.

# "Oral"

## COMPREHENSION

**My Ancestors Were Slave Owners**

www.npr.org/2014/01/15/262431646/a-woman-comes-to-terms-with-her-familys-slave-owning-past

*(0'23 to 2'23)*

1. Watch the video three times and take down notes.
2. Then write a report on it, in French.

## EXPRESSION

### "Myths and heroes"

***How did some extraordinary people manage to survive and fight slavery?***

• **Prepare your presentation in note form**

Step 1 **Introduce the notion of hero.**

"A hero is someone who acts or has acted in service to humanity, in defense of a moral cause…" Explain why slaves who managed to fight slavery were heroes.

Step 2 **Explain what slavery is.**

Explain what a slave is. Say what you know about where American slaves came from; how they arrived in America.

Cultural Background / Sound File

Step 3 **Talk about the living conditions of slaves.**

Sound File / Text File 1 / Text File 2

Step 4 **Talk about slaves who dared.**

Give examples of people who resisted in spite of their condition of slaves.

Sound File / Text File 1 / Text File 2

Step 5 **Conclude.**

Mention cultural events or works of art that help modern-day Americans face the reality of slavery.

Video File / Art Corner

Talk about your feelings when you read or listened to the people's stories.
Say why these extraordinary people can be called "heroes".

• **Train yourself**

Follow the steps above and speak for five minutes.
If possible, add personal comments. Record yourself and listen to your presentation to improve it.

• **Get ready for a conversation**

Listen to the recording of your presentation and prepare yourself to justify, develop, and exemplify what you have said.

# unit 9 Sport Is More Than Just a Game

**"Myths and heroes"**
*What is the social significance of sports culture in the UK?*



To access our audio resources, use our Flashcodes or go to our website:
www.ressources.hachette-education.com/boardingpass/1re/units/unit9.html

Gareth Lloyd Ball,
*Rugby International*,
Wales vs Scotland.

CULTURAL BACKGROUND

# SPORTS IN THE UK

## 1 What Do You Know About... Sports Marketing?

**In small groups, choose the right words to complete statements *a* to *e*.**

a. Sports marketing includes the ... of sports events, the ... of athletes, and the ... of stadiums.
b. Its most important sources of money are: ....
c. The number of people with ... jobs in the UK is estimated at over 400,000.
d. Sport is in the top 15 industry sectors in England, above ....
e. Players get extravagant sums of money to wear clothing, or do TV commercials, or photos for ....

sport-related — construction — advertisements — ticket sales and TV broadcast rights — motor vehicles and telecom services — management — sponsorship

## 2 A Nation of Bookmakers

2 Track 62

A betting office – Dublin, Ireland

1. Pick out the synonym for "bookmakers".
2. Note down the three figures you hear and say what each of them corresponds to.
3. Complete: At a betting shop, you can easily ... on Manchester United. Bets are also taken ....
4. Pick out the sports the British bet on.
5. Give the other examples of events people may bet on.

**Wordbox**

Noun
- outcome: *résultat*

Verbs
- bet: *parier*
- gamble: *jouer (jeu d'argent)*
- place a bet on: *parier sur*

## 3 The Sports They Like

Football is by far the most popular of all sports in the UK. Football as we know it today is as English as fish and chips. It was in London, in 1963, that the rules of modern football were codified. The Football Association was also founded in London. It is the oldest in the world. In the Premier League, twenty teams play each year. The most famous teams are Chelsea, Manchester United, Liverpool, and Arsenal. Football plays a great role in the economy of the UK. For every £1 the central government gives to sports in the UK, it makes £5 in tax.

Popular sports in the UK include rugby, cricket, golf, horseracing, and tennis. London hosts the world's oldest tennis tournament, Wimbledon, first held in 1877. Annual top events for sports in the UK are the F1 British Grand Prix, the Grand National Horse Race, and the Open Championship Golf. There are 2,752 golf courses in the UK—8% of the world's golf courses.

1. What is football compared to? Why?
2. Why do the British think England is football's real home?
3. Give the sports mentioned and the sports events quoted.
4. Find the equivalents for these words: *règles – fondée – équipes* (§1); *courses de chevaux – événements* (§2).

## 4 British Sports by Numbers

| Sport | TV viewing | Participating | Interested in |
|---|---|---|---|
| Football | 46% | 10% | 45% |
| Rugby | 33% | - | 37% |
| Tennis | 20% | 3% | 23% |
| Cricket | 19% | 2% | 19% |
| Athletics | 18% | 2% | 21% |
| Snooker | 17% | 5% | 24% |
| Motor racing | 16% | - | 20% |
| Boxing | 12% | - | 14% |
| Golf | 11% | 6% | 16% |
| Darts | 9% | 3% | - |
| Swimming | - | 9% | - |
| Gym | - | 12% | 17% |

Choose two sports and compare them.

Anne Keothavong (Great Britain)

### Wordbox

Nouns

- darts: *fléchettes*
- snooker: *billard*

### Action! Organize a guessing contest

Play in groups. Prepare slips of paper with one of the numbers from the chart above. Draw lots to choose a slip of paper and make a sentence explaining what the proportion corresponds to: "This is the proportion of people who…". If your sentence is correct, you get one point.

VIDEO FILE

# NUMBER ONE, AT LAST!

## TRAIN YOUR EARS

1. **Listen and repeat. Mind the stress.** 2 Track 63

defeat • cricket • cricketer • official • generation • expect • accept • compete • England • applaud • talent

2. **Listen to these sentences and repeat. Mind the rhythm.** 2 Track 64

It's been a long time coming.
It's the best team in the world.
It's been a long wait.
Make no mistake.

## Before you watch

1. Look at the picture and say what you know—or can guess—about this sport.

## Now watch

B1+ A2+ Use the question sheet in your eWorkbook.

2. Take notes and sum up what you have understood.

## Recap

3. Find out information about the past and recent results of the England cricket team.
4. Say how cricket fans reacted in the past.
5. Explain what may change with the recent title the England cricket team won.

## React

6. Do you agree with the saying "It's not the winning but the taking part that counts"?
7. Do you think a national team's performance has an impact on the country? Give examples.

**Sum up the document in French.**

### Wordbox

Nouns
- defeat: *défaite*
- ranking: *classement*
- title: *titre*

Adjective
- latest: *dernier en date*

### Action! Interview a friend about a sporting event

In pairs, role-play this situation: interview a friend to find out about a sporting event that has made an impact on his/her life.

SOUND FILE

# DO ATHLETES MAKE TOO MUCH MONEY?

TRAIN YOUR EARS

1. Read these words out loud. Then listen and repeat. 2 Track 65
   recent • interviewed • athletes • heroes • refusing • profit • ridiculous • multimillion • salaries • sponsors • revenue • famine
2. Listen and repeat. Mind the stress. 2 Track 66
3. Read the sentences out loud; then listen and repeat. Mind the stress. 2 Track 67
   They deserve the money they get.
   It is a controversial topic.

## Before you listen

1. Look at the photo. Explain what it shows and what the message is.
2. Give examples to illustrate the topic.

## Now listen

B1+

A2+ Use the question sheet in your eWorkbook.

2 Tracks 68 to 70

3. Listen to the document and take notes.

## Recap

4. Developp the question asked in the title.
5. Mention:
   – the arguments for a positive answer;
   – the arguments for a negative answer.

## React

6. Give your own answer to the question in the title of the document.

**Sum up the document in French.**

Action!

### Make a presentation about an athlete

In groups, choose an athlete who makes a lot of money. Make a presentation about him/her and say whether you think they deserve the money they get. Record yourselves.

# TEXT FILE 1

## Before you read

1. Look at the photos and say what aspects of football they illustrate.
2. Read the title of the text and give your own answers to the question.

## Now read

B1+ A2+ Use the question sheet in your eWorkbook.

3. Read the text and check your guesses.

## Recap

4. **Andy Harper** – Say who he is, what he loves in football, and the essential reason why he loves it.
5. **Walled Abu Nada** – Say why he quotes many figures. Say what being a football fan entails. Give the beautiful sides and then the ugly sides of football.
6. **Roy Hodgson** – Say who he is, and why he considers football is so special.

## React

7. Comment on the last sentence. Then read it out loud; what word will you stress particularly?

## Work on Words

1. **Pick out the contrary of these words:** victory – fall – beautiful – clean – proud – cheat (be…).
2. **Find the equivalents for these French words:** *ancien – cinéma – pitreries – partager.*
3. **Observe the word "unfortunately".** Identify the prefix, the root, and the suffix. Then make similar words with these adjectives: natural – pleasant – realistic – willing.
4. **Observe the ending of the word "aesthetics".** Based on your observation, give the English equivalent of *athlétisme.* Then find some words that refer to sciences with the same ending.

> Grammar **Le gérondif (V-*ing*)** See p. 170

## Sum up

1. **Listen to our recorded summary.** 2 Track 72
2. **Use the words below to write your own summary of the text.**
   - Andy Harper – former
   - everything – brings – together
   - Walled Abu Nada – fan
   - football – common – people – world
   - mentions – ugly – beautiful
   - abusive – chants – fixing – cheating – dirty
   - says – life
   - Roy Hodgson – Britain's culture – popular

# Why Do We Love Football? Track 71

I love football. I love the aesthetics of football. I love the movement of the players, the antics of the coaches. I love the dynamism of the fans. I love their passion for their badge and the colour of their team and their country. I love the noise and the buzz, and the electricity in the stadium. I love the songs. I love the way the ball moves and then it flows, and the way a team's fortune rises and falls through a game and through a season. But what I love about football is that it brings people together across religious divides, geographic divides, and political divides.

**Andy Harper, former Newcastle player**

Football is more than just a game, more than just 22 players running after a ball [...]. The only thing that we, the 7 billion people living on earth, share, is our passion and love towards our favourite football team. [...] 1 universe, 8 planets, 204 countries, 804 islands, 7 seas, 7 billion people—and football is what is in common between them. Representing your team, kissing your team's badge after you score when you're playing with your friends, being proud to support your team, being proud but humble after each victory and loyal after each defeat, this is football, this is life. Everyone of us has a favorite football team or club. [...]

Unfortunately, just like any other sport, the beautiful game has an ugly side. Abusive and racist chants, match fixing, cheating, and dirty playing are major factors which can make any normal person hate watching football. But these factors motivate us, football fans around the globe, [to put an end to these ugly acts. Football] is more than just a game, [...] football is life and yes, I absolutely love this life.

**Walled Abu Nada, football fan**

I have always been aware that football is the culture—the mass culture. Films, plays, books, operas are not for everyone but football really is. That is the ultimate for me. Football is cultural and it is our culture.

**Roy Hodgson, manager of the England national football team**

http://footballspeak.com, November 5th, 2011.

**Action!**

## Discuss: why do you/don't you love football?

In pairs, discuss why you love football or not. Use the testimonies above as models.

# Fallen Idols

2 Track 73

Tiger Woods, Lance Armstrong, and Oscar Pistorius. These three sportsmen were once at the top of their respective fields [...]; they were idols who we all looked up to and who could seemingly do no wrong. Yet, in 2009 the world learnt that Tiger Woods, the world's best golfer and renowned family man, had cheated on his wife on various occasions. In 2012 [...], Lance Armstrong, seven-time winner of the Tour de France, was charged with using performance-enhancing drugs. And in 2014, Paralympian and worldwide sporting icon, Oscar Pistorius, [was convicted of homicide in the death of his girlfriend], Reeva Steenkamp. [...]

Like Woods, it has been discovered that footballers, such as Ryan Giggs and Ashley Cole, have cheated on their wives. One might argue that we should turn a blind eye to such cases, as their actions have not affected their ability to perform in their respective sports, [...] and that what goes on in their private lives should stay private. However, this argument is difficult to defend when one considers that Woods and Giggs made vast sums of money through sponsors, who targeted them for their image as two of the biggest role models in world sport, in order to promote their brands.

The Armstrong case is particularly shocking. The American cyclist overcame cancer before going on to win the Tour de France seven times. But his story is a tale of deceit. The illegal substances that he took contributed to all 7 of his Tour de France wins. Armstrong has tarnished not only his own reputation, but that of his sport. [...]

All of these men had achieved greatness as sporting legends, enjoying glorious careers and worldwide fame. Yet they have all eroded some of the public faith in our sportsmen and women.

www.epigram.org.uk, March 5th, 2013.

Tiger Woods

1. Note down the three names in l.1. Say who each person is, and why they are "fallen idols".
2. Say why two footballers are quoted in §2.
3. Rephrase the two arguments developed in §2: *Perhaps we should... but their behaviour is shocking because...*
4. Give details about Armstrong.
5. Should we expect sporting heroes to be irreproachable?

**Now discuss the links between this text and the text on p. 167.**

6. Compare or contrast the topics. Which lines of text 1 does text 2 echo?
7. What do you think Walled Abu Nada would feel when reading about the "fallen idols"?

Grammar Le *past perfect* See p. 170

Action!

## Write a paragraph about a "fallen idol"

Using §3 as a model, write a paragraph about a "fallen idol" of your choice: who he/she is; what he/she did; what is shocking.

# HOW TO DESIGN A HOMEPAGE

Action!

**In groups of two or three, design the homepage of a site promoting a typically British sport.**

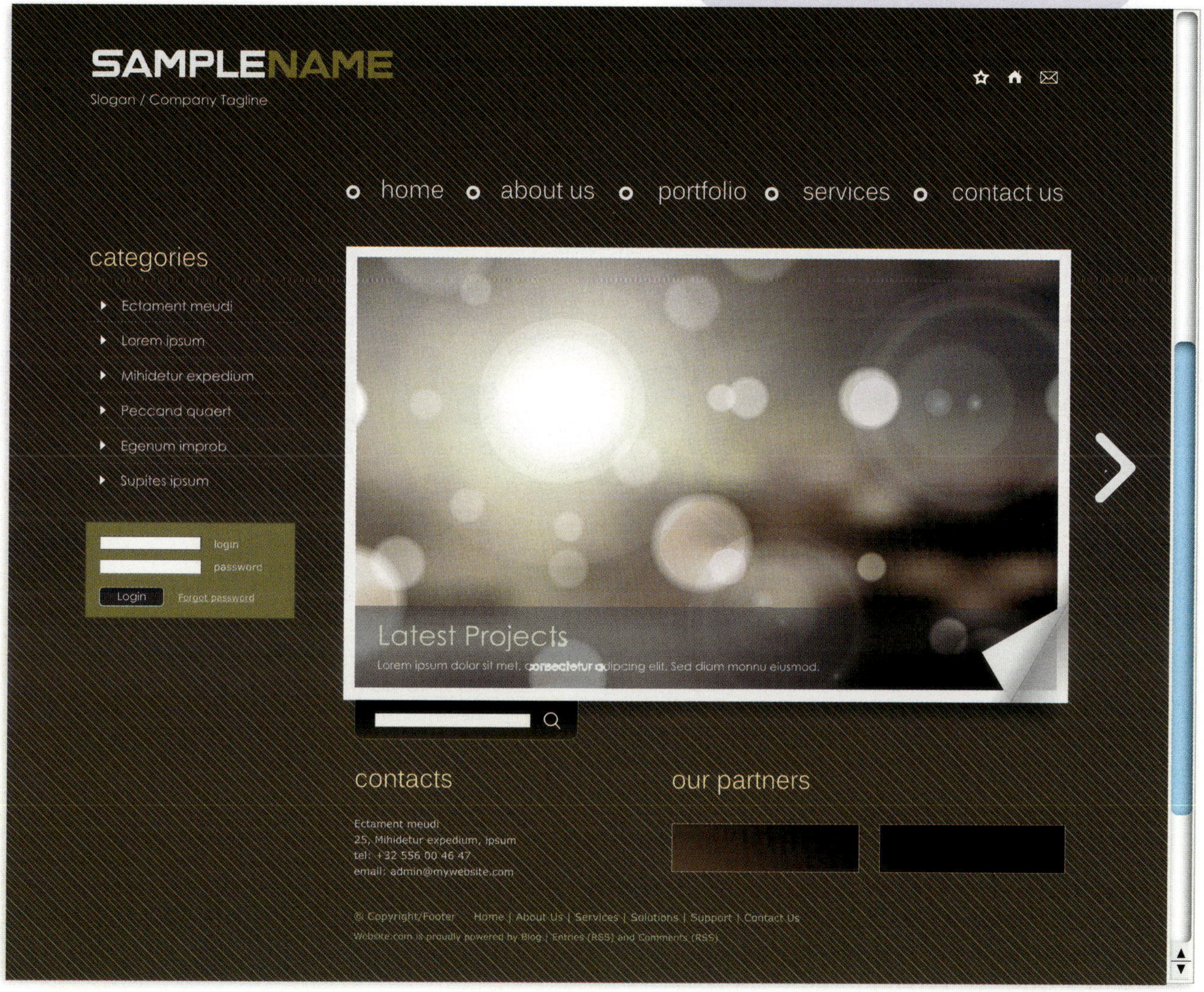


1. **Observe your model.**
   a. Look at the web page above and locate these elements: side panels – header – footer – hyperlinks – general presentation.
   b. Say what the role of each element is.
2. **Prepare your home page.**
   a. Make a list of six or seven typically British sports. You may find ideas on the following sites:
   www.historic-uk.com
   www.englandforever.org
   www.england.costasur.com
   b. Search the web to find more examples of homepages. That will give you ideas on what you want your own homepage to look like.
   c. Find visuals to illustrate the sport you have chosen.
3. **Create your homepage.**
   a. Make a template to organize your home page.
   b. Write one or two lines to introduce each sport you have selected.
   c. Use a word processor or a web editor to create your homepage.

# LANGUAGE WORKSHOP

GRAMMAR

## Le gérondif (V-*ing*) (Text File 1 p. 166)

Précis grammatical p. 214

a. Being proud to support your team is part of life.
b. Match fixing, cheating, and dirty playing can make any normal person hate watching football.
c. The British love supporting their team.

**Rappelez-vous**

Dites comment on transforme un verbe en nom.

**Allez plus loin**

1. Identifiez la fonction grammaticale des formes V-*ing* dans chaque exemple.
2. Dans la phrase *c*, pourquoi peut-on dire que la forme V-*ing* est à la fois un nom et un verbe ?

**Exercises**

**1. Give the gerund form of these verbs; then translate into French.**
*write – (mountain) climb – canoe – smoke – train – camp – shop*

**2. Translate.**
a. J'aime la course à pieds.
b. Je trouve que la boxe est un sport violent.
c. Le ski n'est pas un sport très britannique.
d. Être fier de son équipe est très important.
e. Motiver les supporters est ce qu'Andrew Harper a réussi à faire.

## Le *past perfect* (Text File 2 p. 168)

Précis grammatical p. 196

a. In 2009 the world learnt that Tiger Woods had cheated on his wife on various occasions.
b. In an interview with Oprah Winfrey, Armstrong confessed that he had used illegal drugs.
c. Armstrong's performances were even more amazing as he had fought cancer.
d. In 2014, Oscar Pistorius, who had inspired so many people, was found guilty.

**Rappelez-vous**

Pour mettre un verbe au *past perfect* : auxiliaire ... + ...

**Allez plus loin**

1. Identifiez les deux formes verbales passées dans chaque exemple.
2. Opposez et justifiez le choix de chacune de ces formes.
3. Faites un repérage temporel : dites quelle action intervient en premier ; en second.
4. Expliquez la valeur du *past perfect* : on l'emploie pour parler d'une action qui est ... à un moment passé.

**Exercises**

**1. Elaborate on the situations: write full sentences using the words between brackets.**
a. I went to see a baseball game for the first time. (I / never / see a ball game / before)
b. He arrived late for practice yesterday. (It / already / begin)
c. They played tennis yesterday. They were not very good at it. (They / never / play / before)
d. She invited us to watch the game but we couldn't come. (We / arrange / to do something else)

**2. Put these verbs into the *past perfect*:** They ...
buy – fall – give – have – make – lose – take – write – pay – leave

**3. Put the verbs into the *simple past* or *past perfect*.**
a. For years, many people ... Armstrong's use of performance-enhancing drugs. (suspect)
b. He ... to his basketball practice yesterday but there ... nobody. He ... that the session ... . (go – be – not know – be canceled)
c. The cricket game last weekend ... great. I ... one before. (be – never see)
d. By 2010, Beckham ... everything there ... to win in football, and ... a father for the first time. (win – be – become)

**4. Translate.**
a. À l'âge de 18 ans, elle avait déjà gagné plusieurs coupes.
b. Ils étaient fans de cyclisme avant d'apprendre qu'Armstrong s'était dopé.
c. Avant son procès (*trial*), Oscar Pistorius avait prouvé que les athlètes handicapés (*disabled*) pouvaient devenir des icônes.
d. Il avait joué toute sa carrière à Manchester lorsqu'il a décidé de changer de club.

## GRAMMAR GAME

### Talk about what you did

Work in small groups. In turns, say to your friends (in one sentence) what you had done before you arrived home last Saturday (it does not have to be true!). Continue until you are stuck. The winner is the last student who has found an idea.
Start like this: *When I arrived home, it was ... I had...*

## Exercises

**1. Find the antonyms in the word bank.**

a. win
b. victory
c. the starting line
d. failure

**2. Give as many answers as possible to complete these prompts.**

a. You can win a ... .
b. You can ... a game.
c. Spectators can ... .

**3. Give the nouns that are based on these verbs and give their French equivalents.**

train – support – win – begin – own – start – lose

**4. Make up a word tree.**

Fill in this word tree with as many words as possible.

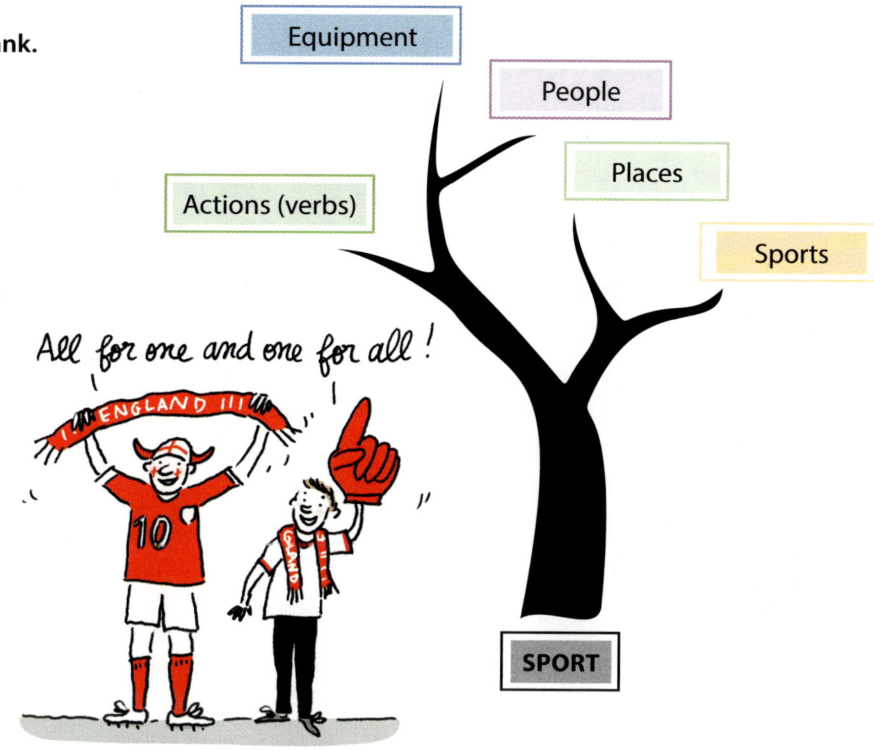


## Word bank

### Nouns

- championship: *championnat*
- contestant: *concurrent*
- defeat: *défaite*
- entry fee: *prix de l'entrée*
- final: *finale*
- finish line: *ligne d'arrivée*
- game, match: *jeu*
- practice: *entraînement*
- prize: *prix (récompense)*
- race: *course*
- referee, umpire: *arbitre*
- rule: *règle*
- spectator: *spectateur*
- stadium: *stade*
- success: *succès*
- supporter: *supporter*
- team: *équipe*
- tournament: *tournoi*
- trainer, coach: *entraîneur*
- victory: *victoire*
- world record: *record du monde*

### Verbs

- applaud: *applaudir*
- beat: *battre*
- be fit: *être en forme*
- compete: *participer, concourir*
- draw, tie: *faire match nul*
- lose: *perdre*
- practise: *entraîner*
- score (a point): *marquer (un point)*
- start: *démarrer*
- target: *viser*
- train: *entraîner*
- use drugs: *se doper*
- win: *gagner*

### Adjectives

- competitive: *qui a l'esprit de compétition*
- keen on: *passioné de*
- sporty: *sportif/ve*

# SKILLS TRAINING

# PRONONCER ET ENTENDRE : L'ACCENTUATION ET L'INTONATION

## L'accentuation

Le rythme de l'anglais vient de la succession de mots accentués — auxquels on accorde du temps et, surtout, de l'énergie — et de mots inaccentués qu'on devine plus qu'on ne les entend.

### 1 L'accent de mot

Tous les mots de plus d'une syllabe comportent une syllabe accentuée.

**Écoutez et répétez ces mots transparents.** 2 Track 74

*America – tradition – culture – imagine – environment – terror – photograph*

### 2 Les mots-clés

Les mots porteurs de sens ou « mots-clés » sont accentués. Vous devez donner de l'énergie à certains mots ou parties de mots et être neutre sur d'autres.

**Écoutez et répétez en respectant le rythme.** 2 Track 75

a. *It's excellent for your body to exercise on a regular basis.*
b. *I heard an athlete refuse to sign an autograph.*
c. *They deserve the money they get.*

### 3 Les mots grammaticaux

Ils sont normalement inaccentués. Ceci concerne les auxiliaires, les prépositions, les articles, les pronoms, les possessifs, etc. On doit les deviner plus que les entendre.

**Écoutez et répétez.** 2 Track 76

a. *He's been with us for forty years.*
b. *It would have been surprising.*
c. *They were at the top of their respective fields.*

### 4 L'accent de phrase

L'accent de phrase signale le mot qui apporte une information nouvelle.

**Choisissez le mot qui apporte une information; puis écoutez et répétez.** 2 Track 77

a. *This is even better than I thought.*
b. *Sports stars are considered as heroes by their fans.*
c. *Sports stars can be inspiring to all of us.*
d. *Why shouldn't athletes make as much money as movie stars?*

### 5 Le choix de l'énonciateur

La place de l'accent principal peut varier en fonction du choix de l'énonciateur : elle fait sens. Par exemple, si vous accentuez *she* dans la phrase *She did it*, celle-ci signifie : " C'est elle qui l'a fait ".

**Écoutez et répétez puis proposez une suite à chacune des phrases.** 2 Track 78

a. *Michael went to Spain last year.*
b. *Michael went to Spain last year.*
c. *Michael went to Spain last year.*

## L'intonation

### 1 Dans les affirmations

L'intonation normale de l'anglais est descendante.

**Écoutez et répétez.** 2 Track 79

a. *Bookmaking is legal in the United Kingdom.*
b. *It is estimated that more than 2 million Britons gamble online.*
c. *Bets are also taken via the Internet or phones.*

### 2 Dans les questions fermées

Les questions commençant par un auxiliaire ou le verbe *be* ont une intonation montante. L'intonation montante : on invite l'interlocuteur à réagir.

**Écoutez et répétez.** 2 Track 80

a. *Is it interesting?*
b. *Are you coming with us?*
c. *Do sports stars make too much money?*

### 3 Dans les questions ouvertes

Les questions commençant par un mot interrogatif ont une intonation descendante.

**Écoutez et répétez.** 2 Track 81

a. *What do you think, Sarah?*
b. *Where did they play last week?*
c. *Who did you go to the match with?*
d. *Why do you love football?*

# Your Project

## Create a website to present typically British sports

Your class is going to make a website presenting different typical British sports.

Epsom Derby,
Great Britain

### Step 1

Divide the class into groups of three or four.
Each group chooses one of the British sports below.
Action! p. 163
Rugby / Cricket / Golf / Hockey / Boxing / Snooker / Curling / Horse racing / Lawn tennis / Polo / University boat race / Darts.

### Step 2

TICE

Search the Internet to find information on the sport you want to present, and classify your information into three or four sections (rules, history, famous stars, etc.). Each section will become a page. Find pictures to illustrate each section.

### Step 3

Prepare your pages. Give a title to each page: use a word processor to write short paragraphs to develop each point you want to present in your pages and insert pictures to illustrate them. The pages will all be saved in the same folder.

Design a homepage for your site and insert hyperlinks that will redirect your reader to your different pages. Writing WORKSHOP p. 169
Do not forget to add a return button on your pages so that readers can come back to the main menu.

### Step 4

Copy the different pages designed by the class in a general folder.
Design a homepage for the class; put a menu so that the readers can have a general idea of the sports presented and access the pages they might want to see.

TICE

You can use a word processor or a free web editor to design your site: WebMatrix, Komodo Edit, NetBeans, BlueGriffon, Bluefish.

*Your site can be inserted into your school website.*

TECHNOLOGY CORNER

From carbon fibre bicycles to electronic taekwondo vests, or high-tech swim suits, technology is everywhere.

# Technologies Are Transforming Sports

## Six sports that have benefited from innovation

**Bowling – Computerized Scoring**
Bowling can be difficult to score. Having a computer keeps the score for you and eases the pain of scoring by 100 percent—and you can keep all your focus on your next ball.

**Hockey – Above the Net Camera**
Having a camera above the net is used to see what goals passed the line. The camera-evidence has changed the outcome of numerous games, all for the better since it gives an indubitable answer whether or not the rubber passed the line.

**Olympic and Animal Racing – Photo Finishes**
Sure electronic timers are helpful, but when two runners finish in the same hundredth of a second the officials go to the cameras, which today shoots 3,000 frames per second. No way to go wrong! This innovation tackles every type of racing, whether it be swimming, running, and horse racing.

**Football – The Headset***
The headset is the best technology football has to offer. The uses can be infinite. Coaches up in the press box can see aerial views of the game, and with the headset they can relay information to the players.

**Tennis – Cyclops**
The Cyclops are a system of six infra-red beams* that rest just a centimeter above the ground. If the ball was hit just outside the court, a sound would project and the play would be stopped. Easy!

**Training – Heart Monitor**
A lifesaver, literally, for the average jogger as well as the elite athlete! These devices play a huge role in progressing in a workout* plan. Without a heart monitor it would be difficult for athletes to track progress and sustainability* of their exercise program.
Some heart monitors also can be used to alert athletes of dehydration and malnutrition.

Matt Sheehan,
http://bleacherreport.com,
June 7th, 2011.

*headset: *casque* – *beam: *rayon* – *heart: *cœur* – *workout: *exercice* – *sustainability: *viabilité*

# The Top 5 Gear and Gadgets

## 1 Ingestible Computers

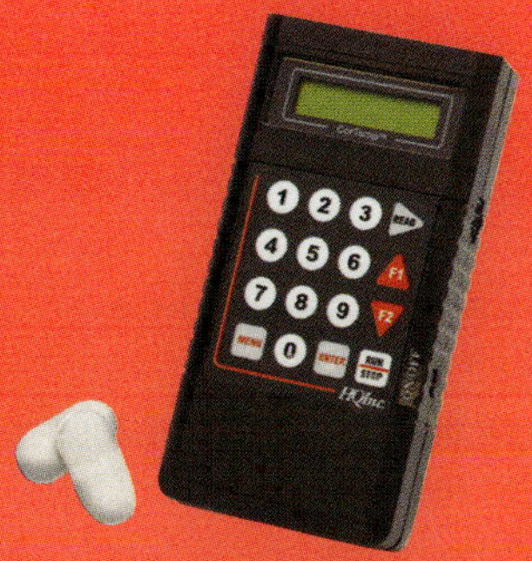

Heat* exhaustion is the second-leading cause of death in athletes. A "thermometer pill*" may save lives. Initially developed by John Hopkins Applied Physics Laboratory, in collaboration with the NASA Goddard Space Flight Center to monitor astronauts from space, the pill contains a quartz crystal sensor and micro-battery wrapped in silicon. Once swallowed, a sensor transmits temperature to the trainer. Athletes in field and track, auto racing, football, hockey, cycling, and soccer have used the "thermometer pill".

## 2 Wearable Computers

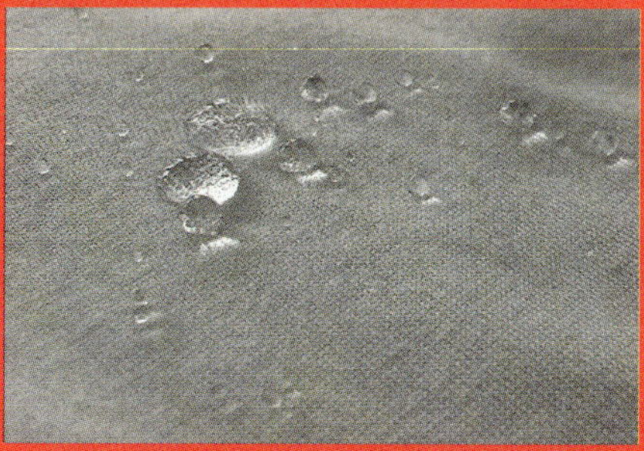

The best sports innovation, ever? Synthetic fibers that dry fast, and are anti-microbial and water- or wind-resistant. The next best thing? "Smart" clothing that uses embedded* microscopic sensors and wireless networks to monitor athletes' heart rate, body temperature, hydration, and more.

## 3 Biomimetics

[E]ngineers are turning to nature for inspiration. Textured fabrics inspired by sharkskin* were one of the many innovations that may have helped Michael Phelps be the swimming champion he was.

In another example, scientists have developed materials that increase in adhesive strength while in motion*—just like the feet of geckos. Coming soon, gecko-inspired non skid* grips and climbing shoes.

## 4 Digital Imaging and Video

It's impossible to imagine a multibillion-dollar global sports industry without television to play (and replay) stunning moments—and generate advertising revenue. Miniature, wireless, and handheld digital cameras that give viewers unbelievable proximity, and put them in the action have transformed the sports-viewing experience.

## 5 Reactive Materials

Until recently, protective clothing that could absorb impact was often bulky* and restrictive. That's changing with the development of materials that flex and move with a body in action but immediately harden upon impact.

Recent applications include gear for downhill skiers and dirt bike* racers, as well as ballet shoes, soccer balls, shorts for equestrians, and protective gear for soldiers and law enforcement agents.

Adaptated from http://news.discovery.com, December 12th, 2012.

*heat: *chaleur*
*pill: *pilule*
*embedded: *intégré*
*sharkskin: *peau de requin*
*motion: *mouvement*
*non skid: *antidérapant*
*bulky: *encombrant*
*gear: *équipement*
*dirt bike: *moto tout terrain*

1. Read the articles and, in small groups, prepare a report in French about what you read.
2. Search the Internet for information and make a short presentation for the class:
   – Find other examples of gadgets or gear that are changing a sport of your choice.
   – Explain how the technology of the gadget or gear you have chosen works and what benefit(s) people draw.

# EXAM TRAINING Written

## COMPREHENSION

### 1 Mom, I'm Going To Be a Star

"Mom, I'm going to be a star."
"I love you child for what you are."
"But I will make a million dollars,
Generating hoots and hollers*!
All the fans will shout my name!"
"Maybe child, and all the same,
I will love you all my days,
If you do or don't win praise."
"Mom, I'll build a house for you,
And it will have an ocean view."
"That, my child, would be quite grand.
Now sit with me and hold my hand,
And know in case you don't succeed,
It's time for you to learn to read."

Bill Littlefield, *Take me Out*, 2014.

*hoots and hollers: *huées et braillements*

**Questions Doc. 1**

1. This document is:
   ☐ an extract from a blog ☐ a newspaper article
   ☐ a poem ☐ a speech
2. Who are the characters? How are they related? Justify your answers by quoting from the text.
3. Find two quotes that show one of the characters is young.
4. What is the conversation about? Explain in one sentence.
5. Right, wrong or doesn't say? Justify by quoting from the text.
   – The child wants to be a millionaire.
   – The child wants to be a very famous football player.
   – The child wants to become a pop star.
6. How does the second character react to the child's words? Why? Explain in your own words.

### 2 A Career? Just Make Us Stars, Say Children in New Survey

When their parents were children, they imagined a future standing in front of a class of pupils or doing the rounds as a doctor. But today's youngsters seem to have set their sights only on being the next Leona Lewis or Wayne Rooney.

According to a survey, they dream of a celebrity lifestyle, perhaps after finding fame through shows such as *The X Factor*, and of being actors or sports stars.

[The] survey found that emulating the likes of Rooney and David Beckham was the top career ambition of today's pre-teens, cited by 12%. Almost as many, 11%, want to be pop stars, and the same proportion dream of being actors. [...]

A quarter of a century ago teaching was the top career choice, cited by 15%. These days the profession is chosen by only 4%. [...]

Many parents blame [...] TV, with some saying it is rivalling their advice as the biggest influence on their children's choice of career. [...]

Child psychologist Laverne Antrobus said the findings reflected today's celebrity culture and cautioned children against unrealistic dreams.

"Children see footballers [...] on TV and their lives look exciting, glamorous, and fun," she said. "It is hard for them to realize that they are the end product of a lot of ingredients including talent and hard work. Wayne Rooney is not on the pitch at Old Trafford by chance. He has incredible talent, determination and has put in years of hard work. There is absolutely nothing wrong with children having big dreams but these have to be based on reality."

Laura Clark, *The Daily Mail*,
October 2nd, 2009.

## Questions Doc. 2

1. Choose and write down the right answer.
This article deals with:
☐ celebrity kids
☐ parents who choose their children's career
☐ children's career ambitions
2. Fill in the table below with the right numbers and jobs when the information is available in the text.

| Career dream | Before | Nowadays |
|---|---|---|
| ... | ... | 4% |
| ... | | 12% |
| ... | | ... |
| ... | | ... |

3. According to parents and the child psychologist, what is the biggest influence on children's career ambitions? Justify by quoting from the text (2 quotes).
4. Right, wrong or doesn't say? Justify by quoting from the text.
a. Wayne Rooney is the living example that anybody can be a sports star.
b. Kids often don't realize what it takes to be a sports celebrity.

## Questions Docs 1 and 2

1. Write down the title that corresponds to both documents.
– Parents' advice to children
– How to become a celebrity
– Children's dreams
2. What do you think the child in doc. 1 would answer to the questions of the survey mentioned in doc. 2?

## EXPRESSION

**Choose one of the following subjects.**

**A. Write a dialogue**

A ten-year old kid explains to his/her parents why he/she wants to become a celebrity. The parents try to warn him/her against unrealistic dreams. Write out the conversation.

**B. Write an essay**

What influences our career choices?

# "Oral"

## COMPREHENSION

**Sport Is Great**

http://learnenglish.britishcouncil.org/en/britain-great/sport-great-part-1
*(0'00 to 1'40)*

1. Watch the video three times and take down notes.
2. Then write a report on it, in French.

## EXPRESSION

### "Myths and heroes"

***What is the social significance of sports culture in the UK?***

• **Prepare your presentation in note form**

Step 1 **Introduce the notion: "Myths and heroes."**
"A hero is a person who is regarded as a model or ideal. Great sportmen ..."

Step 2 **Talk about the economics of sports.**
Talk about sports marketing and the tradition of bookmaking. ▶ Cultural Background
Talk about the money athletes make.
▶ Sound File / Text File 2
Say what these two aspects show about the British.

Step 3 **Explain what "sports culture" is.**
Talk about what the British feel for football; or the importance of cricket competition. ▶ Video File / Text File 1

Step 4 **Talk about the ugly sides of the game.**
What they are; what the consequences are; how fans react. ▶ Text File 1 / Text File 2

Step 5 **Conclude.**
Give your opinion about sports in general and about the various documents you have studied in this unit. Then answer the question that started your presentation: "What is the social significance of sports culture in the UK?"

• **Train yourself**

Follow the steps above and speak for five minutes. If possible, add personal comments. Record yourself and listen to your presentation to improve it.

• **Get ready for a conversation**

Listen to the recording of your presentation and prepare yourself to justify, develop and exemplify what you have said.

# LE BAC EN LIGNE DE MIRE

Vous êtes en classe de 1re et le baccalauréat n'est pas pour cette année. Cependant, il est important que vous sachiez à quoi vous attendre pour avoir les meilleures chances de réussite l'année prochaine.
Pour vous entraîner, vous avez, à la fin de chaque chapitre, un sujet d'écrit (compréhension et expression), un document pour la compréhension de l'oral ainsi qu'un guidage pour vous permettre de développer la problématique du chapitre, en préparation pour l'épreuve d'expression orale.

## L'ÉPREUVE « orale »

**Elle se déroulera en deux temps, au sein de votre établissement.**

### LA COMPRÉHENSION

**Durée de l'épreuve :** 10 minutes (après l'écoute).

L'évaluation aura lieu au cours du deuxième trimestre de terminale. Elle s'appuie sur un ou deux document(s) enregistré(s), lié(s) aux notions du programme, non étudié(s) en classe. Il peut s'agir d'un monologue, d'un dialogue, d'un discours ou d'une discussion (durée : 1 minute 30).
Le document peut être un enregistrement audio ou une vidéo.
Le titre de l'enregistrement vous sera communiqué.
Vous aurez trois écoutes, séparées chacune d'une minute.
Vous pourrez prendre des notes pendant chaque écoute.
Vous aurez ensuite 10 minutes pour rendre compte par écrit en français de ce que vous avez compris.
Le professeur établira son évaluation à partir d'une fiche d'évaluation.

### L'EXPRESSION

**Durée de l'épreuve :** 10 minutes (après 10 minutes de temps de préparation).

L'évaluation est organisée au troisième trimestre de l'année de terminale.
Elle comporte **deux parties** de 5 minutes chacune.
**a.** Prise de parole en continu
Vous tirerez au sort une des notions du programme : « Lieux et formes de pouvoir », « L'idée de progrès », « Espaces et échanges », « Mythes et héros ». Vous devrez faire un exposé de 5 minutes à propos de cette notion.
**b.** Interaction
À partir de votre exposé, le professeur conduira une conversation pour évaluer votre capacité à réagir de manière spontanée à des questions non préparées. Cette phase d'interaction durera 5 minutes.

Pour chacune des parties, le professeur établira son évaluation à partir d'une fiche d'évaluation (▶ couverture).

# L'ÉPREUVE écrite

**Durée de l'épreuve :** 2 heures.
**Pendant ces 2 heures, vous devrez répondre au questionnaire de compréhension et traiter le ou les sujets d'expression. Il vous appartient de bien gérer votre temps.**

## LA COMPRÉHENSION

L'épreuve prend appui sur un ou deux documents en anglais, en lien avec les notions du programme.
Les documents seront accompagnés d'un questionnaire semblable à ceux que nous vous proposons dans les sujets qui figurent à la fin de chaque chapitre de ce manuel.

Vous allez devoir montrer que vous êtes capable de comprendre le texte, c'est-à-dire sa thématique générale, repérer et comprendre les informations essentielles, les liens logiques, chronologiques ou thématiques, les motivations et réactions des personnages, du narrateur ou de l'auteur, et les conclusions d'une argumentation.
Si vous êtes en LV1, vous devez également être capable de comprendre les détails et de percevoir les points de vue développés dans le texte.

L'épreuve de compréhension est notée sur 10 points.

## L'EXPRESSION

En LV1, vous aurez deux sujets à traiter : un sujet de niveau B1 et un sujet de niveau B2.
En LV2, vous aurez un sujet de niveau B1 à traiter.

**Sujet 1**
Le sujet sera en lien avec les événements, faits, ou prises de position que vous avez identifiés dans le texte de l'épreuve de compréhension.
Le correcteur évaluera votre aptitude à rédiger, dans une langue correcte, un texte cohérent et clairement articulé. (Niveau B1)

**Sujet 2**
Le sujet vous demandera une argumentation personnelle en relation avec le document de l'épreuve de compréhension. Le correcteur évaluera votre aptitude à exprimer, de façon nuancée et argumentée, une opinion ou un avis, en présentant clairement, dans une langue correcte aussi précise que possible, les avantages ou les inconvénients d'une proposition, les points forts et les limites d'une prise de position. (Niveau B2)

## Le niveau CECRL attendu

**En LV1 : niveau B2**
(utilisateur indépendant, niveau avancé)
Vous pouvez comprendre le contenu essentiel de sujets concrets ou abstraits dans un texte complexe et communiquer avec un anglophone avec un certain degré de spontanéité.
Vous pouvez vous exprimer de façon claire et détaillée sur une grande gamme de sujets, émettre un avis sur un sujet d'actualité et exposer les avantages et inconvénients de différentes possibilités.

**En LV2 : niveau B1**
(utilisateur indépendant, niveau seuil)
Vous pouvez comprendre les points essentiels quand un langage clair et standard est utilisé et s'il s'agit de sujets familiers.
Vous pouvez vous débrouiller dans la plupart des situations rencontrées en voyage, produire un discours simple et cohérent sur des sujets familiers et dans vos domaines d'intérêt, raconter un événement, une expérience ou un rêve, décrire un espoir ou un but et exposer brièvement des raisons ou explications pour un projet ou une idée.

## Sommaire

1

# Adjectifs

## A Règles générales

- Les adjectifs sont invariables. Ils ne s'accordent ni en genre ni en nombre.
- Les adjectifs épithètes se placent toujours devant le nom qu'ils qualifient.
- Les adjectifs attributs se placent après les verbes d'état comme *be – become – get*.
- Les adjectifs suivis d'une préposition introduisant un complément sont le plus souvent employés comme attributs : *proud of*

*Jane is proud of her daughter because she is good at maths.*

## B L'ordre des adjectifs

On place toujours au plus près du nom, c'est-à-dire en dernier, l'adjectif qui lui est le plus intrinsèque tandis que les adjectifs appréciatifs sont placés en tête, le plus loin du nom. L'ordre généralement adopté est celui-ci : appréciation, taille, âge, couleur, origine, matière.

*A strange old black lady is at the door.*
Une vieille femme noire étrange est à la porte.

## C Les verbes qui nuancent l'adjectif

*very – so (much) – too – rather – quite – a little – almost* se placent à gauche de l'adjectif, *enough* à sa droite.

*She is very pretty, but not tall enough to be a model.*

## D Les adjectifs en *-ed* ou *-ing*

On peut former un adjectif en ajoutant à certains verbes une terminaison *-ed* (sens passif) ou *-ing* (sens actif).

*interested* intéressé – *interesting* intéressant

## E Les adjectives substantivés

Certains adjectifs peuvent être utilisés comme noms pour désigner l'ensemble de la catégorie.
Ils sont précédés de *the*, sont invariables, mais sont suivis d'un verbe au pluriel.
Pour parler d'un seul ou de quelques individus, on utilise *man*, *woman*, *person*, etc.

*The English* (les Anglais). *Some English people* (des Anglais).
*An English man* (un Anglais).

## Exercises

**1. Mettez les mots dans l'ordre.**

a. I / big / wooden / have / a / house / blue / new /.
b. dress / She / beautiful / has / a / wedding / white / old /.
c. We / puppy / a / new / friendly / brown / young / have /.
d. gave / He / horrible / her / a / box / chocolates / big / of / cheap /.
e. some / gave / She / him / woolen / pink / socks / trendy /.

**2. Choisissez la forme de l'adjectif qui convient.**

a. The film we saw yesterday was very … (bored – boring).
b. The sequel however was very … (entertained – entertaining).
c. We weren't at all … (bored – boring).
d. We were … (interested – interesting) from beginning to end.
e. I always go to the cinema when I feel a bit … (depressed – depressing).

**3. Traduisez en anglais.**

a. Je connais un Anglais qui est professeur de français.
b. Il n'est pas assez strict avec ses élèves.
c. Mais il est assez sympathique.
d. Les Anglais voyagent beaucoup.

2

# Adverbes

## A Fonction

Avec un adverbe, l'énonciateur nuance le sens d'un verbe, d'un adjectif, d'un autre adverbe ou d'une phrase entière pour préciser son opinion, une manière, un lieu, un moment, une fréquence, etc.

## B Forme

Les adverbes en *-ly* sont formés à partir d'un adjectif. Cette terminaison donne des adverbes de manière ou d'appréciation correspondant souvent à la terminaison française « -ment ».

*nicely* agréablement – *frequently* fréquemment.

**Modifications orthographiques**

- Adjectifs terminés par *-y* > *-ily*. *angrily.*
- Adjectifs terminés par *-ble* > *-ibly*. *possibly.*

**Attention !**

Quelques adjectifs terminés en *-ly* ne sont pas des adverbes.

*friendly – silly – lonely.*

Certains adverbes ont la même forme que l'adjectif qui leur correspond.

*fast – late – daily.*

Certains adverbes ne correspondent à aucun adjectif.

*always – almost.*

## C Place dans la phrase

En règle générale, les adverbes se placent devant le mot ou groupe de mots qu'ils modifient. Mais on ne sépare jamais un verbe de son complément.

*I like tea very much.* J'aime beaucoup le thé.

### 1. Les adverbes de manière

Ils se placent après le complément mais parfois aussi en position médiane (entre le sujet et le verbe à un temps simple ou après le premier auxiliaire).

*She speaks English fluently. She quietly went away.*

### 2. Les adverbes de modalité

*apparently – certainly – undoubtedly – obviously*, etc., se placent comme les adverbes de manière.

*It would certainly be easy.*

### 3. Les adverbes de fréquence

*never – rarely – sometimes – occasionally – frequently – often – usually – always*. Ils se placent avant le verbe à une forme simple, après le premier auxiliaire à une forme composée, après *be*.

*He never came though he'd been invited.*

Les locutions adverbiales comme *every day – every two days – once a week – twice a month – three times a year* se placent en fin de phrase.

### 4. Les adverbes de lieu et de temps

*here – there – downstairs – yesterday – tomorrow – today*, etc., se placent généralement à la fin de l'énoncé ou, plus rarement, en début de phrase.

*We'll go there tomorrow.*

## Exercises

**1. Trouvez l'adverbe correspondant au mot entre parenthèses et placez-le au bon endroit dans la phrase.**

a. "Will you be coming with me?" I asked. (hope)
b. "I won't, unless you do what I want," she said. (angry)
c. I started to feel afraid. (serious)
d. So, I decided what I'd do. (quick)

**2. Mettez les mots dans le bon ordre.**

a. I / tea / very / much / like.
b. She / fluently / English / speaks.
c. He / so / quietly / speaks.
d. I / go / always / to / Spain / in / the / summer.
e. I / to / the / gym / go / daily.

**3. Récrivez les phrases en utilisant *hardly*.**

a. I don't know Pat very well at all.
b. I almost never see her.
c. We don't often talk on the phone.
d. She has almost no friends.

**5. Les adverbes de degré**

*too – very – more – totally – nearly – extremely*, etc. se placent immédiatement avant l'adjectif ou l'adverbe qu'ils modifient.

*She is totally wrong.*

*Enough* se place après un adjectif ou un adverbe, mais avant un nom.

*I'm not rich enough but I have enough time.*

**6. Les adverbes négatifs**

*hardly – barely – scarcely* (à peine, presque pas), ayant un sens négatif, ne peuvent être associés qu'à un verbe à la forme positive.

*We could hardly see anything.* On ne voyait presque rien.

3

# Article Ø

## A Valeur

L'article Ø renvoie à la notion, c'est-à-dire directement au concept. Il reflète l'absence de détermination.

## B Emplois

- **Devant les noms dénombrables pluriels,** l'article Ø exprime une généralité.

  *Vegetables are good for you.* (On parle des légumes en général.)

- **Devant les noms indénombrables,** l'article Ø indique le renvoi à la notion. Il s'utilise devant :

  – les noms abstraits ;

  *Experience is essential.*

  – les noms de matières ou matériaux ;

  *Oil is expensive.*

  – les noms de repas ;

  *Lunch is served at 12:30.*

  – les noms de couleur ;

  *I like green.*

  – les noms de langue, etc.

  *I can speak Japanese.*

- **Dans certaines expressions figées :**

  – *go to school/hospital/university/church/work/bed* ;

  – *by car/plane/bus/train*, etc.

  **Attention !** Cette règle ne s'applique pas s'il y a détermination par *of* + nom ou une relative.

  *The school I go to is in the city centre.*

- **Devant les noms propres au singulier :**

  – les noms de personnes, y compris s'ils sont précédés d'un titre ;

  *Queen Elizabeth – Prince William – Doctor Smith.*

  – les noms de lieu singuliers et non suivis de *of.*

  *Africa – England – Lake Michigan – Oxford Street – Buckingham Palace.*

- **Devant les noms de jours et de mois :**

  *I hate November and I hate Mondays.*

### Exercises

**1. Complétez avec *train, a train* ou *trains*.**

a. It was the first time I'd been on … .

b. I decided to go to London by … .

c. … are a real problem. They never get in on time.

d. What's the use of taking … if you spend a long time waiting for it to arrive.

**2. Il y a une faute dans chaque phrase. Corrigez-la.**

a. My favorite colour is the yellow.

b. I go to the school at 8 a.m. every day.

c. What time do you go to the bed?

d. I stay at the home on Saturdays.

e. I love the August best of all the months.

**3. Traduisez en français.**

a. Le Canada est un pays magnifique.

b. Elle aime le bleu. C'est la couleur de ses yeux.

c. Le bois est une matière très noble.

d. À quelle heure le déjeuner est-il servi ?

e. Est-ce que tu es à la maison demain soir ?

4

## Article *a/an*

### A Forme : *a* ou *an* ?

- On utilise *a* devant un nom singulier commençant par une consonne et *an* devant un nom singulier commençant par un son vocalique. *A clock. An alarmclock.*
- On tient compte de la prononciation et non de l'orthographe. *A uniform. An umbrella.*
- Quand un nom commence par la lettre « h », on utilise *a* si le « h » est aspiré et *an* s'il ne l'est pas. *A hot cake. An hour.*

### B Valeur

Avec *a/an*, l'énonciateur isole un élément et le présente comme non connu du co-énonciateur.

*I met a young woman. She is a teacher.* (L'énonciateur n'a pas encore mentionné la jeune femme. Il isole une personne dans la classe des professeurs.)

### C Emplois

*A/An* ne peut introduire qu'un nom dénombrable au singulier.
Il peut renvoyer à l'ensemble d'une classe.

*A dog is a domestic animal.* (C'est vrai de tous les chiens.)

Il peut avoir un emploi distributif.

*He works 30 hours a week.* Il travaille 30 heures par semaine.

### D *A/An* ou *one* ?

Si on veut insister sur la quantité, on utilise plutôt *one*, qui est un nombre.

*How many sandwiches do you want? – One sandwich.*

**Exercises**

**1. Complétez avec *a* ou *an*.**

a. ... uniform
b. ... hotel
c. ... house
d. ... hour
e. ... university
f. ... dog
g. ... ugly dog
h. ... eye
i. ... boy
j. ... intelligent boy

**2. Complétez avec *a*, *an* ou *one*.**

a. Would you like ... apple?
b. Yes please. Will you eat ... apple too?
c. There is only ... apple.
d. I'll have ... orange.
e. I make sure I eat ... apple at least, every day.

5

## Article *the*

### A Forme

L'article défini *the* est invariable et s'emploie pour les noms pluriels et singuliers, masculins, féminins ou neutres. *The woman. The men.*

### B Emplois

L'article *the* fait référence à du « déjà connu » ou « déjà repéré ». Il a une valeur de détermination plus forte que celle de l'article défini français.

- *The* s'utilise devant un nom dénombrable, singulier ou pluriel, désignant un ou plusieurs éléments déjà mentionnés.
  *Salisbury has an old cathedral. The cathedral was built in the 13th century.* (La cathédrale dont je viens de parler.)
- *The* renvoie à un élément identifié par la situation présente.
  *Close the door.* (La porte de la pièce où nous sommes.)
- *The* s'utilise devant un nom, même indénombrable, déterminé par un groupe prépositionnel (notamment *of* ou *in*), ou une proposition relative.
  *You'll have the calcium you need if you drink milk.*

**Exercises**

**1. Complétez avec *the* ou Ø.**

a. ... weather is awful today.
b. Normally it's sunny in ... August.
c. ... seaside resorts are terrible when it rains.
d. ... seaside resort I go to has lots of things to do.
e. ... holidaymakers who are here are fed up.

**2. Il y a une faute par phrase. Corrigez-la.**

a. What do you do? – I'm teacher.
b. Do you teach the English?
c. No, I don't. I teach the maths.
d. Is it difficult job?

- *The* renvoie à ce qui est connu de tous.

  *The sun rises in the East.*

- *The* s'emploie devant les noms de pays au pluriel ou bien formés à partir de noms communs. L'accord se fait généralement au singulier.

  *The USA – the United Kingdom – the Netherlands.*

- *The* s'emploie devant les noms de montagnes, mers, fleuves, etc.

  *The Alps – the Mediterranean – the Thames.*

- *The* s'emploie devant les noms propres pluriels pour désigner une famille.

  *The Gordons.* Les Gordon/la famille Gordon.

**3. Traduisez en anglais.**

a. Je préfère voyager par le train.
b. La reine Élizabeth II fut couronnée en 1952.
c. J'irai soit en Afrique, soit aux États-Unis cet été.
d. Le lundi, j'ai un cours d'anglais, puis je fais du tennis.

# 6 Avenir (référence à l')

L'anglais ne dispose pas de temps futur. On a recours à différentes structures : présent simple ou *be* + V-*ing*, modalité (*will* ou *shall*) ou expression contenant le *to* de visée (*be going to*).
On choisit la structure selon ce que l'on veut exprimer : prédiction, intention, programme, imminence, etc.

## A *Will*

*Will* est la forme la plus fréquemment utilisée pour faire référence à l'avenir. Avec *will*, l'énonciateur fait une prédiction : il déduit ce qui va se passer d'après ce qu'il sait ou d'après ce qu'il décide au moment où il parle.
On traduit généralement la forme en *will* par un futur, mais on peut aussi utiliser le verbe « aller » ou le verbe « vouloir ».

*I'll help you. I'm sure you'll need help.* Je vais vous aider. Je suis sûr que vous allez avoir besoin d'aide (d'après ce que je sais de la situation).

On utilise souvent *Will you* pour demander à quelqu'un de faire quelque chose.

*Will you help me, please?*

**Attention !** Une subordonnée introduite par *when* ou *as soon as* est au présent avec une principale qui fait référence à l'avenir.

*I'll be away when you arrive.* Je serai parti quand tu arriveras.

## B *Shall*

Comme *will*, *shall* fait référence à une action à venir mais il exprime une contrainte ou une nécessité imposée par l'énonciateur.
À la première personne, comme le sujet grammatical est *I* ou *we*, la contrainte est forcément atténuée : c'est celle que se donne l'énonciateur à lui-même. On utilise souvent *shall* à la forme interrogative pour proposer un service.

*What shall we do? Shall I help you?*

Aux autres personnes, *shall* est couramment employé dans les règlements, lois et contrats — chaque fois qu'une contrainte physique ou légale est implicite.

*You shall not modify the software.* Il est interdit de modifier le logiciel.

### Exercises

**1. Choisissez entre *will* ou *shall*.**

a. I have a headache.
... I get you an aspirin?
b. The phone's ringing.
... I answer it for you?
c. You are making too much noise.
... you be quiet now please.
d. ... you have some more coffee?
e. It's late. Do you think he ... get here soon?
f. I've lost my handbag.
What ... I do?

**2. Complétez avec *be going to*.**

a. Why are you turning on the television?
I (watch) the news.
b. I have lost my wallet. I don't have any money.
I (lend) you some.
c. Why are you carrying that ladder?
I (paint) my house.
d. Everything is planned.
I (be) on holiday for a few weeks.
e. That's a great idea.
I (come) with you.

**3. Réagissez aux situations suivantes en utilisant *'ll* et la suggestion donnée entre parenthèses.**

a. It's too cold here! I ... (window)
b. – I haven't got a cardigan.
– No problem. I ... (lend)
c. If it rains, I ... (umbrella)
d. I am tired. I ... (bed)

## C *Be going to* + V

L'énonciateur exprime l'intention du sujet ou fait une prévision liée à la présence d'indices qu'il constate.

*We're going to start early. It's going to rain.*

Cette structure peut s'utiliser au prétérit.

*I was going to tell you.* J'allais vous le dire.

## D Présent *be* V-*ing*

Avec le présent *be* V-*ing* associé à un marqueur de temps futur, l'énonciateur annonce un projet pour lequel le sujet a pris ses dispositions.

*We're flying to England tomorrow.* (Nous l'avons décidé.)

## E Présent simple

Le présent simple avec un marqueur de temps approprié exprime un futur indépendant de la volonté de l'énonciateur.

*Our train leaves at 10.* (C'est l'horaire du train.)

## F *Be to* + V

C'est le *to* de visée qui renvoie à l'avenir.

**Une disposition convenue**, par exemple dans un règlement ou un contrat.

*The loan is to be repaid.* Le prêt est/sera à rembourser.

**Un ordre ou une instruction émanant de quelqu'un d'autre.**

*You are to go to the headmaster's office after school.*

**Un projet dans le révolu** (au prétérit) ; on ne sait pas s'il s'est réalisé.

*We were to meet after school.* (Nous devions nous rencontrer.)

## G *Be about to*

Cette structure insiste sur l'imminence de l'événement annoncé (présent ou prétérit).

*I was about to call the police.* J'allais appeler la police.

**4. Associez chaque phrase (*a* à *g*) à la définition (*1* à *7*) qui lui correspond.**

a. Everything is OK. They'll get here at 5.
b. Will you do that for me?
c. Shall I get it for you?
d. I'm leaving at six.
e. Now, what shall I do?
f. With all that money, I'm going to buy a new car.
g. Hurry up. Your plane leaves in four minutes.

1. Un projet pour lequel on a pris des dispositions.
2. Une prédiction liée à ce que l'on sait.
3. Un horaire.
4. Une intention.
5. Une demande à quelqu'un de faire quelque chose.
6. Une offre très polie.
7. Une demande de conseil.

# 7 *Be*

## A Forme

### 1. Présent

- Forme affirmative : sujet + *be*

*I am – You are – He/She/It is – We are – You are – They are.*

Contractée : *I'm – You're – He's/She's/It's – We're – You're – They're.*

- Forme négative : sujet + *be* + not

*I am not – You are not – He/She/It is not – We are not – You are not – They are not.*

Contractée : *I'm not – He isn't – They aren't.*

- Forme interrogative : *be* + sujet

*Am I? – Are you? – Is he/she/it? – Are we? – Are you? – Are they?*

### Exercises

**1. Posez les questions qui ont amené ces réponses.**

a. Yes, he is very tall.
b. No, she wasn't here yesterday.
c. No, there isn't a dog in the house.
d. Yes, my grandmother is very old.
e. Yes, I'm 16.

**2. Prétérit**

- Forme affirmative :

*I was – You were – He/She/It was – We were – You were – They were.*

- Forme négative :

*I was not – You were not – He/She/It was not – We were not – You were not – They were not.*

Contractée : *wasn't – weren't.*

- Forme interrogative :

*Was I? – Were you? – Was he/she/it? – Were we? – Were you? – Were they?*

## B Emplois

**1. *Be*, auxiliaire**

Comme tous les auxiliaires, il n'a pas de sens propre mais sert à indiquer le temps ou l'aspect d'un autre verbe, comme dans la forme *be* V-*ing* ou la voix passive.

*He is smiling.* Il sourit. *He was injured.* Il a été blessé.

**2. *Be*, verbe d'état**

- *Be* indique une propriété du sujet.
  Il équivaut souvent au verbe français « être » mais, dans certains emplois, on le traduit par « avoir », « aller » ou « mesurer ».
  – Description. *They are tall.*
  – Identification. *She is American.*
  – Âge. *He is 14.*
  – Couleur. *It's red.*
  – Taille/poids. *She is 5 feet tall.* Elle mesure cinq pieds.
  – État physique. *How are you?* Comment allez-vous ?

  *I am hungry/cold.* J'ai faim/froid.

  – Métier. *She is a doctor.*
  – Autres états.

  *He is afraid/right/wrong/lucky.* Il a peur/raison/tort/de la chance.

- *Be* situe le sujet dans le temps ou l'espace.

  *Our house is close to the city centre.* Notre maison est proche du centre-ville.

- *Be* s'emploie dans des expressions impersonnelles.

  *It's cold/warm/hot.* Il fait froid/chaud/très chaud.

- *Be* sert à former *there is* (+ nom singulier)/*there are* (+ nom pluriel) pour signaler l'existence de quelque chose, comme « il y a ».

  *There's a problem but there are solutions.*
  Il y a un problème mais il y a des solutions.

  Cette expression peut se mettre au passé ou se combiner avec n'importe quel auxiliaire pour rendre compte d'un aspect ou d'une modalité.
  **Attention !** Elle ne sert pas à exprimer la durée. ▶ 12
  – *There was* (+ nom singulier)/*there were* (+ nom pluriel) : il y avait.
  – *There is going to be* : il va y avoir.
  – *There used to be* : il y avait.
  – *There will be* : il y aura.
  – *There would be* : il y aurait.
  – *There must be* : il doit y avoir.
  – *There could be* : il se pourrait qu'il y ait.

**2. Peut-on utiliser *there* + *be* pour traduire ces phrases ?**

a. Il y a des centaines de choses à faire.
b. Il est arrivé il y a environ quatre mois.
c. Il doit y avoir trois ans que je ne l'ai pas vue.
d. Il se pourrait qu'il y ait des problèmes.

**3. Traduisez en anglais.**

a. Est-ce qu'il y a une chaise dans la pièce ? – Oui.
b. Est-ce que tu as froid ? – Non.
c. Votre chien est-il dangereux ? – Oui.
d. Ta mère a-t-elle faim ? – Oui.
e. Quel âge as-tu ? – J'ai 18 ans.

**4. Dans chaque phrase, dites si *be* est auxiliaire ou verbe.**

a. This is a nice blue hat.
b. Are you being stupid?
c. We've been away for two weeks.
d. Are you 19 or 20?
e. Were they allowed to enter the building?

**5. Traduisez en anglais.**

a. Je sais que tu as raison.
b. Tu as toujours raison – du moins, c'est ce que tu dis.
c. Tu as de la chance.
d. Allons déjeuner. J'ai très faim.

8

# Comparaison

## A Le comparatif de supériorité (plus… que)

### 1. Comparaison portant sur un adjectif ou un adverbe

- Adjectif/adverbe court : adjectif/adverbe + *-er* + *than*
  On appelle « adjectif court » un adjectif composé d'une seule syllabe ou de deux syllabes s'il est terminé par *-y* .

  *short > shorter – heavy > heavier.*

- Adjectif long : *more* + adjectif/adverbe + *than*
  On appelle « adjectif long » un adjectif comportant plus d'une syllabe ou plus de deux s'il se termine par *-y.*

  *comfortable > more comfortable – quietly > more quietly.*

- Modifications orthographiques
  Si le mot se termine par une voyelle suivie d'une seule consonne, celle-ci est doublée. *big > bigger.*

  Si le mot se termine par une consonne suivie de *-y*, la terminaison est *-ier.* *pretty > prettier.*

### 2. Comparaison portant sur d'autres éléments

- Sur un nom : *more* + nom *I have more friends than enemies.*
- Sur un verbe : verbe + *more* *I work more than my friend (does).*

### 3. Comparatifs irréguliers

*good* > ***better*** – *bad* > ***worse*** – *far* > ***further*** – *old* > ***elder*** (personnes d'une même famille).

### 4. Pour traduire « de plus en plus… »

- Avec un adjectif ou un adverbe
  Adjectif ou adverbe court : … + ***-er and…*** + ***-er***
  Adjectif ou adverbe long ou nom : ***more and more…***

  *He gets richer and richer everyday… and more and more eccentric!*

- Avec un nom : *more and more*

  *He gives me more and more trouble.*

## B Le comparatif d'égalité (aussi… que)

Il indique l'équivalence entre deux éléments, objets ou personnes :
***as*** **+ adjectif/adverbe +** ***as***

*She is as clever as her sister.*

## C Le comparatif d'infériorité (pas aussi/moins… que)

Il permet de comparer des personnes, des objets ou des ensembles entre eux : ***not as*** **+ adjectif/adverbe +** ***as***
***less*** **+ adjectif/adverbe +** ***than***

*My cell phone is not as sophisticated as John's / less sophisticated than John's.*

## D Le superlatif de supériorité (le plus…)

- Adjectifs courts : ***the*** **+ adjectif +** ***-est***

  *This laptop is the smallest we have.*
  Ce portable est le plus petit que nous ayons.

- Adjectifs longs : ***the most*** **+ adjectif**

  *It is also the most sophisticated we have.*
  … le plus perfectionné que nous ayons.

## Exercises

**1. Mettez les adjectifs entre parenthèses au comparatif.**

a. My sister, Mandy, is … than me. (old)
b. But she is … at school than I am. (good)
c. My brother Bill is … than I am. (young)
d. He is … than me and my sister. (noisy)
e. He is … than we are. (fast)

**2. Il y a une faute dans chaque phrase. Corrigez-la.**

a. My computer is moderner than yours.
b. My house is not as big than yours.
c. My new sofa is more comfortable as yours.
d. This book is gooder than *Harry Potter.*
e. You are more nice than I am.

**3. Complétez les phrases avec un adjectif au double comparatif, choisi en fonction du sens.**

a. Our town used to be clean. Now, it's getting … .
b. Computers used to be expensive, but now they're getting … .
c. Our neighbour used to be very nice, but now he's getting … .
d. Cars used to be slow, but now they are … .

**4. Choisissez l'adjectif qui convient dans la liste et mettez-le au comparatif ou au superlatif.**

energetic – sad – funny – fit – bad

a. He is the … boy I know. He is always crying.
b. She does a lot of running. She is … than I am.
c. It was the … holiday I ever had. It was awful.
d. I laughed for two hours. It was the … film I had ever seen.

- Pour traduire « le plus… des deux », on utilise un comparatif.

*He has two dogs. Miro is the bigger (of the two).*
Miro est le plus gros (des deux).

### E Le superlatif d'infériorité (le moins…)

Pour tous les adjectifs : ***the least*** **+ adjectif**

*This is the least interesting aspect of your document…*
le moins intéressant.

### F Le complément du superlatif

Il est introduit par *in* s'il s'agit d'un lieu ; par *of* dans les autres cas.

*It's the best restaurant in the city. The chef is the best of all.*

### G Comparatifs et superlatifs irréguliers

*good, better, the best.*
*bad, worse, the worst.*
*far, further, the furthest.*
*old, elder, the eldest* (personnes d'une même famille).

**5. Complétez avec un superlatif de supériorité ou d'infériorité.**

a. He is bad. He is … person I know.
b. She is good. She is … person I know.
c. That woman is old. She is … woman I know.
d. That dog is dangerous. It is … dog I have ever seen.

**6. Traduisez en anglais.**

a. C'est la fille la plus brillante de la classe.
b. Ce livre est le meilleur (des deux).
c. C'est la tâche la moins intéressante que je dois faire.
d. C'est le plus petit chien que j'aie jamais vu.
e. Il est moins joli que mon chien.

## 9 ▶ Démonstratifs

**Les démonstratifs sont *this/these* et *that/those*.**

### A Valeurs

L'énonciateur présente un élément par rapport à lui-même.
*This/These* marquent la proximité, *that/those* l'éloignement ou la rupture.
**Espace :** *this/these* indiquent que l'élément introduit est lié à la situation d'énonciation (*this world* = notre monde) ; *that/those* indiquent une rupture (*that world* = un autre monde).
**Temps :** *this* renvoie au présent (*this year* = l'année en cours), *that* au passé (*that year*).
**Affectivité :** avec *that/those*, l'énonciateur peut indiquer un jugement, généralement négatif. *Look at those girls!*

### B Quelques emplois

*This* s'utilise pour présenter quelqu'un ou pour prendre contact au téléphone.

*This is Camilla. – Hello, this is Mark speaking.*

*This* peut servir à introduire un énoncé (il est tourné vers l'avenir), alors que *that* peut reprendre un énoncé (il est tourné vers le passé).

*This is what he said: "Don't go alone!" "Don't go alone!" that's what he said.*

### C *This/These* et *that/those* pronoms

*This/These* et *that/those*, pronoms, ne peuvent désigner que des inanimés.

*Look at this/that!*

On peut aussi employer *this one/that one* et *these ones/those ones* pour éviter une répétition.

*Which is your favorite photo? This one or that one?*

**Exercises**

**1. Complétez cette conversation avec *this* ou *that*.**

a. I'm sure … is going to be a great film.
b. Look, John. … boy in front of you is eating sweets.
c. … is going to make a terrible noise during the film.
d. … is it! The film is going to start.
e. Oh, no! I've already seen … film.

**2. Complétez avec *these* – *those* – *this* – *that*.**

a. … dresses are really ugly.
b. I prefer … dresses over there.
c. Ah, yes, … are the ones I saw in the fashion magazine.
d. They are … year's finish.
e. They are exactly what trendy people are wearing … days.

**3. Traduisez en anglais.**

a. Regarde ce gâteau. Il a l'air magnifique.
b. J'ai mangé un gâteau comme ça la semaine dernière et ce n'était pas très bon.
c. Un gâteau au chocolat, voilà ce que je veux.

# 10 Discours indirect

## A Les verbes introducteurs

Les verbes qui servent à rapporter les paroles de quelqu'un sont : *add – answer – exclaim – explain – hope – protest – reply – report – say – tell – think – write*, etc.

***Say* ou *tell*** ?
Ces deux verbes se traduisent par « dire » mais leur emploi est différent :
– avec *tell*, l'interlocuteur est cité et le nom ou pronom est placé immédiatement après *tell* ;
– avec *say*, l'interlocuteur n'est pas nécessairement cité et, s'il l'est, il est introduit par *to* : *You tell somebody something – You say something (to somebody)*.

*She says (that) she is coming. She tells me (that) she is coming.*

*Tell* s'emploie dans quelques expressions figées sans mention d'un interlocuteur : *tell the truth – tell a story – tell the time*.

## B Les modifications

- **Temps et aspect**
Si le verbe introducteur est au présent, il n'y a pas de changement de forme verbale. *"I'm tired," Bill says. > Bill says he's tired.*
Si le verbe introducteur est au passé, l'énonciateur signale le changement de moment d'énonciation en appliquant la concordance des temps.
**Présent > prétérit.** Cela concerne aussi les modaux : *will*, *can* et *may* deviennent *would*, *could* et *might*.
*Sam said, "I'm tired and I'll have a rest" > Sam said he was tired and he'd have a rest.*
**Prétérit simple et *present perfect* > *past perfect*.**
*"I did a lot of things," Sam said. > Sam said he had done a lot of things.*

- **Pronoms, possessifs, déterminants, marqueurs spatiaux et temporels**
L'énonciateur rapportant les paroles de quelqu'un d'autre signale le changement d'énonciateur en modifiant les pronoms personnels, possessifs et déterminants, ainsi que les repères spatiaux et temporels.
*me* > ***he/she***; *we* > ***they***; *my* > ***his/her***; *our* > ***their***; *this* > ***that***, etc.
*Sam said, "I'll give you my ticket." > Sam said he would give me his ticket.*
*here* > ***there***; *now* > ***then***; *yesterday* > ***the day before***; *tomorrow* > ***the day after***, etc.
*Sam said, "I arrived yesterday." > Sam said he had arrived the day before.*

## C Les questions

- **Verbes introducteurs :** *ask, wonder, want to know*, etc.
Les règles de concordance des temps sont les mêmes que celles décrites ci-dessus. L'ordre des mots est celui de la phrase affirmative : sujet (+ auxiliaire) + verbe, et l'auxiliaire *do/does/did* est supprimé.

- **Pour les questions fermées** (sans mot interrogatif)
On utilise *if* ou *whether*.
*"Do you like tea?" She asked. > She asked if/whether I liked tea.*

## Exercises

**1. Mettez ces paroles au style indirect.**
a. I am proud to be among you today.
> *He said* ...
b. I'm coming from my hometown.
> *He said* ...
c. I spoke to a group of protesters yesterday.
> *He said* ...

**2. Retrouvez les paroles qui ont été prononcées.**
a. He told us his parents had bought a nice new house.
b. He said it was very close to where we were.
c. He said they were moving in the next day.
d. He added he would be able to come and visit us easily.
e. He promised he would take us out often.

**3. Rapportez les questions qui vous ont été posées à l'aéroport lors de votre voyage aux États-Unis.**
a. How long are you going to stay here? > He asked me ...
b. Where do you come from?
> He asked me ...
c. Do you know anybody here?
> He asked me ...
d. Who is going to put you up?
> He asked me ...
e. Do you have any goods to declare?
> He asked me ...
f. Are you aware that you cannot import fresh fruit?
> He asked me ...

**4. Rapportez les suggestions de l'ami à qui vous allez rendre visite à Toronto en plein hiver.**
a. "Take your warmest clothes," he advised me.
b. "Send me a photo of your family," he asked me.
c. "Don't forget to bring your camera," he reminded me.
d. "Don't tell your friend I'm coming," he asked me.

Si l'auxiliaire est un modal, il est maintenu pour conserver le sens.

*Jane asked, "What can you do for me?"*
*> Jane asked what I could do for her.*

S'il y a un mot interrogatif au discours direct, on le garde au discours indirect.

*She asked, "When will you come?" > She asked me when I would come.*
*He asked, "Who came?" > He wanted to know who had come.*

- **Pour les questions ouvertes** (*wh- questions*)
On conserve les mots interrogatifs du style direct.

*Jane asked, "Who rang, and why did you go?"*
*> Jane asked who had rung and why we had gone.*

### D Les ordres et interdictions

- Verbes introducteurs : *tell, order, forbid, ask*, etc. On utilise une construction infinitive avec *to* ou *not to* pour rapporter les énoncés à l'impératif.

*"Come in," he said. > He told me to come in.*

## 11 *Do*

### 1. *Do*, auxiliaire

- Il sert d'opérateur pour mettre les verbes lexicaux (sauf *be*) aux formes interrogatives et négatives du présent (*do/does*) et du prétérit (*did*).

*Why does she go now? – I don't know.*

- Il sert d'opérateur pour renforcer une affirmation.

*I do understand.* Je comprends très bien/Mais si, je comprends.

- Il sert pour les réponses courtes ; il complète *Yes* ou *No*.

*Do you know him? – Yes, I do.*

- Il évite de répéter le verbe dans les *question tags* (n'est-ce pas ?).

*I love chocolate. – So do I.* Moi aussi.

### 2. *Do*, verbe lexical

Il se construit comme tous les verbes. *He doesn't do much.*

### *Do* ou *make* ?

- *Do* correspond à « faire ». C'est l'emploi le plus courant.

*What are you doing? I never do the washing-up. He does his best.*

- *Do* correspond à un emploi particulier de « aller ».

*How are you doing?* Comment allez-vous ? *It will do!* Ça ira !

**Quelques emplois :** *do one's room, one's homework, the shopping, the ironing, the accounts, sports, competitions, one's duty, business*, etc. Faire sa chambre, ses devoirs, les courses, le repassage, les comptes, etc.

- *Make* correspond aussi au verbe « faire », notamment (mais pas seulement) dans le sens de « fabriquer ».

*Make tea. Make a cake.*

**Quelques emplois :** *make a noise, a bed, a fire, war, peace, a journey, a phone call, a mistake, an effort, money, a decision*, etc.
Faire du bruit, un lit, du feu, la guerre, etc.

### Exercises

**1. Mettez ces phrases à la forme interrogative, puis à la forme négative.**
Ex. : *Hilary plays tennis.*
*> Does Hilary play tennis?*
*– No, she doesn't play tennis.*
a. Hilary cooks fantastically.
b. She makes lots of cakes.
c. She likes cooking.
d. She made a chocolate mousse yesterday.
e. She does her job very well.

**2. Complétez avec *do* ou *make*.**
a. Maria ... very nice clothes.
b. She always ... a very good job.
c. Her French is not good. She always ... mistakes.
d. But she has ... a lot of progress.
e. She works at French but she doesn't ... housework.

**3. Traduisez en anglais.**
a. Je vais faire le thé.
b. Est-ce que tu fais beaucoup de sport? – Oui.
c. Mes voisins font trop de bruit.
d. Léo ne fait jamais sa chambre.

12 ▶

# Durée

## 1. *Since*

- *Since* indique le point de départ d'une action ou d'un état. Il implique un bilan (durée écoulée depuis ce point), donc l'emploi, dans la principale, d'un *present perfect* ou d'un *past perfect* si le point de référence est passé, tandis que le français utilise un présent.
- *Since* peut être une préposition (introduire un nom) se traduisant par « depuis ».

  *He has lived here since 2013.* Il vit ici depuis 2013.
- *Since* peut être une conjonction (introduire une proposition) se traduisant par « depuis que ».

  *He has lived here since he married.* Il vit ici depuis qu'il est marié.

## 2. *For*

*For,* dans sa valeur temporelle, est une préposition introduisant un nom indiquant une durée : *hour – day – week – month – year,* etc.

- Avec le *present perfect*, ou le *past perfect*, si le point de référence est passé, *for* indique la durée d'une action ou d'un état non terminé. Il se traduit par « depuis ». En français, le verbe est au présent.

  *He has lived here for five years.* Il vit ici depuis cinq ans.
- Avec le prétérit, *for* indique la durée d'une action ou d'un état révolus, sans lien avec le présent. Il se traduit par « pendant » et le verbe est au passé.

  *He lived here for five years.* Il a vécu ici pendant cinq ans.

  **Attention !** Il ne faut pas confondre *for* et *during,* qui se traduit également par « pendant » mais n'indique pas une durée : il situe une action ou un état dans une période.

  *He lived here during war.* Il a vécu ici pendant la guerre.

## 3. *Ago*

*Ago* est une préposition qui se place après le nom qui exprime la durée écoulée entre l'événement et le moment d'énonciation.
Il indique que l'événement s'est déroulé à une période révolue et implique donc un verbe au prétérit. Il se traduit en français par « il y a »

*He went home two years ago.* Il est retourné chez lui il y a deux ans.

## 4. Poser une question

Pour interroger sur la durée d'une action, on utilise l'expression interrogative *how long* :
– avec le *present perfect* si l'action n'est pas terminée ;
– avec le prétérit si l'action est terminée.

*How long has he lived here?* Depuis combien de temps vit-il ici ?
*How long did he live here?* Combien de temps a-t-il vécu ici ?

## Exercises

**1. Complétez avec *for* ou *since*.**

a. He has lived here ... two years.
b. Julia lived in London ... five years.
c. They have been together ... 2005.
d. She has been working with us ... she got married.

**2. Traduisez en vous interrogeant sur le sens de « il y a ».**

a. Il y a douze mois dans une année.
b. Il y a trois mois, je suis allé à la mer.
c. Il y a deux mois que j'attends son retour.
d. Il y a deux ans, elle a changé de travail.

**3. Traduisez en anglais.**

a. Depuis quand connais-tu Benji ?
b. Je le connais depuis cinq ans.
c. En fait, depuis qu'il est arrivé en France.
d. Avant de venir, il a vécu en Angleterre pendant deux ans.
e. Nous travaillons ensemble depuis le début de l'année.

# Énoncés à deux verbes

**1. Verbe 1 + *to* verbe 2**
La forme *to* + V fait référence à l'avenir. Elle s'utilise après des verbes exprimant une opinion, une volonté ou une cause puisqu'on projette la réalisation d'une action dans l'avenir :
*advise – agree – ask – cause – choose – decide – expect – force – hope – oblige – promise – refuse – want*

*I want to go to the cinema.*

**2. Verbe 1 + verbe 2-*ing***
La forme V-*ing* fait référence à une action déjà commencée ou déjà mentionnée.
Elle s'utilise après les verbes et expressions *can't bear – can't stand – can't help – imagine – give up – keep on – prevent from – stop*, etc.

*Stop talking! I can't help crying.* Je ne peux pas m'empêcher de pleurer.

**3. Verbe 1 + verbe 2 = *let, make* et *have***

- ***Make* + nom/pronom + V :** « faire faire quelque chose à quelqu'un ».
  Le sujet exerce une action sur quelqu'un d'autre (nom ou pronom à la forme complément). Le verbe à l'infinitif a un sens actif.

  *She made Sue dance, which made me laugh.* Elle a fait danser Sue, ce qui m'a fait rire.

  Quand la pression est effectuée sur le sujet de la phrase par un agent inconnu, la tournure est employée à la forme passive : sujet + *be made to* + V. On la traduit avec un impersonnel : « On m'a fait faire/dire, etc. »

  *He was made to sleep.* On l'a fait dormir.

- ***Have* + nom/pronom + participe passé :** « faire faire quelque chose ».
  La pression exercée par le sujet porte sur le verbe à l'infinitif qui a un sens passif.

  *We had the house painted.* Nous avons fait peindre la maison.

- ***Let* + nom/pronom + V :** « laisser faire quelqu'un ou quelque chose ».

  *My parents let me go out but they don't let my brother do the same.*

  *Let* peut être utilisé à l'impératif. *Let him go.*

  Il sert à former la première personne de l'impératif avec *us*.
  *Let's go now!*

### Les verbes à deux constructions

**4. Verbe 1 + verbe 2-*ing* ou Verbe 1 + verbe 2**
Certains verbes, en particulier les verbes de perception (*hear – listen – see – watch*, etc.), peuvent accepter les deux constructions. On choisit l'une ou l'autre selon que l'on s'intéresse plutôt à l'action perçue ou au résultat de cette action.

*I saw him eating. I saw him eat the sandwich.*

**5. Verbe 1 + verbe 2-*ing* ou Verbe 1 + *to* + verbe 2**
Certains verbes admettent ces deux constructions.
On choisit l'une ou l'autre selon que l'on se réfère à l'avenir ou à une action passée ou déjà mentionnée : *be afraid – forget – hate – like – love – notice – regret – remember – start – try.*

*Remember to lock the door!* Pense à fermer la porte.
*I remember locking the door.* Je me souviens avoir fermé la porte.

## Exercises

**1. Ces verbes sont-ils suivis de *to* + V ou de V-*ing* ?**
a. agree
b. avoid
c. can't stand
d. decide
e. expect
f. feel like
g. give up
h. want
i. enjoy
j. promise

**2. Complétez les phrases en mettant le verbe entre parenthèses à la forme qui convient.**
a. Jane enjoys ... in the sea. (swim)
b. Bill can't stand ... sport. (do)
c. He prefers ... mountains. (climb)
d. He wants Jane ... with him. (come)
e. But she refuses ... dangerous sports. (do)

**3. Traduisez en anglais.**
a. Je ne supporte pas d'attendre.
b. Je lui ai demandé de m'aider.
c. Il a refusé de porter mes bagages.
d. Il adore prendre l'avion.
e. Il ne se souvient pas avoir fermé sa voiture.

14

# Exclamation

**1. *What* (que, quel, quelles)**
*What* s'emploie lorsque l'exclamation porte sur un nom, modifié ou non par un adjectif.
Devant un dénombrable au pluriel : *What* + Ø (+ adjectif) + nom + !

*What nice dogs!*

Devant un dénombrable au singulier : *What* + *a/an* (+ adjectif) + nom + !

*What a strange idea! What an idiot!*

Devant un indénombrable : *What* + Ø + (adjectif) + nom + !

*What exceptional courage!*

Devant un indénombrable précédé de *a* dans des expressions figées.

*What a pity! What a shame! What a mess!*

**2. *How* (que, comme)**
*How* peut porter :
– sur un adjectif seul ; *How nice you are!* Que vous êtes aimable!
– sur un adverbe ; *How fast he drives!* Comme il conduit vite !
– sur un énoncé entier. *How he loves you!* Qu'est-ce qu'il t'aime !

## Exclamatives et interrogatives

**Attention !** Il ne faut pas confondre *how* et *what* exclamatifs avec *how* et *what* interrogatifs : dans les phrases exclamatives, il n'y a pas d'inversion entre l'auxiliaire et le sujet.

*How long this story is!* Que cette histoire est longue !
*How long is this story?* Combien de temps dure cette histoire ?

## Traduction de « si », « tellement », « aussi »

**1. *So***
*So* traduit « si » devant un adjectif ou un adverbe.
Il peut aussi modifier un quantifieur. *She is so nice! She has so many friends!*

**2. *Such***
*Such* s'emploie devant un groupe nominal. Si le nom est un dénombrable singulier, il est précédé de *a/an*.

*They're such nice people! She is such a nice girl.*

## Exercises

**1. Restituez la ponctuation en vous demandant si ces phrases sont des interrogations ou des exclamations.**
a. What are you talking about
b. What a lot of money they have
c. How much money do they have
d. How fast he's driving

**2. Complétez avec *how* ou *what* suivis d'un article si nécessaire.**
a. ... horrible weather!
b. ... expensive these clothes are!
c. ... bad quality they are!
d. ... strange!
e. ... lovely person!

**3. Complétez avec *so* ou *such*.**
a. He is ... nice.
b. He is married to ... a beautiful girl.
c. They get on with each other ... well.
d. They have ... a big dog.
e. They have ... many friends.

15

# *Have*

## A Forme

### 1. Forme affirmative

**Présent** : *I have – You have – He/She/It has – We have – You have – They have.*
Contractée (pour l'auxiliaire uniquement) : *I've – You've – He/She/It's – We've – You've – They've.*
**Prétérit** : *had* à toutes les personnes.
Contractée (pour l'auxiliaire) : *'d.*

### 2. Formes interrogative et négative

***Have*, auxiliaire,** se place devant le sujet à la forme interrogative ; il est suivi de *not* à la forme négative. Contractée (pour l'auxiliaire uniquement) : *haven't – hasn't – hadn't.*

*Have you seen him? No, I haven't seen him.*

***Have*, verbe lexical,** se conjugue avec l'auxiliaire *do/does/did.*

*Do you have a sister? – No, I don't have a sister.*

## B Emplois

- ***Have*, auxiliaire** indique l'aspect avec le participe passé d'un verbe (forme *have* V-*en*).

  *She's worked a lot.* Elle a beaucoup travaillé.

- ***Have*, verbe lexical** exprime la possession ou le lien de parenté, comme le verbe « avoir ».
  En anglais britannique, on utilise souvent *get* au *present perfect* : *have got.*

  *Do you have a sister? – No, I don't have one. Have you got a computer? – Yes, I've got one.*

  *Have* se traduit par « prendre », « faire » ou d'autres verbes dans certains emplois :
  – *Have breakfast/lunch/dinner/a pizza/a drink* : prendre le petit déjeuner/le déjeuner/le dîner/une pizza/un verre.
  – *Have a bath/a shower* : prendre un bain/une douche.
  – *Have a walk* : faire une promenade.
  – *Have a good time* : s'amuser.

## Exercises

**1. Écrivez les réponses courtes.**

a. Are you cold? Yes, …
b. Is he hungry? No, …
c. Have you got a bike? Yes, …
d. Did your parents have a good time? Yes, …
e. Are there a lot of people in the restaurant? No, …

**2. Traduisez en français.**

a. I've had a very good time.
b. He's always wrong.
c. I have a shower every morning.
d. She never has breakfast.
e. My brother is 16.

16

## *Have + V-en*

L'expression « formes *have* + V-*en* » désigne toutes les formes composées de l'auxiliaire *have* et du participe passé.
On symbolise le participe passé par « V-*en* », alors que sa terminaison régulière est -*ed* pour ne pas le confondre avec le prétérit.
Par convention, les grammairiens ont choisi la terminaison -*en* de *been* – *beaten* – *eaten*, etc.

### A Formes

**Le *present perfect* : *have/has* + V-*en*.**
**Le *past perfect* : *had* + V-*en*.** *They had left.*
**La forme infinitive : *to have* + V-*en*.** *They were supposed to have left.*
**La forme V-*ing* : *having* + V-*en*.** *Having left early, they arrived early.*

### B Emplois

**1. Le *present perfect***
Le *present perfect* n'est pas un temps mais un **aspect**. L'énonciateur ne s'intéresse pas au moment où l'événement s'est déroulé, mais à son lien avec le présent.
Le *present perfect* sert à **expliquer le présent**.

*We've had a lot of rain. That's why the lawn is so green.*

Le *present perfect* sert à faire le **bilan** de ce qui vient de se passer.

*It has rained a lot—much more than last year.*

Le *present perfect* peut indiquer que l'événement s'est passé à un moment indéterminé, auquel on ne s'intéresse pas.

*They have moved to Paris.* (Peu importe la date ; ce qui importe est qu'ils soient à Paris.)

**2. Le *present perfect be* + V-*ing***
Le *present perfect be* + V-*ing* signale que l'énonciateur s'intéresse plus à l'activité du sujet grammatical qu'au résultat.

*Tim has been working for hours. He is tired.* (On s'intéresse à Tim.)
*Tim has worked on this report for hours. It must be good.*
(On s'intéresse à son rapport.)

**3. Le *past perfect***
Cette forme équivaut au *present perfect* mais le moment de référence est révolu. Elle marque l'antériorité. On attend souvent *when* ou *before*.
*He had left when I arrived.* Il était parti quand je suis arrivé.

**Exercises**

**1. Classez ces expressions en deux catégories : celle que l'on utilise avec le *present perfect* et celle que l'on utilise avec le prétérit.**
a. yesterday
b. 10 years ago
c. already
d. yet
e. this morning
f. this year
g. last year
h. at half past five

**2. Traduisez en anglais.**
a. Qu'est-ce que tu as fait hier soir ?
b. Depuis combien de temps habites-tu ici ?
c. Ça fait combien de temps qu'il pleut ?
d. Je n'ai jamais vu cela quand j'étais à New York.
e. Il travaille ici depuis vingt ans.

**3. Mettez les verbes au prétérit ou au *past perfect*.**
a. He (lose) the book I (give) him for Christmas.
b. I (go) to the concert you (tell) me about.
c. John already (be) there for two hours when I (arrive).
d. He (tell) me he would come, but he (not turn) up.
e. The next day she (leave), as she (plan).

17

## Hypothèse

Il n'y a pas de conditionnel en anglais. On utilise le modal *would*.
***Would* + V** annonce ce qui arriverait si une condition, exprimée ou non exprimée, se réalisait. Si la condition est exprimée dans une subordonnée en *if*, le verbe de cette subordonnée est au prétérit.

*I would be happy if he came.* Je serais heureux s'il venait.

*Would* + *have* V-*en* évoque un irréel dont on sait qu'il ne se réalisera pas.

*I would have told you.* Je vous l'aurais dit.

*Could* et *might* peuvent aussi exprimer une hypothèse.

*They might help us.* Il se pourrait qu'ils nous aident.

**Exercises**

- **Traduisez en anglais.**

a. Je serais surpris s'ils venaient.
b. Il se pourrait qu'ils soient en retard.
c. J'aimerais tellement te voir demain.
d. Si elle avait su, elle ne serait pas venue.

18

# Impératif

## A À la deuxième personne

L'énonciateur donne un ordre ou une consigne à d'autres personnes.

- **Forme affirmative : base verbale.** *Listen.* Écoute/Écoutez.
- **Forme d'insistance : *do* + base verbale.**
  *Do come in.* Je vous en prie, entrez.
- **Forme négative : *do not* + base verbale.**
  *Do not worry/Don't worry.* Ne vous faites pas de souci.
- **Les adverbes *always* et *never* se placent devant la base verbale.**
  *Always be polite. Never answer back.*

## B À la première personne

L'énonciateur s'implique dans la consigne : il invite une ou des personnes à faire la même chose que lui.

- **Forme affirmative : *let us/let's* + base verbale.**
  *Let's go.* Allons-y. Et si nous partions ?
- **Forme négative : *let's not* + base verbale.**
  *Let's not forget it!* Ne l'oublions pas !

### Exercises

1. **Complétez les phrases avec les verbes suivants :**
   *eat – have – give – sit down – take off.*
   a. If you are hungry, ... a sandwich.
   b. If you are tired, ... a rest.
   c. If you are hot, ... your jumper.
   d. If your feet hurt, ... .
2. **Utilisez l'impératif pour formuler ce que dit le médecin.**
   a. The doctor asks Mr. James to listen to him.
   b. He tells him to stop smoking.
   c. He tells him not to eat sweets.
   d. He tells him not to cook in butter.
3. **Traduisez en anglais.**
   a. Essayons de faire cet exercice.
   b. Maintenant, corrigez votre travail.
   c. Partez tout de suite.
   d. N'oubliez pas votre livre.

19

# Modaux

Les modaux sont : ***must* – *can* – *could* – *may* – *might* – *shall* – *should* – *will* – *would*.**
Avec les modaux, l'énonciateur exprime son point de vue :
– il indique à quel point il est sûr de quelque chose ;
– il porte un jugement ou fait pression sur le sujet.

## A Forme

Les modaux n'ont pas de forme infinitive, pas de temps composé, pas de *-s* à la troisième personne.
Les modaux sont suivis de la base verbale (infinitif sans *to*).
Les modaux servent d'auxiliaire pour les formes interrogative et négative.

*Can Lena come with us? – No, she can't.*

Les formes contractées s'utilisent couramment, surtout à l'oral : *can't – mustn't – 'll – won't – 'd – wouldn't.*

## B Valeurs 1 : les degrés de certitude

C'est la modalité épistémique. On choisit le modal en fonction du degré de certitude. Voici la liste, classée du « presque certain » au « presque impossible » : *must – will – should – may – could/might – mustn't/can't.*
En français, on utilise souvent des formes impersonnelles pour exprimer la modalité : « il se peut que », « il se pourrait que », « il est impossible que ».

*Tim must be 16.* Tim doit avoir 16 ans. (On en est pratiquement certain.)
*Tim may be 16.* Il se peut que Tim ait 16 ans.
(On le pense, mais on n'est pas sûr.)

### Exercises

1. **Complétez avec *can* ou *can't*.**
   a. You've just eaten. You ... go swimming now. But you ... play on the beach if you like.
   b. ... I go shopping? – Of course, you ... go shopping.
   c. ... I borrow your car? – No, you ... . You ... drive.
2. **Complétez avec *must* ou *have to*.**
   a. You ... finish your homework before you watch television.
   b. I don't have time now. I'll ... finish it tomorrow.
   c. She doesn't ... do it if she doesn't want to.
   d. If you want more pocket money, you'll ... work better at school.
   e. They ... be getting here soon. It's very late.
   f. Look at his house. It's beautiful. He ... have a lot of money.

*Tim could/might be 16.* Il se pourrait que Tim ait 16 ans. (On n'est pas sûr du tout.)
*Tim can't be 16.* Il est impossible que Tim ait 16 ans. (On est certain du contraire.)

La modalité peut aussi s'exprimer avec :
– des adverbes : *probably – certainly – perhaps*, etc. ;
– des expressions : *be certain – likely – unlikely*, etc.

*He is likely to be late.* Il est probable qu'il sera en retard.

Les modaux peuvent être suivis de *have* + participe passé ; en français, c'est le modal qui prend la marque du passé.

*He must have been angry.* Il a dû être en colère.

## C Valeurs 2 : la contrainte

C'est la modalité radicale. L'énonciateur indique le degré de liberté ou de contrainte dont jouit le sujet grammatical pour réaliser l'événement exprimé par le verbe.

- **La capacité : *can***
  L'énonciateur donne son avis sur la capacité du sujet de faire quelque chose.
  *Can, cannot/can't* au présent. *Could, could not/couldn't* au prétérit.
  *He can ski but I can't.* Il sait skier mais moi je ne sais pas.
  *Could/couldn't* a aussi une valeur d'irréel.
  *You could do that.* Tu pourrais faire cela.
- **La permission : *can* ou *may***
  L'énonciateur autorise le sujet grammatical à faire quelque chose.
  *You can/may go now.* Tu peux partir maintenant.
  *Might* a aussi une valeur d'irréel. *You might go.* Tu pourrais y aller.
- **L'obligation : *must***
  L'énonciateur dit qu'il pense que le sujet grammatical doit faire quelque chose.
  *You must stop.* Il faut que tu arrêtes/Tu dois arrêter.
- **L'interdiction : *must not/mustn't***
  L'énonciateur interdit au sujet grammatical de faire quelque chose.
  *You mustn't go.* Tu ne dois pas y aller.
- **Le conseil ou la recommendation : *should***
  *You should do that.* Tu devrais faire cela.
- **L'absence d'obligation : *needn't***
  *You needn't go now.* Tu n'as pas besoin d'y aller maintenant.

## D Les substituts des modaux

Ils remplacent les modaux pour les temps et formes qui leur manquent. Mais l'effet de sens est différent : l'énonciateur constate, il ne porte pas de jugement.

- **La capacité : *be able to***
  *You won't be able to see them.* Vous ne pourrez pas les voir.
- **La permission ou l'interdiction : *be allowed to***
  *I was not allowed to see her.* Je n'ai pas eu le droit de la voir.
- **L'obligation : *have to***
  *I'll have to tell him.* Il va falloir que je lui dise.
- **L'absence d'obligation : *do not have to/haven't got to***
  *You don't have to pay.* Tu n'as pas besoin de payer.

**3. Complétez avec *can – can't – must* ou *mustn't*.**

a. Your aunt … be happy living in Florida. It's lovely there.
b. She … be happy there. She's coming back tomorrow.
c. You look exhausted. You … have been working too hard.
d. You … give your credit card number to anyone. It's dangerous.

**4. Traduisez en employant un modal.**

a. S'il n'est pas ici il doit avoir un problème. J'en suis absolument sûr.
b. Il se peut qu'il ait oublié. Mais c'est peu probable.
c. Il se pourrait qu'il soit malade. Cela peut arriver à tout le monde.
d. Il se pourrait qu'il ait gagné au loto et qu'il n'ait plus besoin de travailler.
e. C'est impossible qu'il ait gagné le gros lot. Il ne joue pas.

# Nombres

## A Les nombres cardinaux

Ils indiquent une quantité. Comme tous les adjectifs, ils sont invariables.

- **Les nombres de 1 à 10**
  *one – two – three – four – five – six – seven – eight – nine – ten.*
- **Les dizaines**
  *twenty – thirty – forty – fifty – sixty – seventy – eighty – ninety.*
- **Les centaines, milliers, etc.**
  *hundred – thousand – million – billion, etc.*
  Ces mots sont invariables lorsqu'ils sont précédés d'un nombre ou de *several* (car ce sont des adjectifs numéraux) mais ils prennent un *-s* au pluriel quand ils sont employés comme noms et sont suivis de *of.*
  *Five hundred people. Hundreds of people.*
- **Les combinaisons**
  Nombres en chiffres : une virgule sépare les milliers des centaines et les décimales sont précédées d'un point qui se prononce.
  Nombres écrits en lettres : il y a un trait d'union entre les dizaines et les unités ; on met *and* entre les dizaines ou les unités et *hundred.*
  4,589.5 = *four thousand five hundred and eighty-nine point five.*
- **Le zéro**
  0 = *nought* (en américain *zero*). Il se lit comme la lettre « o » dans les numéros de téléphone, les numéros de bus et de chambres d'hôtel. Il ne se prononce pas dans les nombres décimaux.
  "*0.7 per cent*" se lit "*point seven per cent*".
- **Les pourcentages : *per cent*** 25% = *twenty-five per cent.*
  Les adjectifs *last, first* et *next* s'insèrent avant les nombres et non après.
  *In the next two years…*

## B Les nombres ordinaux

Ils servent à indiquer le rang d'un élément dans l'ensemble auquel il appartient. Ils sont généralement précédés de *the.*

- **Les nombres 1, 2 et 3** ont une terminaison spécifique : *the first (the 1st) – the second (the 2nd) – the third* (*the 3rd*). Cette particularité se retrouve dans les nombres composés : *the twenty-third* (*the 23rd*).
- **Les autres nombres :**
  On ajoute *-th* au nombre cardinal. *The fourth (the 4th).*
  La graphie de *five* et *nine* est affectée par la terminaison *-th* : *the fifth – the ninth.*
  Les dizaines ont pour terminaison *-eth. The twentieth.*
- **Les fractions :** on utilise la forme ordinale des adjectifs numéraux (1/3 – *one third*) et on introduit le complément avec *of.*
  *Four fifths of all American children…*
  *Half* est couramment suivi de *a* ou de *the* + nom, avec omission de *of.*
  *Half a pint of beer.*
- **La date :** on utilise les adjectifs ordinaux. On peut l'écrire avec ou sans virgule.
  *July 14, 1789 – 14 July, 1789 – July 14th 1789* (à l'oral : *the fourteenth of July*).
- **Les noms de rois et reines :** on les écrit comme en français mais on prononce le numéro sous sa forme ordinale.
  *Queen Elizabeth II.* (On prononce "*Elizabeth the second*".)

## Exercises

**1. Écrivez en toutes lettres.**
a. 40,635.
b. 876,923.
c. 9,738,931.
d. 421,928,581.
e. 979,863,785,972.

**2. Écrivez en toutes lettres les chiffres en gras.**
a. Can you put me through to room **404** please.
b. He's not in. You're the **9th** person to call him.
c. Try room **901**.
d. Well, ask him to call me back on **309 852 3001**.
e. Tell him he owes me **£765,348**.

**3. Traduisez en anglais.**
a. J'aimerais avoir deux millions de livres.
b. J'ai dix mille livres à la banque.
c. Ils ont économisé des centaines de dollars.
d. Je voudrais la moitié de ce gâteau.
e. Deux tiers des élèves ne sont jamais allés aux États-Unis.

**4. Écrivez ces heures en toutes lettres (utilisez *a.m.* et *p.m.*, *to* et *past*).**
a. 9:45
b. 10:50
c. 8:15
d. 15:27
e. 20:20
f. 22:32
g. 19:59

21

# Noms

## A Genre

Il y a trois genres qu'il est utile de déterminer pour choisir les pronoms personnels, les adjectifs et pronoms possessifs :
– **le masculin** (les hommes et les garçons) ;
– **le féminin** (les femmes et les filles) ;
– **le neutre** (animaux et objets).
Certains mots sont différents pour le masculin et pour le féminin.

*boy/girl – father/mother – actor/actress.*

D'autres noms servent à la fois pour le féminin et le masculin.
On peut spécifier que l'on parle d'un homme ou d'une femme en faisant des noms composés avec *man/woman* ou en ajoutant l'adjectif *male/female.*

*a man servant – a woman doctor – a male nurse.*

(Précision inutile si le contexte suffit.)

## B Nombre

- **Règle générale :** un singulier correspond à une personne, un ensemble ou un objet. Un pluriel correspond à plusieurs personnes, ensembles ou objets : nom singulier + *-s*. *books – computers.*
- **Prononciation :** le *-s* final se prononce toujours. Il y a trois prononciations. Le choix dépend de la facilité de la prononciation :
  – **[z]** : *boys – ladies – tables – papers – families – cars* ;
  – **[s]** : *books – sports – banks – discs – boots* ;
  – **[iz]** : *glasses – watches – clashes.*
- **Orthographes particulières :**
  Noms terminés par ***-s***, ***-x***, ***-ch***, ***-sh*** : terminaison ***-es*** *churches – glasses.*
  Noms terminés par ***-f*** ou ***-fe*** : terminaison ***-ves***. *knives – leaves.*
  Noms terminés en ***-o*** : terminaison ***-oes***. *potatoes – tomatoes.*
- **Pluriels irréguliers :** peu nombreux, ils concernent des mots courants. *children – men – women – feet – teeth – mice.*

## C Accords particuliers

- **Noms ayant plusieurs possesseurs :** ils se mettent au pluriel, contrairement au français.

  *All the houses had red roofs.* Toutes les maisons avaient un toit rouge.
- **Noms toujours au pluriel** et accompagnés d'un verbe au pluriel : les noms correspondant à des objets « doubles » (*glasses – trousers – jeans – pyjamas – shorts).*

  *My jeans are dirty.* Mon jean est sale.
- **Noms singuliers terminés par un *-s* :** *news – physics – mathematics – economics – politics – customs* (douane), etc.

  *This is good news.* C'est une bonne nouvelle.
- **Noms désignant un groupe de personnes :** ils sont suivis d'un verbe au pluriel. *The police are investigating.*

## D Dénombrables et indénombrables

La distinction entre nom dénombrable et nom indénombrable est indispensable pour le choix du déterminant.

- **Un nom dénombrable** désigne un élément ou une classe d'éléments que l'on peut compter. Il peut être précédé de *a/an* au singulier et peut être mis au pluriel.

  *A cup > three cups. An answer > several answers.*

## Exercises

**1. Classez ces noms en trois catégories selon la façon de prononcer les terminaisons : [z], [s], [iz].**
aunts – books – boots – boys – clashes – cousins – glasses – houses – papers – parts – passes – phones – races – sports – tables.

**2. Mettez tous les groupes nominaux au pluriel.**
a. I have bought a beautiful pair of jeans.
b. The child had a nice white mouse in his pocket.
c. The lady gave me one penny.
d. The man took my knife to cut a tomato.

**3. Traduisez en anglais.**
a. Mes bagages sont lourds !
b. Auriez-vous d'autres informations à son sujet ?
c. Elle a les cheveux blonds.
d. Tu as entendu la dernière nouvelle ?
e. J'aime bien les fruits en dessert.

**4. Traduisez en anglais.**
a. Donnez-moi vos bagages.
b. Les nouvelles à la télévision ne sont pas bonnes.
c. J'aime beaucoup vos meubles.
d. Les légumes sont bons pour la santé.
e. Je vais vous donner une information.

- **Un nom indénombrable** désigne quelque chose de concret (*milk*) ou d'abstrait (*courage*) qu'on ne peut pas compter.
Il ne peut pas être mis au pluriel. Il n'est jamais précédé de l'article *a/an* ni d'un adjectif numéral (*one, two, three*…).

*Milk is good for you.* Le lait est bon pour vous.

Il n'est pas précédé de *the*, sauf s'il est déterminé par un complément de nom, une relative, ou parfois par le contexte.

*The milk she drinks is boiled.* Le lait qu'elle boit est bouilli.
(Milk est déterminé par une relative.)

- **Noms indénombrables singuliers** correspondant à des mots français au pluriel : *luggage* (des bagages) – *fruit* (des fruits) – *advice* (des conseils) – *furniture* (des meubles) – *information* (des informations), etc.

*Her advice is always useful.* Ses conseils sont toujours utiles.

Pour désigner un élément dans un de ces ensembles, on utilise des expressions comme *a piece of*. *A piece of furniture.* Un meuble.

22

# Passif

## A Forme

### 1. *Be* + participe passé

*Be* se conjugue ou se combine avec un modal pour marquer le temps ou l'aspect. Le participe passé est invariable.
**Présent :** *am/is/are* + participe passé *It is broken.* C'est cassé.
**Prétérit :** *was/were* + participe passé *It was broken.* C'était cassé.
***Present perfect* :** *has/have been* + participe passé

*It has been broken.* Ça a été cassé.

***Past perfect* :** *had been* + participe passé

*It had been broken.* Ça avait été cassé.

### 2. Forme *be* + V-*ing*

*Am/is/are/was/were* + *being* + participe passé.
L'auxiliaire *be* est utilisé deux fois : il se conjugue, au présent et au prétérit, comme dans toutes les formes passives et il apparaît avec la terminaison *-ing*.

*Do not enter while the animals are being fed.*
N'entrez pas pendant qu'on nourrit les animaux.

### 3. Forme *be going to*

*Be going to be* + participe passé.

*You are going to be invited.* Vous allez être invité.

### 4. Modal

Modal + *be* + participe passé
Pour exprimer le futur : *will*. *You will be invited.* Tu seras invité.
Pour exprimer une condition : *would*.

*You wouldn't be invited.* Tu ne serais pas invité.

Pour exprimer une éventualité : *may/could/might*.

*You might be invited.* Il se pourrait que tu sois invité.

Pour exprimer obligation, conseil ou degré de certitude : *must/have to/should*.

*You should be invited.* Tu devrais être invité.

## Exercises

**1. Identifiez les phrases qui sont au passif.**
a. He was going to see a film.
b. The film had been showing for two months.
c. It was made in the USA.
d. It has been well received by the critics.
e. He has been waiting in the queue for 20 minutes.

**2. Mettez ces phrases à la forme passive.**
a. Somebody has found the body of Lord Arthur in the lounge.
b. They called the police at 7.
c. They will arrest the murderer soon.
d. Someone must have followed Lord Arthur on his way home.
e. They did not tell me the truth.

**3. Traduisez ces phrases en utilisant un passif.**
a. On a vu Jenny dans une voiture blanche ce matin.
b. Elle était conduite par un grand homme noir.
c. On m'a dit que c'était son père.
d. Il paraît qu'il est très riche.
e. La vaisselle doit être faite avant son retour !

### B Emplois

Le passif est beaucoup plus fréquent en anglais qu'en français.
Il permet d'attirer l'attention sur le sujet grammatical. La réalité est la même qu'avec une forme active mais le point de vue de l'énonciateur est différent.

*Julian was selected by Don Hallward to play with the national team.* (On raconte la vie de Julian.)
*Don Hallward selected Julian to play with the national team.* (On raconte la vie de l'entraîneur.)

Le passif est souvent employé en langage technique car on s'intéresse davantage aux processus ou aux actions et à leurs conséquences qu'aux personnes qui agissent.

*Then the water is heated.* Ensuite, on chauffe l'eau.

On trouve souvent des passifs avec ellipse de l'auxiliaire dans des notices, affiches ou titres de journaux.

*English spoken here.* Ici, on parle anglais.

### C Le complément d'agent

Quand l'agent est évident, inconnu ou sans importance, il n'est pas mentionné. C'est le cas le plus fréquent.

*A strange object was seen in the sky yesterday.* (Peu importe qui l'a vu.)

Si l'identité de l'agent constitue une information, il est mentionné et introduit par *by*.

*This rare bird was given to the zoo by Mr. Smithson.*

### D Traduction

Le passif se traduit souvent en français par une tournure avec « on » ou une structure impersonnelle ou pronominale.

*I was told (that) this was dangerous.* On m'a dit que ceci était dangereux.
*Something must be done to save the planet.* Il faut faire quelque chose pour sauver la planète.
*English is spoken in many countries.* On parle anglais dans beaucoup de pays.

**4. Rédigez des phrases au passif avec les mots proposés. Mettez les verbes à la forme indiquée entre parenthèses.**
a. My brother / be happy / invite / at your birthday party. (expression de l'hypothèse)
b. Yesterday, he / interview / for a Summer job. (prétérit)
c. He / offer / a permanent job in September. (expression de l'éventualité)
d. If everything works out all right, he / pay / well. (expression du futur)

## 23 Possessifs

### A Les adjectifs possessifs (mon, ma, mes...)

***My – your – his – her – its – our – your – their*** sont des déterminants du nom indiquant un lien de parenté ou de possession. Ils s'accordent uniquement avec le possesseur.

*Sammy and her sister are coming.* (On sait que Sammy est une fille.)

On utilise un adjectif possessif devant les noms désignant les parties du corps, les vêtements ou les objets portés.

*He had a hat on his head.*

### B Les pronoms possessifs (le mien, le tien...)

***Mine – yours – his – hers – its – ours – yours – theirs*** s'accordent avec le possesseur et ne sont pas précédés d'un article.

*His car is green but hers is red...* la sienne est rouge.

*Of* + pronom possessif

*A friend of mine.* Un ami à moi.

**Exercises**

**1. Complétez avec des adjectifs possessifs.**
a. Nick lived with ... mother until he was 17.
b. But his sister lived with ... father.
c. But they spent their holidays together at ... grandparents'.

**2. Remplacez les mots en gras par des pronoms possessifs.**
a. Leila's brother is younger than **my brother.**
b. I've lost my pen. Can you lend me **your pen?**
c. This is our car. It's older than **their car.**

24

# Prépositions

En anglais, les prépositions introduisent soit un nom, soit un gérondif (une forme verbale en *-ing*).

| | |
|---|---|
| *above* : au-dessus de | *in front of* : devant |
| *across* : à travers, de l'autre côté de | *into* : dans |
| *along* : le long de | *near, close to* : près de |
| *among* : parmi | *next to* : à côté de |
| *around* : autour de | *off* : au large de, éloigné de |
| *at* : à | *on* : sur, dans (un bus, un train…) |
| *behind* : derrière | *opposite* : en face de |
| *below* : au-dessous de | *over* : par-dessus |
| *between* : entre | *to* : à |
| *down* : en bas de, vers le bas | *towards* : vers |
| *from* : (en provenance) de | *under* : sous |
| *in* : dans | *up* : en haut de, vers le haut de |

## A Les prépositions de lieu

- ***In* ou *into* ?**
  *in* : dans, quand on localise quelqu'un ou quelque chose.
  *into* : dans, quand on indique qu'on pénètre dans un lieu.

  *He worked in the city. He went into a shop.*

- ***At* ou *to* ?**
  *at* : à, quand il n'y a pas de mouvement.
  *to* : à, quand il y a un mouvement (*to* indique une visée).

  *He goes to the office at 8:45.*
  *He's at the office before 9.*

- ***To* ou *from* ?**
  *from* : de, quand on se réfère à la provenance.
  *to* : de, quand on se réfère à la direction.

  *The train from London is late.*
  *I met him on the train to London.*

- **Avec les verbes de mouvement**
  L'anglais précise le moyen avec le verbe tandis que le français donne la priorité au déplacement.

  *He sailed across the Atlantic.* Il a traversé l'Atlantique à la voile.
  (*Sailed* est traduit par « à la voile », *across* est traduit par le verbe « a traversé ».)

## B Les prépositions de temps

| | |
|---|---|
| *after* : après | *since* : depuis |
| *at* : à (+ heure) | *in* : en |
| *before* : avant | *within* : en, avant |
| *during* : pendant | *until* : jusqu'à |
| *for* : pendant, depuis | *still* : encore |
| *from* : à partir de | *on* : le (+ jour) (avec limite de temps) |

*From 9 o'clock until 6 o'clock. In the afternoon.*

*On Monday* = lundi (prochain).
*On Mondays* = le lundi (tous les lundis).

## Exercises

**1. Choisissez la réponse qui convient.**

a. He was looking … me. (at – on – in – from)
b. She's busy, she is listening … the news. (at – to – upon – into)
c. She doesn't believe … working hard. (to – at – on – in)
d. You'd better put your raincoat … . (at – on – up – over)
e. It depends … what they really want. (of – on – at – for)
f. This book does not belong … me. (at – on – in – to)
g. It was different … what I expected. (of – for – in – from)

**2. Complétez avec les prépositions qui conviennent.**

a. She's afraid … empty spaces.
b. Why did you say that? I'm ashamed … you!
c. I apologize … being late.
d. Stop laughing … his silly jokes!
e. No, I'm not jealous … his success!
f. I'm just tired … hearing the same old stories.
g. I know he is mad … me, but I don't care.

**3. Traduisez en anglais.**

a. Je n'ai pas pu répondre au professeur.
b. J'ai besoin de vous voir cet après-midi.
c. En quoi consiste l'épreuve d'examen ?
d. Je dépends de mes parents en ce moment.
e. Elle ressemble à sa mère.

## C Autres prépositions

*by* : par
*with* : avec
*for* : pour
*instead of* : au lieu de
*because of* : à cause de
*except for* : excepté
*thanks to* : grâce à
*like* : comme
*as* : en tant que
*about* : à propos de, sur

## D La place de la préposition

Une préposition se place devant le complément qu'elle introduit mais elle est rejetée après le verbe (et son complément éventuel) dans les relatives et dans les questions commençant par *who*, *which* et *what*.

*Who are you talking to? – I'm talking to Janet.*

## E Les verbes : transitifs ou intransitifs ?

- **Construction indirecte en anglais, directe en français**

*approve of* : approuver
*comment on* : commenter
*cut down on* : réduire
*listen to* : écouter
*look at* : regarder
*look for* : chercher
*pay for* : payer

- **Construction directe en anglais, indirecte en français**

*address* : s'adresser à
*answer* : répondre à
*discuss* : discuter à propos de
*enter* : entrer dans
*need* : avoir besoin de
*obey* : obéir à
*remember* : se souvenir de
*phone* : téléphoner à
*trust* : faire confiance à
*use* : se servir de

- **Prépositions différentes du français**

*consist of* : consister en
*depend on* : dépendre de
*laugh at* : rire de
*live on* : vivre de
*look after* : s'occuper de
*look like* : ressembler à
*speak about* : parler de
*suffer from* : souffrir de
*think about/of* : penser à

**Attention !**
Il ne faut pas confondre les prépositions avec les particules adverbiales : *about, across, away, back, down, in, off, on, out, over, round, through, together, up*.
Celles-ci n'introduisent pas un complément mais elles appartiennent au verbe dont elles modifient le sens.

*Turn* (tourner) ; *turn off* (éteindre) ; *turn up* (arriver inopinément).
*She gets on well with her cousin. On* est une particule qui modifie le sens (*get on* = s'entendre) ; *with* est une préposition.

**4. Récrivez les phrases en rejetant la préposition après le verbe (et son complément).**

a. The friend with whom I play tennis can't play today.
b. So I'm going to try and call the boy about whom I talked to you last time.
c. You know, the one who has a racket of which he was so proud.
d. This is a game in which I am not at all interested.

25

# Présent simple

## A Forme

- **Forme affirmative : sujet + V** (+ -*s* à la 3e personne du singulier).

  *I work – You work – He/She/It works – We work – You work – They work.*

- **Forme interrogative : *do/does* + sujet + V ?**
  C'est l'auxiliaire qui prend la marque de la 3e personne : *does*.

  *Do I work? Does he work?*

- **Forme négative : sujet + *do/does not* + V.**
  C'est l'auxiliaire qui prend la marque de la 3e personne : *does*.

  *I do not work. He/she/it doesn't/does not work.*

### Orthographe de la 3e personne

**Règle générale :** on accole le -*s* à la base verbale. *makes.*
**Verbes terminés par -*s*, -*sh*, -*ch*, -*o* :** on accole -*es*. *catches – goes.*
**Verbes terminés par -*y* :** le -*y* se transforme en -*ies*. *carries.*
Attention ! Cette modification ne s'applique pas aux verbes terminés en -*ay*, -*ey* ou -*uy*.
*says – obeys – buys.*

## B Emplois

Avec le présent simple, l'énonciateur donne une information objective, sans commentaire. Il définit une **caractéristique** du sujet.

*She works in a hospital.* Elle travaille dans un hôpital. (= Elle est infirmière.)

Il exprime une **habitude**, un fait habituel.

*I always go there by train.* J'y vais toujours en train.

Il exprime une **vérité générale**.

*The sun rises in the East.* Le soleil se lève à l'est.

Il présente une **succession d'événements** rapides.

*X passes the ball to Y. Y shoots.* X passe la balle à Y. Y tire.

Il fait référence à l'avenir avec un marqueur de temps futur pour parler d'un événement indépendant de la volonté de l'énonciateur.

*The train leaves at 5.* Le train part/partira à 5 heures.

Il s'emploie avec les verbes exprimant **un état, un sentiment, une opinion**. *It seems nice. I think it is nice.*

### Exercises

**1. Écrivez une phrase définissant le métier de ces personnes.**
a. John is a taxi driver. > He …
b. Sarah is a romantic novel writer.
c. Julie is a maths teacher.
d. My father is a software programmer.
e. My mother is a dressmaker.

**2. Complétez ces mini dialogues.**
Ex. : Mark is a footballer.
— Oh, does he play in London?
a. Kevin is a teacher.
— Oh, (work / your school)?
b. Sam is a fireman.
— Oh, (often / save / people)?
c. My sister is a typist.
— (work / office)?
d. My friends are nurses.
— Oh, (like it)?
e. Brian is a baker.
— Oh, (make / good cakes)?

**3. Mettez les mots dans le bon ordre pour obtenir des phrases correctes.**
a. do / does / what / Sundays / he / on / ?
b. works / he / in / cinema / a / in / London / big / .
c. tickets / ice-cream / sells / and / he / .
d. home / he / get / time / does / what / ?
e. morning / he / gets / at / in / 3 / the / home / .

26

# Présent *be* + V-*ing*

## A Forme

L'auxiliaire *be* se conjugue.

- **Forme affirmative : sujet + *be* + V-*ing***

  *I'm working – He/she/it is working – They're working.*

- **Forme interrogative : *be* + sujet + V-*ing* + ?**

  *Am I working? – Are you working? – Is he/she/it working?*

### Exercises

**1. Classez ces verbes en deux catégories : ceux que l'on peut employer aux deux présents et ceux que l'on emploie seulement au présent simple.**

| | | |
|---|---|---|
| a. believe | d. hate | g. walk |
| b. do | e. meet | h. prefer |
| c. eat | f. like | i. run |

- **Forme négative : sujet + *be* + *not* + V-*ing***

  *I am not working. He/she/it is not working.*

  Contractée : comme pour *be* ▶ 7. On dispose de deux formes (sauf avec *I*).

  *I'm not going – You aren't/You're not going – He's not/He isn't going.*

  **V-*ing* : modifications orthographiques**
  Règle générale : on ajoute *-ing* à la base verbale. *looking.*
  Terminaison *-e* : le *e* disparaît. *driving.*
  Verbes monosyllabiques terminés par une consonne : la consonne est doublée. *getting.*

### B Emplois

L'énonciateur **décrit** ou **commente** ce qu'il voit, entend ou sait.

*Listen! She is singing.*

Il fait référence à **l'avenir** pour exprimer un projet ou une intention avec un marqueur de temps futur. *He's leaving tomorrow.*

Il est généralement utilisé avec les **verbes exprimant une attitude** : *lie – sit – stand*. *They're sitting on the beach.*

Il indique l'irritation ou l'admiration avec *always*.

*She is always talking.* Elle n'arrête pas de parler.

**Attention !** Il ne s'emploie pas avec les verbes indiquant une pensée, un sentiment, etc. *I'm thinking* signifie « je réfléchis » (action).

**2. Quelle phrase (A, B ou C) peut compléter les expressions *a* à *j* ?**

A. He's watching television.
B. He watches television.
C. Is he watching television?

a. Look! …
b. What is he doing? …
c. Every day, …
d. Tell him to answer the door. …
e. In the evenings, …
f. After school, …
g. Sometimes, …
h. Not at the moment. …
i. … Yes, he is.
j. When he gets home, …

**3. Traduisez en anglais.**

a. Que font les gens dans la rue ?
b. Ils attendent le bus.
c. Ils prennent le bus tous les jours.
d. Je travaille beaucoup en ce moment.
e. Je pars en vacances la semaine prochaine.

## 27 ▶ Prétérit simple

### A Forme

Le prétérit a la même forme pour toutes les personnes (sauf *be*).

**1. Forme affirmative**
**Verbes réguliers : sujet + V + *-ed*.**
*work > I worked.*

**Verbes irréguliers :** voir la liste dans la couverture.

*go > went ; think > thought.*

**Le verbe *be* :**

*I was – You were – He/She/It was – We/You/They were.*

**2. Forme interrogative**
***Did* + sujet + V :** le verbe retrouve sa forme nue puisque c'est l'auxiliaire qui porte la marque du prétérit.

*Did they work here? Did they go to London?*

**Le verbe *be*** se place avant le sujet.

*Are you in London?*

**3. Forme négative**
**Sujet + *did not* + V :** le verbe retrouve sa forme nue.
*We did not work.*

**Le verbe *be*** est suivi de *not*.
*I was not/wasn't – We weren't.*

**Exercises**

**1. Écrivez ces verbes au prétérit.**
begin – break – drive – leave – sleep – speak – start – think – want – work.

**2. Mettez ces phrases à la forme interrogative.**

a. Brendon taught mathematics.
b. Jenny spoke English.
c. Candy flew to Washington.
d. The situation became worse.
e. Mary stole a bag.

**3. Répondez par des réponses négatives courtes.**

a. Were you aware of the situation? No, I …
b. Did he arrive early?
c. Was she surprised?
d. Were you and your brother at home?
e. Did they buy food for tonight?

**4. Modifications orthographiques**
**Verbes terminés par –*e* :** V + *-d*. *loved.*
**Verbes terminés par une consonne + *-y* :** *-y* devient *-ied*. *carried.*
**Attention !** Cette modification ne s'applique pas aux verbes terminés par deux voyelles. *played.*
**Verbes terminés par une seule consonne précédée d'une seule voyelle :** on double la consonne si la syllabe est accentuée. *stopped.*

## B Emplois

- **Rupture avec le présent**
  L'énonciateur parle, de manière objective, de faits ou d'états passés, terminés, généralement datés explicitement ou implicitement. C'est le temps du récit.

  *They lived in New York and then moved to Paris.*

- **Rupture avec le réel**
  L'énonciateur parle de faits, d'actions ou d'états imaginaires, par exemple, après les verbes *imagine*, *suppose*, *fancy*, ou après la conjonction *if* lorsque l'on sait que la condition énoncée ne se réalisera pas. Dans cet emploi, le verbe *be* prend la forme *were* à la première personne du singulier en anglais britannique.

  *Imagine you were the richest man in the world!*
  (Il n'y a aucune chance que cela arrive.)

**4. Choisissez la bonne réponse: prétérit ou *present perfect*.**

a. Here I am.
1. You're late. I've been waiting for hours.
2. You're late. I waited hours.

b. I'm sorry.
1. Was your train late?
2. Has your train been late?

c. I tried to call you but your weren't in.
1. I was upstairs. I haven't heard the phone.
2. I was upstairs. I didn't hear the phone.

d. There's no supper left.
1. I've eaten it all.
2. I ate it all.

e. Shall we order a pizza?
1. I already did that.
2. I've already done that.

# 28 Prétérit *be* + V-*ing*

## A Forme

Le prétérit *be* + V-*ing* se construit comme le présent *be* + V-*ing* mais l'auxiliaire *be* est au prétérit : *was/were*.
**Forme affirmative : sujet + *was/were* + V-*ing***
**Forme interrogative : *was/were* + sujet + V-*ing* + ?**
**Forme négative : sujet + *was/were* + *not* + V-*ing***

## B Emploi

L'énonciateur indique son point de vue ; il décrit ce qu'il voyait ou savait à un moment du passé. Cette forme est souvent employée en contraste avec un prétérit simple pour indiquer qu'une action était en déroulement au moment de référence, ou qu'elle servait de cadre à une autre action qui constitue l'événement.

*He was sleeping when the phone rang. He was sleeping* (action en déroulement, circonstances : prétérit *be* + V-*ing*). *The phone rang* (événement : prétérit simple).

Cette forme est couramment employée avec les verbes exprimant une attitude comme *stand* – *sit* – *lie*.

*I was standing in the rain.*

## Exercises

**1. Mettez les verbes au prétérit simple ou *be* + V-*ing*.**

a. I (sleep) when a noise (wake) me up.
b. I was sure that someone (walk) in the room upstairs.
c. I (switch) the light on and the noise (stop) immediately.
d. I thought it was some pigeons that (walk) on the roof.
e. I (feel) relieved and (go) back to sleep at once.

**2. Traduisez en anglais.**

a. Quand je suis arrivé, il se préparait à sortir.
b. Quand il m'a vu, il a ouvert la porte.
c. Pendant que je faisais mon travail, il jouait avec l'ordinateur.
d. Je nettoyais la maison quand quelqu'un a sonné à la porte.

29 ▶

# Pronoms personnels

## A Les pronoms sujets

*I – you – he – she – it – we – you – they.*

## B Les pronoms compléments

*Me – you – him – her – it – us – you – them* sont toujours placés après le verbe.

*I love him. I love them too.* Je l'aime. Je les aime aussi.

## C Les pronoms réfléchis

*Myself – yourself – himself – herself – itself – ourselves – yourselves – themselves* et la forme impersonnelle, *oneself*, sont toujours placés après le verbe.

*Enjoy oneself.* S'amuser.

Les équivalents de certains verbes pronominaux français ne prennent pas de pronom réfléchi sauf pour insister sur un aspect inhabituel : *dress – wash – shave – wake up*, etc.

*I like the way she dresses.* J'aime la façon dont elle s'habille.
*Though she is only 3, she can dress herself.* Bien qu'elle n'ait que trois ans, elle s'habille toute seule.

## D Les pronoms réciproques

*Each other/One another* sont invariables et toujours placés après le verbe. Comme ils indiquent une réciprocité, ils sont toujours employés avec un sujet et un verbe au pluriel.

*They love one another/each other.*

Certains verbes n'ont pas besoin de pronoms réciproques car ils portent en eux la réciprocité : *fight – meet – kiss*, etc.

*They often fight.* Ils se battent souvent.

**Attention !** Ne pas confondre pronoms réfléchis et pronoms réciproques.

*They look at themselves* (eux-mêmes).
*They look at each other* (l'un l'autre).

### Exercises

**1. Complétez avec des pronoms personnels.**

a. Fred is a lovely guy. ... is very generous.
b. I like ... a lot. What about ... ?
c. I like his wife more. ... is very friendly.
d. ... is in the USA at the moment.
e. Fred misses ... a lot.

**2. Complétez avec des pronoms réfléchis.**

a. I really enjoy ... when I clean the house.
b. My husband works in a Do It ... supermarket.
c. He never calls a plumber. He does the plumbing ...
d. Rachel and Sammy are only 3 and 4 years old but they dress ..., which saves their mother a lot of time.

**3. Complétez avec des pronoms réfléchis ou réciproques.**

a. My brothers play with ... in their room at night.
b. My sister likes to look good and takes great care of ...
c. We really enjoyed ... at the party yesterday.
d. We all gave ... presents. I got a crossword puzzle book.

30 ▶

# Propositions circonstancielles

Elles précisent les circonstances dans lesquelles l'action a lieu : temps, lieu, manière, cause, etc. Elles sont introduites par des conjonctions.
**Temps :** *when – while – as – until – after.*
**Lieu :** *where.*
**Cause :** *because – since – as.*
**Manière :** *as.*
**Contraste :** *whereas – though/although.*
**Condition :** *if – unless* (= *if not*) *– provided* (*that*).
**Conséquence :** *so that – so.*
**Opposition :** *but – yet.*
**But :** *to – so that.*

*When we come back, she'll be off.*

### Exercises

- **Complétez avec *when – so that – because – though* ou *where*.**

a. I cooked a meal ... you wouldn't be hungry.
b. He never spends any money ... he has a lot.
c. I put your books ... you normally keep them.
d. I came here ... I heard the news.
e. I am hungry ... I didn't have breakfast.

31 ▶

# Propositions complétives

Elles dépendent du verbe de la principale.

## A Les complétives en *that*

On les trouve en particulier après :
– les verbes exprimant un état de pensée, comme *think – believe – claim – know – hope – fear* ;
– les verbes impliquant une réalisation à venir comme *suggest – propose – decide – arrange* ;
– les expressions comme *it's natural that – it's surprising that*.

*I believe (that) there's life in the universe.*

- ***That* ou Ø ?**

*That* est obligatoire lorsque la complétive est attribut du sujet de la principale ou est apposée à un nom.

*The strange thing is that he likes me.* (Complétive attribut du sujet.)
*I hate the idea that he is my cousin.* (Complétive apposée à *the idea*.)

*That* est souvent omis lorsque la complétive est complément du verbe de la principale.

*I thought Ø you were ill.*

- ***Should***

L'ajout de *should* indique que l'événement n'est pas considéré comme allant de soi.

*It is surprising that he should like me.*

## B Les complétives en *wh-*

On les trouve après des verbes comme *ask – know – tell – wonder*, etc.

*I told him what had happened. I wonder how I can thank him.*

### Exercises

**1. Dans quelles phrases peut-on omettre *that* ?**
a. He said that he loved her.
b. The strange thing is that he doesn't like chocolate.
c. This is the person that came here last night.
d. She is the woman that gave me the money.
e. The only thing that changes is the price.

**2. Complétez avec *who, what, when*.**
a. I told him ... had happened.
b. He asked me ... he should do.
c. She told me ... she had talked to.
d. They told me ... they would arrive.
e. I wondered ... had called when I was out.

**3. Traduisez en anglais en utilisant *should*.**
a. C'est étonnant qu'il arrive si tôt.
b. Si jamais vous le voyez, dites-lui de me téléphoner.
c. C'est incroyable qu'il dise cela.

32 ▶

# Propositions infinitives

## A Forme

La proposition infinitive est une subordonnée composée d'un sujet et d'un verbe à l'infinitif qui peut avoir un complément :
sujet + verbe 1 + GN sujet + (*not*) *to* + verbe 2.
Si le sujet de la subordonnée est un pronom, il est à la forme complément (*me – you – him – her – it – us – you – them*).

*I wanted her/my mother to come with me.* (Le verbe de la principale, *wanted*, est conjugué. Le verbe 2, *come*, est à l'infinitif et a pour sujet le groupe nominal complément, *my mother* ou *her*.)

## B Emploi

La proposition infinitive s'utilise après les verbes marquant une pression du sujet grammatical sur autrui : *advise – allow – ask – expect – force – help – oblige – offer – persuade – tell – want –* (*I*) *would like –* (*I*) *would prefer*, etc.

### Exercises

**1. Reformulez avec une proposition infinitive.**
Ex. : She wants me to do it now.
a. He said, "Sit there." (tell me)
b. The twins said, "Do we look alike?" (ask us)
c. Their mum said, "Clean up this mess." (expect them)
d. Susie asked her sister, "Can you tidy up?" (persuade her)
e. Mum said, "You can't go out tonight." (not allow me)

**2. Traduisez en anglais.**
a. Dis à ton père de faire les courses.
b. Je veux que tu fasses la vaisselle.
c. Ils vont t'obliger à travailler dur.
d. Demandez à votre professeur de vous expliquer encore.

# 33 Propositions relatives

Elles dépendent d'un nom : l'antécédent. Elles sont introduites par un pronom relatif qui reprend cet antécédent et a les fonctions d'un nom dans la proposition relative : sujet, complément, attribut.

*I don't like the girl who is standing over there.* (Who est sujet.)

## Choix du relatif

Pour choisir le pronom relatif, on doit se demander s'il est sujet ou complément, et s'il a comme antécédent un humain ou un non-humain.

| Antécédent | Relatif sujet | Relatif complément |
|---|---|---|
| • humain | *who/that* | *who/whom/that/Ø* |
| • non-humain | *which/that* | *which/that/Ø* |

### 1. *Who/which* ou Ø ?

*Who* et *which* sont indispensables quand ils sont sujets de la relative.

*Meghan, who is Irish, is my best friend.* (Who est sujet, il est obligatoire.)

Ils sont le plus souvent omis quand ils sont compléments.

*Meghan is the girl we saw this morning.*
(Who est complément, il peut être omis.)

### 2. *Who/which* ou *that* ?

*That* est préférable à *who/which* pour introduire une proposition « déterminative » (indispensable car elle identifie l'antécédent), surtout après *all – nothing – everything – the only – the first*, les superlatifs, etc.

*The only thing that matters is…*

*Who/Which* introduisent une proposition « descriptive » (qui ajoute une précision non indispensable), précédée d'une virgule.

*My mother, who is 54, lives in London.*

### 3. *Whose*

*Whose*, génitif de *who*, est complément de nom et indique une relation de possession ou de parenté. Il est directement suivi du nom possédé, sans article.

*The girl whose father is a clown…* La fille dont le père est clown…

**Attention !** En français, « dont » a d'autres emplois qui se traduisent de façon différente : il peut être complément d'un adjectif ou d'un verbe.

*The thing I am most proud of.* La chose dont je suis le plus fier.

### 4. *When*

Il signifie « où », « le moment où ». Il reprend un antécédent indiquant un moment : *day – time – night – year*, etc.

*The day when I was born.* Le jour où je suis né.

### 5. *Where*

Il signifie « où ». Il reprend un antécédent indiquant un lieu.

*The city where I was born.* La ville où je suis né.

### 6. *Why*

Il signifie « pourquoi », « pour laquelle ». Il reprend un antécédent indiquant une cause : *reason*. *This is the reason why we left.* C'est la raison pour laquelle nous sommes partis.

### 7. *What* et *which* sans antécédent (« ce qui », « ce que »)

*What* annonce ce qui suit. *What he says is true.* Ce qu'il dit est vrai.

*Which*, précédé d'une virgule, reprend ce qui précède.

*He says he met my father, which is impossible.*

**Attention !** « Tout ce qui/que » se traduit par *all that*.

*All that he had said was true.*

## Exercises

**1. Reliez les phrases en utilisant un pronom relatif.**

a. Robert Hanssen was an American spy. He has had a very quiet life.
b. Robert Hanssen is an American citizen. His wife is Russian.
c. Robert Hanssen was never proved guilty. His own children never suspected anything.
d. His house has a nice front garden. His house is very large.

**2. Mettez les relatifs qui conviennent.**

a. It all started on the day … I read a book about Helen Keller.
b. Louis Braille had invented a system … would enable blind people to read.
c. … I decided to do was improve the system … Braille had invented.
d. It took me a long time during … I learnt a lot.
e. I am very thankful to all the people … trusted me.
f. I must say some people did not trust me, … I can understand.

**3. Traduisez en portant votre attention sur la traduction de « dont ».**

a. J'ai rencontré l'homme dont vous m'avez raconté l'histoire.
b. L'étudiant dont les notes sont les meilleures recevra le prix.
c. C'est un prix dont vous pouvez être fiers.

**4. Traduisez en anglais.**

a. Je suis arrivé un mardi, le jour où les Américains votaient.
b. La Maison Blanche est l'endroit où vit le Président.
c. La Californie est un état où vivent beaucoup de Mexicains.
d. C'est la raison pour laquelle on parle espagnol dans beaucoup d'endroits.

34 ▶

# Quantifieurs indéfinis

## A *Some* et *any*

***Some*** (du, des, de la) indique que le nom qu'il détermine existe. Il est donc privilégié dans les phrases affirmatives. Il peut aussi être pronom.

*There's some water. Give me some, please.*

***Some*** peut être utilisé dans une phrase interrogative si la question ne porte pas sur l'existence du nom qu'il détermine.

*Could you give me some water?* (On sait qu'il y a de l'eau.)

***Any*** (du, des, de la) indique que le nom qu'il détermine peut ne pas exister. On le privilégie dans les phrases négatives ou interrogatives. Il peut aussi être pronom.

*Have you seen any animals in this park? No, there aren't any.*
(Sous-entendu, je ne suis pas sûr qu'il y en ait.)

**Avec un dénombrable au singulier,** *some* et *any* ne se réfèrent pas à la quantité mais soulignent le caractère indéfini.

*We'll meet again some day...* un jour ou l'autre.
*You can come any day...* n'importe quel jour.

## B *No*

*No* a un sens négatif. Comme il ne peut jamais y avoir deux négations dans une phrase, il est associé à un verbe positif. *No* équivaut à *not any*.

*There are no animals here/There are not any animals.*

## C Les composés de *some, any, no*

*Somebody/someone – anybody/anyone* : quelqu'un.
*Nobody/no one* : personne. *Something/anything* : quelque chose.
*Nothing* : rien. *Somewhere/anywhere* : quelque part.
*Nowhere* : nulle part.

## D Les autres quantifieurs

Certains quantifieurs peuvent être employés uniquement devant un indénombrable ou uniquement devant un dénombrable.

| | **Indénombrables** | **Dénombrables** |
|---|---|---|
| pas de/aucun | *no/not any* | *no/not any* |
| peu de | *little* | *few* |
| un peu de | *a little* | *a few* |
| des/quelques | *some/any* | *some/any* |
| plusieurs | | *several* |
| assez de | *enough* | *enough* |
| beaucoup de | *much/a lot of – lots of* | *many/a lot of – lots of* |
| une bonne quantité de | *plenty of* | *a number of* |
| la plupart | *most of the* | *most (of the)* |
| tout le/la/les tous/toutes les | *all the* | *all the/each/every* |

***A lot of*** est plutôt employé dans les phrases affirmatives.
***Much/many*** sont préférés dans les phrases négatives.
*Each* et *every* sont suivis d'un nom au singulier. Ils correspondent à « chaque » mais *every* se traduit souvent par « tous les/toutes les ».

*Every day.* Tous les jours.

## E Les adverbes modifiant les quantifieurs

*Very* (très) et *too* (trop) s'emploient devant *much, many – few – little*.

*I have very little time and too much work.* ... très peu de temps... trop de travail.

## Exercises

**1. Remplacez *no* par *not any*.**

a. We have had no dinner.
b. There is no sun today.
c. There are no children in our group.
d. We have no money.
e. They have no friends.

**2. Mettez ces phrases à la forme négative et ajoutez *much* ou *many* devant les noms.**

a. I eat vegetables.
b. I drink beer.
c. I have time at the weekends.
d. I have friends in this city.
e. You can find information on this website.
f. There's furniture in this house.

**3. Complétez avec *some, any, no* ou leurs composés.**

a. There are ... very strange stories about Ricardo.
b. Do you know ... about him?
c. No, I know absolutely ...
d. I'm not sure ... knows where he is.
e. He must be ... around here.
f. But in fact, he could be ... for all I know.

35

## Questions

### A Les questions fermées

La seule réponse possible est « oui » ou « non ». Elles ne comportent pas de mot interrogatif mais le verbe est à la forme interrogative. L'ordre des mots est : auxiliaire + sujet + verbe + compléments + ? Au présent ou au prétérit, on utilise *do(es)* ou *did* et le verbe est la simple base verbale. Le verbe *be* se comporte comme un auxiliaire et se place devant le sujet.

*Is she working? Does she know we are here?*

### B Les questions ouvertes

Elles commencent par un pronom, adverbe ou locution adverbiale interrogatifs. Comme ces mots comportent tous les lettres *w* et *h,* on les appelle souvent les *wh- questions*. L'ordre des mots est le suivant : *wh-* + auxiliaire + sujet + verbe + compléments + ?

*What does she do? Where did you meet him?*

Lorsque le pronom interrogatif est sujet, il n'y a pas besoin d'auxiliaire.

*Who came first?*

Lorsque la question porte sur un complément introduit par une préposition, celle-ci est rejetée en fin d'énoncé.

*Who were you talking to?*

### C Les mots interrogatifs

Ils permettent de préciser l'information que l'on veut obtenir. Voici les plus courants.

*Who* : l'identité d'un être humain
*What* : la nature d'un objet inanimé
*When* : le moment
*Where* : le lieu
*Why* : la cause
*Which* : un choix entre deux éléments
*Whose* : l'identité du possesseur
*How* : la manière
*How old* : l'âge
*How far* : la distance
*How long* : la durée
*How often* : la fréquence

### Exercises

**1. Mettez le ou les mot(s) interrogatif(s) nécessaire(s).**

a. ... were you born? – In London.
b. ... were you born? – Before World War II.
c. ... are you? – I'm 98.
d. ... sons do you have? – I have four.
e. ... have you lived in the States? – For 57 years.
f. ... decision was it to emigrate? – My father's.
g. ... came here first? – My father did.

**2. Posez des questions commençant par *how* pour obtenir les réponses en gras.**

a. We go to Michigan every year.
b. It's about 1,000 miles from here.
c. The flight is only about one hour and thirty minutes.
d. Well, about $100 per person. It's not too bad.
e. We've met our cousins there about five times.

**3. Traduisez en anglais.**

a. Qu'est-ce que tu écoutes ?
b. Avec qui es-tu allé ?
c. De quoi es-tu le plus fier ?
d. Qu'est-ce qui t'attire le plus dans ce projet ?
e. De quoi parles-tu ?
f. Qui vous a appelé ce matin ?
g. Qui allez-vous emmener avec vous ?

36

## Relations entre les noms

**1. Nom + *of* + nom**

On peut relier deux noms au moyen d'une préposition (notamment *of*).

*The end of the story. An excerpt from a novel by Sharon Gilbert.*

**2. Nom composé**

Cette construction correspond à une relation reconnue comme stable : identité, lieu, usage, matière, cause, etc.

- **Nom + nom**

*A school teacher. The town centre. A cotton skirt.*

- **Verbe + *-ing* + nom**

*A sewing machine. A dancing club.*

### Exercises

**1. Reliez chaque mot de la colonne de gauche à un mot de la colonne de droite pour faire un nom composé.**

| | |
|---|---|
| a. airport | A. park |
| b. car | B. driver |
| c. building | C. building |
| d. garden | D. site |
| e. town | E. furniture |
| f. bus | F. center |

• **Pronom + nom**

*A she-goat.* Une chèvre. *A he-goat.* Un bouc.

• **Verbe + particule**

*A checkout.* Une caisse (de supermarché).

Les éléments peuvent être juxtaposés, accolés ou reliés par un trait d'union. Le nom principal vient en dernier ; on traduit en commençant par lui, puis on remonte mot par mot. Le pluriel se forme en ajoutant un *-s* au dernier élément. Si un adjectif porte sur le mot principal, on l'insère avant le groupe.

*Young San Francisco county police officers.* De jeunes officiers de police du comté de San Francisco. (L'adjectif porte sur *officers*.)

On utilise une structure avec *of* et non un nom composé pour désigner une partie d'un indénombrable.

*A cup of tea* = une tasse de thé (mais *a tea cup* = une tasse à thé).

**3. Le génitif**

• **Possesseur au singulier + *'s* + nom**
• **Possesseur au pluriel terminé par *-s* + *'* + nom**
• **Possesseur au pluriel irrégulier + *'s* + nom**

*My father's car. My parents' car. The men's car.*

Le génitif jouant le rôle d'un déterminant, il ne peut y avoir d'article, de démonstratif ni d'adjectif possessif devant l'objet possédé.

*The man's car.* La voiture de l'homme.

Un adjectif peut s'intercaler devant le nom qu'il qualifie.

*The old man's car.* La voiture du vieil homme.
*The man's old car.* La vieille voiture de l'homme.

Le génitif peut exprimer :
– la possession lorsque le possesseur est une personne, un animal ou un groupe humain (*country*, *city*, etc.) ;

*My father's red car. Australia's climate.*

– le lien de parenté ;
*Sally's sister.*

– la date, la durée, la distance.

*Yesterday's paper. A two hours' drive.*

**2. Choisissez un nom dans la liste pour compléter les noms composés.**
*bed – ground floor – front*
a. The robber walked across the ... garden.
b. He threw a brick through a ... window.
c. He went upstairs to the ... room.

**3. Traduisez en anglais.**
a. Un verre de vin. Un verre à vin.
b. Un verre à eau. Un verre d'eau.

**4. Choisissez la bonne solution pour compléter les phrases.**
a. I've found ... under this armchair.
Anne's blue jumper / the blue Anne's jumper
b. I don't really like ... .
her friend's dress / her friends' dress
c. I had never seen anything like ... before!
her pink boyfriend's trousers / her boyfriend's pink trousers

**5. Complétez avec des génitifs.**
a. She is driving ... (car – her parents)
b. He is playing ... (piano – his girlfriend)
c. They are going on ... (holiday – a week)

**6. Chaque phrase comporte une faute. Corrigez-la.**
a. I'm wearing the John's new coat.
b. Everybody likes clothes' John.
c. You should try mums cake. It's delicious.

## 37 ▶ *Used to* + V

Cette forme s'applique au révolu, comme le prétérit, mais elle souligne la rupture avec le présent. On la traduit par l'imparfait et on peut ajouter « jadis ».

*There used to be a restaurant here.* Jadis, il y avait un restaurant ici.

**Exercises**

• **Transformez les phrases avec *used to*.**
Ex. : He's stopped studying hard.
> He used to study hard.
a. She's stopped smoking.
b. They've stopped spending a lot of money.
c. I've stopped running every morning.
d. Jenny and Mark have stopped going out with each other.

# 38 V-*ing*

Cette forme, d'un emploi très courant en anglais, a des emplois divers qu'il est important d'identifier.

## A *Be* + V-*ing*

La forme V-*ing* peut être le deuxième élément du présent, du prétérit ou du *present perfect be* + *-ing*.

26 • 28 • 16

*She is training for the Olympics.* Elle s'entraîne pour les Jeux Olympiques.

## B La forme nominale du verbe

Comme un nom, le gérondif V-*ing* peut être sujet ou complément.

*Smoking is bad for athletes.* Fumer est mauvais pour les athlètes. (*Smoking* est le sujet de is.) *She hates driving.* Elle n'aime pas conduire. (*Driving* est le complément d'objet de *hates*.)

Comme un verbe, le gérondif V-*ing* peut avoir des compléments.

*Smoking cigarettes is not recommended.* Il n'est pas recommandé de fumer des cigarettes. (Le sujet de is est *smoking cigarettes*.)

## C Les constructions à deux verbes

La forme V-*ing* s'utilise dans de nombreuses constructions à deux verbes. Voici quelques-uns des emplois principaux.

**Après les verbes exprimant l'appréciation,** par exemple *like*, *appreciate*, *enjoy*, *hate*, etc.

*I like playing tennis.* J'aime jouer au tennis.

**Après les verbes de perception,** quand l'énonciateur veut insister sur le fait qu'il a vu ou entendu l'événement en train de se dérouler.

*I saw him playing against the world champion.*
Je l'ai vu jouer contre le champion du monde.

**Après le verbe *need*.**

*My racket needs repairing.* Ma raquette a besoin d'être réparée.

**Après le verbe *go*,** pour parler des sports et activités.

*Let's go swimming after the match.* Allons nager après le match.

## D Après une préposition

Le gérondif est obligatoire lorsqu'on veut mettre un verbe après une préposition.

*After winning the first set, he was defeated.*
Après avoir gagné le premier set, il a été battu.

## E Proposition

Comme en français, le participe présent V-*ing* peut remplacer une proposition de cause.

*Being sick, he gave up in the middle of the second set.*
Étant malade, il a abandonné au milieu du deuxième set.
(Cette phrase est équivalente à *Because he was sick*, ...)

## F Adjectif

À partir de certains verbes, on peut créer des adjectifs en leur ajoutant une terminaison *-ing* ou *-ed*.
Attention, les adjectifs en *-ing* ont un sens actif tandis que les adjectifs en *-ed* ont un sens passif !

*It's boring.* C'est ennuyeux. *I was bored.* Je me suis ennuyé.

## Exercises

**1. Répondez à ces questions en utilisant *by* + V-*ing*.**
joining a gym club – cook healthy food – work hard in the evenings – go to bed early – do the housework

a. How can I get a good score in my exams?
b. How can I eat properly?
c. How can I feel better in the morning?
d. How can I get my house clean?
e. How can I get more exercises?

**2. Complétez avec : *to* – *of* – *in* – *on* (x2)**

a. He is very interested ... cooking.
b. He insisted ... my coming with him.
c. She is thinking ... studying to become a lawyer.
d. You can count ... his arriving early.
e. I'm looking forward ... going to the USA.

**3. Complétez avec : *surprise* – *bore* – *tire* (+ *-ed* ou *-ing*).**

a. I was ... to see my father there. I hadn't been expecting him.
b. I fell asleep during the film. It was really ... .
c. I often get ... if the film is too long.
d. I'm ... because I went to bed late last night.
e. It's ... revising all night long.

# Crédits photographiques

## Couverture

**Vancouver :** Dan Breckwoldt/Shutterstock.com ; **campagne :** Pierre Leclerc/Shutterstock.com ; **étudiants :** Monkey Business Images/Shutterstock.com ; **épices :** curioso/Shutterstock.com ; **jeunes :** Syda Productions/Shutterstock.com.

## Intérieur

**P. 11 :** William Perugini/Shutterstock.com ; **p. 12 :** Dmitry Kalinovsky/Shutterstock.com ; **p. 14 :** Karol Kozlowski/Shutterstock.com ; **p. 15 :** Syda Productions/Shutterstock.com ; **p. 17 :** Archives du 7e Art/Walt Disney Pictures/Photo12 ; **p. 18 :** Nicholas Greenaway/Shutterstock.com ; **p. 19a :** Nebojsa Bobic/Shutterstock.com ; **p. 19b :** ayelet-keshet/Shutterstock.com ; **p. 20 :** University Robert Morris, Illinois ; **p. 21 :** Dikiiy/Shutterstock.com ; **p. 22 :** The Advertising Archives/Rue des Archives ; **p. 23 :** Stefano Tinti/Shutterstock.com ; **p. 24a :** Stockbyte/Getty ; **p. 24b :** Gazlast/Shutterstock.com ; **p. 26 :** art4all/Shutterstock.com ; **p. 29 :** Bruno DELESSARD/Challenges-REA ; **p. 30a :** Manuel Cohen/AFP ; **p. 30b :** Stefano Tinti ; **p. 31 :** Nicolas TAVERNIER/REA ; **p. 35 :** Kathrin HARMS/LAIF-REA ; **p. 36 :** Canadapanda/Shutterstock.com ; **p. 37 :** Mohammad Asad/Pacific/SIPA ; **p. 38a :** Tra To Nha/Shutterstock.com ; **p. 38b :** Vladimir Gjorgiev/Shutterstock.com ; **p. 39 :** think4photop/Shutterstock.com ; **p. 40a :** © Floydine/Fotolia.com ; **p. 40b :** Clynt Garnham Food & Drink/Alamy/ Photo 12 ; **p. 41 :** Image Courtesy of The Advertising Archives ; **p. 42 :** © Buy Nothing Day ; **p. 43 :** Tous Droits Réservés ; **pp. 47 et 49a :** Photos©The Ethical Consumer Group - www.ethical.org.au ; **p. 48 :** Robert Kneschke/Shutterstock.com ; **p. 49b :** Hiroshi Watanabe/Getty ; **p. 53 :** "Blue Tile With Ice Water", © copyright 2015, Ralph Goings, all rights reserved ; **p. 55a :** Bettmann/CORBIS ; **p. 55b :** Pixelbliss/Shutterstock.com ; **p. 55c :** Yulia Davidovich/Shutterstock.com ; **p. 55d :** D. Kucharski K. Kucharska/Shutterstock.com ; **p. 55e :** Suzana Marinkovic/Shutterstock.com ; **p. 56a :** MWB/ZO6/WENN.COM/SIPA ; **p. 56b :** Laura Eisenberg/Getty ; **p. 57 :** Kim Kulish/Corbis ; **p. 58a :** Igor Golovniov/ZUMA-REA ; **p. 58b :** Isabelle Tramoy ; **p. 59a :** All Rights Reserved ; **p. 59b :** Liubou Yasiukovich/Shutterstock.com ; **p. 60 :** Richard Levine/Alamy/Hemis ; **p. 61 :** All Rights Reserved ; **p. 63 :** Scotellaro/Getty ; **p. 64 :** Tonu/Cartoonbase/Photononstop ; **p. 65a :** PaCondryx/Getty ; **p. 65b :** Corbis ; **p. 66 :** Patti McConville/Alamy /Hemis ; **p. 67a :** Tyler Olson/Shutterstock.com ; **p. 67b :** wisawa222/Shutterstock.com ; **p. 71 :** RosalreneBetancourt 1/Alamy/Photo12 ; **p. 72a :** All Rights Reserved ; **p. 72b :** Ken Wolter/Shutterstock.com ; **p. 73a :** Asif Islam/Shutterstock.com ; **p. 73b :** ALTIZER DREW/SIPAUSA/SIPA ; **p. 74a :** Hattanas Kumchai/Shutterstock.com ; **p. 74b :** Giuseppe Costantino/Shutterstock.com ; **p. 75 :** PETER ENDIG/DPA/dpa Picture-Alliance/AFP ; **p. 76a :** loreanto/Shutterstock.com ; **p. 76b :** Solis Images/Shutterstock.com ; **p. 77 :** PETER DASILVA/The New York Times-REDUX-REA ; **p. 78a :** arosoft/Shutterstock.com ; **p. 78b :** Bloomua/Shutterstock.com ; **p. 78c :** eko Photo Studio/Shutterstock.com ; **p. 79 :** Jamie Rhodes/Norton Hea/REX/SIPA ; **p. 83 :** Halfpoint/Shutterstock.com ; **p. 84 :** 360b/Shutterstock.com ; **p. 85a :** Jamie Rhodes/Norton Hea/REX/SIPA ; **p. 85b :** PETER DASILVA/The New York Times-REDUX-REA ; **p. 89 :** Picture Alliance/Rue des Archives ; **p. 90a :** Burlingham/Shutterstock.com ; **p. 90b :** Mark PETERSON/REDUX-REA ; **p. 91a :** Superstock/Rue des Archives ; **p. 91b :** All Rights Reserved ; **p. 92 :** © Paresh Nath – 2015 ; **p. 94 :** FRANCES M. ROBERTS/NEWSCOM/SIPA ; **p. 95 :** Maryna Pleshkun/Shutterstock.com ; **p. 96 :** Sascha Burkard/Shutterstock.com ; **p. 97 :** REUTERS/Jim Young ; **p. 101 :** IxMaster/Shutterstock.com ; **p. 102a :** Wyatt Earp and the Battle of the OK Corral, English School, (20th century)/Private Collection/© Look and Learn/Bridgeman Images ; **p. 102b :** © Dickinson Research Center, National Cowboy and Western Heritage Museum, Oklahoma City, Oklahoma ; **p. 102c :** akg-images/Interfoto/Sammlung Rauch ; **p. 103a :** Rue des Archives/RDA ; **p. 103b :** IAM / akg-images ; **p. 103c :** Archives du 7e Art/EuropaCorp/Ithaca/ Photo12 ; **p. 107 :** Bloomberg/Getty ; **p. 108a :** Vasin Lee/Shutterstock.com ; **p. 108b :** bikeriderlondon/Shutterstock.com ; **p. 108c :** Kobal/The Picture Desk/AFP ; **p. 109a :** Ecelop/Shutterstock.com ; **p. 109b :** Kodda/Shutterstock.com ; **p. 110 :** Andrey_Popov/Shutterstock.com ; **p. 111a :** jesadaphorn/Shutterstock.com ; **p. 111b :** Monkey Business Images/Shutterstock.com ; **p. 112a :** Lucian Milasan/Shutterstock.com ; **p. 112b :** 360b/Shutterstock.com ; **p. 112c :** 360b/Shutterstock.com ; **p. 112d :** charnsitr/Shutterstock.com ; **p. 112e :** 360b/Shutterstock.com ; **p. 112f :** 360b/Shutterstock.com ; **p. 113 :** Paul Hudson/Getty ; **p. 114a :** Vasin Lee/Shutterstock.com ; **p. 114b :** Vasin Lee/Shutterstock.com ; **p. 115 :** Frances Roberts/Alamy/Hemis ; **p. 118 :** 360b/Shutterstock.com ; **p. 119a :** wavebreakmedia/Shutterstock.com ; **p. 119b :** Kutsyi Bohdan/Shutterstock.com ; **p. 121a :** Newnow/Shutterstock.com ; **p. 121b :** 1000 Words/Shutterstock.com ; **p. 125a :** Targn Pleiades/Shutterstock.com ; **p. 125b :** steschum/Fotolia.com ; **p. 126a :** duchy/Shutterstock.com ; **p. 126b :** Stephen McCluskey/Shutterstock.com ; **p. 127 :** Jeremy Sutton-Hibbert/Getty Images ; **p. 128 :** Esteban De Armas/Shutterstock.com ; **p. 129a :** akg-images/De Agostini Picture Library ; **p. 129b :** Dave Head/Shutterstock.com ; **p. 129c :** Christopher Elwell/Shutterstock.com ; **p. 130 :** Francois Loubser/Shutterstock.com ; **p.131 :** Gail Johnson/Shutterstock.com ; **p. 132 :** kornilov007/Shuterstock.com ; **p. 133a :** Roman Sigaev/Fotolia.com ; **p. 133b :** Mondadori Portfolio/Rue des Archives ; **p. 137 :** Heartland Arts/Shutterstock.com ; **p. 138a :** © Culture and Sport Glasgow (Museums)/Bridgeman Images ; **p. 138b :** The Yellow Dress, c.1908-9 (oil on canvas), Peploe, Samuel John (1871-1935)/Private Collection/Bridgeman Images ; **p. 138c :** The Drambuie Collection, Edinburgh, Scotland/Bridgeman Images ; **p. 138d :** Polarpx/Shutterstock.com ; **p. 138e :** DSQ/WENN.COM/SIPA ; **p. 139a :** Iberfoto/Photoaisa/Roger-Viollet ; **p. 139b :** The advertising Archives/Rue des Archives ; **p. 139c :** Kobal/The Picture Desk/AFP ; **p. 139d :** COLLECTION CHRISTOPHEL © Thorn EMI Screen Entertainment ; **p. 139e :** Collection Christophel © Sony Pictures ; **p. 143 :** Hope at Sunrise, 2007 (acrylic on canvas), Brintle, Patricia/Private Collection/Bridgeman Images ; **p. 144 :** Everett Historical/Shutterstock.com ; **p. 145 :** Everett Historical/Shutterstock.com ; **p. 146 :** Archives du 7e Art/Regency Enterprises/Photo12 ; **p. 147 :** Everett Historical/Shutterstock.com ; **p. 148 :** Brenda Kean/Alamy/Photo 12 ; **p. 149 :** Rue des Archives/BCA ; **p. 150 :** Sabena Jane Blackbird/Alamy/ Photo12 ; **p. 151a :** Everett Historical/Shutterstock.com ; **p. 151b :** Bettmann/Corbis ; **p. 155 :** geliatida/Shutterstock.com ; **p. 156a :** Superstock/Rue des Archives © ADAGP 2015 ; **p. 156b :** The Washington Family, 1789-1796 (oil on canvas), Savage, Edward (1761-1817)/National Gallery of Art, Washington DC, USA/Bridgeman Images ; **p. 156c :** Everett Historical/Shutterstock.com ; **p. 157a :** Ullstein Bild/Roger-Viollet ; **p. 157b :** Artwork © Marcus Lyon/Used by arrangement with The Random House Group Limited ; **p. 157c :** Collection Christophel © MGM ; **p. 157d :** COLLECTION CHRISTOPHEL © DreamWorks SKG ; **p. 157e :** Collection Christophel © Columbia pictures/ANdrew Cooper/Sony pictures releasing ; **p. 161 :** Rugby International, Wales V Scotland (w/c on paper), Ball, Gareth Lloyd (Contemporary Artist)/Private Collection/Bridgeman Images ; **p. 162 :** Martin Good/Shutterstock.com ; **p. 163a :** Vlad1988/Shutterstock.com ; **p. 163b :** Adam Fraise/Shutterstock.com ; **p. 164 :** Lance Bellers/Fotolia ; **p. 165 :** Refat/Shutterstock.com ; **p. 166 :** Andreas Pollok/Getty ; **p. 167 :** CHEN WS/Shutterstock.com ; **p. 168 :** Debby Wong/Shutterstock.com ; **p. 169 :** yienkeat/Shutterstock.com ; **p. 173 :** REUTERS/Michael Crabtree ; **p. 174 :** Brues/Shutterstock.com ; **p. 175a :** Lee Carbonelli/HQ Inc. ; **p. 175b :** Threadsmiths/Lewis Pitchford/REX/SIPA ; **p. 175c :** Gines Romero/Shutterstock.com ; **p. 178a :** Ross Petukhov/Shutterstock.com ; **p. 178b :** Shvaygert Ekaterina/Shutterstock.com ; **p. 178c :** mimagephotography/Shutterstock.com.

Imprimé en Italie par «La Tipografica Varese Srl» Varese
Dépôt légal : juin 2017 - Collection n° 3 - Édition n° 03
23/2226/4